JCSS Study no. 24

Israel and Syria: Peace and Security on the Golan

Aryeh Shalev

Routledge
Taylor & Francis Group
LONDON AND NEW YORK

First published 1994 by Westview Press

Published 2018 by Routledge
52 Vanderbilt Avenue, New York, NY 10017
2 Park Square, Milton Park, Abingdon, Oxon OX14 4RN

Routledge is an imprint of the Taylor & Francis Group, an informa business

Library of Congress Cataloging-in-Publication Data

Shalev, Aryeh, 1926-
[Shalom u-vitahon ba-Golan. English]
Israel and Syria: peace and security on the Golan / by Aryeh Shalev.
p. cm.
Includes bibliographical references.
ISBN 0-8133-2222-7
1. Israel—Foreign relations—Syria. 2. Syria—Foreign relations—Israel. 3. Golan Heights—International status. 4. Israel—Politics and government. I. Title.
DS119.8.S95S513 1994 94-22074
327.569405691—dc20 CIP

ISBN 13: 978-0-367-00926-7 (hbk)
ISBN 13: 978-0-367-15913-9 (pbk)

This book is dedicated

to

BERNARD DENBURG

of blessed memory

Contents

Preface

This book had its genesis a few years before the Madrid Conference, which ushered in peace talks between Israel and its neighbors, including of course Syria. Guided by the assumption that the differences between Syria and Israel could be bridged only by political negotiations, I felt that issues such as the strategic importance of the Golan Heights and possible security arrangements within a peace treaty framework were already then relevant.

The negotiations with Syria and on the future of the Golan Heights are basically political in character. So it is politicians, rather than army officers, who will make the final decisions. Security considerations, though, will be of major importance.

For some years I was directly involved in events concerning the security relations between Israel and Syria. From 1949 until the end of 1952 I represented Israel in the Syria-Israel Mixed Armistice Commission. During that period we held direct talks on security affairs with Syrian officers representing their country. Later (1957-1959) I served as chief intelligence officer in the Northern Command, which was responsible for the Syrian front. These experiences undoubtedly served me in writing this book as they did with a previous study, *The Israel-Syria Armistice Regime 1949-1955* (JCSS Study no. 21, 1993), which drew primarily on archival material and dealt with relations between the two countries in the first half of the 1950s.

The present book consists of five parts. **Part I, Political and Historical Background**, asks what can be gleaned from the security relations between Israel and Syria in the past. **Part II, Major Obstacles in Peace Negotiations**, examines the difficulties the sides have to overcome in their peace talks. Next, **Part III, Topography and the Balance of Forces** looks at the main elements directly affecting Syria's options for attacking Israel. **Part IV, Security Risks for Israel**, examines the dangers that emerge from an analysis of topography and the balance of forces. Finally **Part V, Security Arrangements**, looks at the security measures that could be determined parallel to the peace arrangements, and offers a proposal for ensuring that security is preserved and consolidated along with the peace.

I drew upon a wide range of sources in preparing this book:

* Books and documents dealing with Syria and other Arab countries and their security arrangements with Israel in the past, e.g., the Israeli-Syrian separation of forces agreement and the Israeli-Egyptian peace treaty.
* Statements by Israeli, Syrian and American leaders formulating their interests and positions on peace negotiations, a potential agreement and security arrangements.
* Conversations with Israeli politicians, IDF (Israel Defense Forces) senior officers (regular army and reserves), experts on the Middle East in Israel and abroad, including Syrian experts, western diplomats who were stationed in Syria, representatives of the Jewish settlements on the Golan Heights, and others.

One of the most difficult problems I had to contend with was an assessment of the two principal parties' probable stands at the end of the negotiating process. While opening positions are easily enough known, final positions are an unknown--indeed, it is unlikely that even the leaders of the two states themselves know in advance what these will be. This is a topic for which the sources offer no clear answers; an appraisal has to be based on knowledge of the basic interests of each country, an assessment of possible developments and a sense of the drift of the Israel-Arab dynamic.

Certainly one crucial factor, particularly with respect to Syria, will be the identity of the country's leader at the time--yet another imponderable. Even the position that President Hafez al-Assad adopts at the end of the negotiating process (assuming that it is concluded during the period of his leadership) is a riddle: as far as we know, Assad does not disclose his strategy regarding Israel and peace talks even to his confidants. Obviously, the position of a post-Assad regime in Syria cannot even be guessed at. Still, experts believe that if peace is achieved and its practical implementation begun during Assad's period of rule, his successor will probably pursue the same course, albeit cautiously.

In short, then, an assessment of final positions must be grounded in a large number of unknowns and uncertainties. Similarly, although an attempt has been made here to address the question of whether Syria would be willing to sign a peace treaty with Israel before a full Israeli-Palestinian agreement is reached, a definitive answer is problematic. It is difficult to predict what the international, regional and internal Syrian situation will be when the time comes to make a decision; nor do we know how Damascus will view its possible alternatives at that time. Meanwhile, the advent of an Israeli-PLO interim agreement in September 1993 has not clarified the issue: Damascus' initial attitude toward the agreement was ambivalent.

In any event a book dealing with future situations leaves the author no choice but to make certain basic assumptions, which are described according to the subjects under discussion. This, I hope, will facilitate the reader's ability to follow the arguments that are adduced. Certainly the inability to predict final positions does not seriously affect the core of the book, namely the bottom-line security arrangements which Israel will have to insist on during negotiations with Syria. Those arrangements will have to ensure security for Israel, the development of normalization between the two countries, and the upholding of the agreement itself.

I owe a special debt of gratitude to my colleagues in the senior research team at the Jaffee Center for Strategic Studies, whose comments were on-target and very beneficial; to Ralph Mandel for his adept translation; and to JCSS Director Joseph Alpher for his efforts in producing this updated and adapted English edition.

Aryeh Shalev
Tel Aviv University
January 1994

Introduction

Until October 1991 there were no direct peace negotiations between Israel and Syria. The issue had been moribund since the two states signed an armistice agreement in July 1949 in the aftermath of Israel's War of Independence. However, there were several occasions when Syria considered the possibility of making peace with Israel:

In 1919-1920, when King Faisal still ruled in Syria, the Arab and Jewish national movements cooperated in Damascus. The prime agent of that cooperation was Eliahu Sasson, who was active in both movements. There was even a newspaper dedicated to promoting partnership between the two groups. Cooperation was based on political support given by the Jewish national movement to the Syrians in their struggle to throw off French rule and, in a complementary fashion, on the Syrians' political support for the Jews in their dealings with British rule in Palestine.

In 1949 the Syrian dictator, Hosni al-Zaim, offered to meet with Israeli Prime Minister David Ben-Gurion and to discuss a peace treaty and a military alliance between the two countries. Syria would absorb 250,000 to 300,000 Palestinian refugees, while Israel, for its part, would cede half of Lake Tiberias (Kinneret) to Syria.

During the period 1951-1953 Syrian ruler Adib Shishaqli indicated his readiness for a non-belligerency agreement with Israel during secret negotiations he held with the United States. Syria viewed such an agreement as a way to improve its relations with Washington.

After the 1967 Six-Day War, the two most relevant issues between Syria and Israel were peace and the future of the Golan Heights. After the signing of a separation of forces agreement in May 1974, in the aftermath of the Yom Kippur War the previous October, little attempt was made to deal with them.

Then, in October 1991 Israel began talks on peace with three Arab states (Syria, Jordan, Lebanon), and on an autonomy arrangement with the Palestinians in the Administered Territories.

In September 1993 the Labor government, which had come to power in Israel in June 1992, reached an interim accord with the PLO through secret negotiations. Syria perceived this agreement as undermining its position, and as isolating it from an inter-Arab standpoint.

Over the years, neither Syria nor Israel had looked for shortcuts or shown a propensity to make substantial concessions in order to resolve the two major problems of peace and borders. The process which began with the Madrid Conference in late 1991 may have signaled a change. At the least, those negotiations must be seen as a breakthrough, against the backdrop of decades in which no talks were held. As of early 1994, however, little progress had been made beyond the presentation of opening stands and disputes over procedural matters. Little of substance was discussed. Nor was it possible to assess when, or whether, substantial issues would be raised.

This book is based on the supposition that peace negotiations between Israel and Syria will be extraordinarily difficult, lengthy and punctuated by frequent crises. Nevertheless, the possibility exists that at the end of the process the two sides will agree, or will be constrained, to make wrenchingly painful concessions as the prelude to signing a peace agreement.

Yet even if the Israeli-Syrian negotiations produce an understanding, it is not certain whether Syria will sign an agreement before a comprehensive Israeli-Palestinian peace is achieved. In other words, Damascus may not view the interim agreement on autonomy between Israel and the Palestinians as enabling it to sign a treaty with Israel, even one that deals favorably, from Syria's point of view, with the disposition of the Golan Heights. This would be perceived by the current Syrian leadership, and almost certainly by Assad's successor as well, as a separate agreement, to which Damascus has traditionally objected. This, despite President Assad's clear show of dissatisfaction with the Israeli-PLO agreement.

Whoever may follow Assad, it is unlikely that Syria will reverse its policy in the direction of insularity and abandonment of its pan-Arab line, and condone a separate peace. The Syrians' slogan "Palestine before the Golan" does not mean that Syria places the Palestinians' interests above its own or that it seeks the creation of a Palestinian state which would not be dependent on Damascus. Its point is that Syria, as it strives for dominance in the Levant, feels obligated, even at this early stage, to take into account and help fulfill the interests of the Palestinians. Ideologically (the Ba'th Party's pan-Arab approach), the Syrians consider themselves the Palestinians' patrons.

The negotiations will also be affected by international developments: the end of the Cold War, the collapse of the Soviet Union which had supported regional conflicts, and the emergence of the United States as the world's only superpower. To this must be added Washington's desire to bring about a political settlement in the Middle East and to prevent wars in the region, and the increasing dependence of Middle Eastern countries on the United States, but also America's growing preoccupation with domestic rather than external affairs. The rise or decline of Islamic fundamentalism in the Arab world, and the growing strength and influence of Iran, are also factors of potential influence.

We have noted that this book takes as its point of departure the possibility that Israeli-Syrian negotiations will produce a peace treaty. If so, it will be a comprehensive treaty, encompassing the two key intractable issues: the contents of the peace and a territorial settlement. According to this assumption, which is itself scrutinized in the book, any interim settlements will stem from the comprehensive agreement and will be stages in its implementation, not separate elements. As for the contents of peace, Syria wants them to be as limited as possible while Israel seeks a broad, all-embracing accord. With regard to a territorial settlement, Syria demands a full Israeli withdrawal from the Golan Heights while Israel may be ready to make certain concessions, but will insist on long-term security arrangements to ensure its safety and the protection of its water sources.

An Israeli-Syrian peace treaty will not totally eliminate security risks for Israel for a long time--indeed, until a Western European-style peace prevails in the Middle East. In the light of this, the book attempts to answer the key interim questions: What effect do topography and balance of forces have on the security question? What security risks is Israel liable to face during the lengthy period until a Western European model evolves in the Middle East? How effective are agreed means for reducing security risks (downsizing the Syrian regular army, deploying part of it far from the Israeli border, etc.) likely to be? And, finally, what are the possible stages of implementing an agreement in terms of territory, security arrangements and the evolution of peace?

Part I

Political and Historical Background

Chapter 1. Political Background

At the end of October 1991, in Madrid, Israel began negotiations on a peace settlement with its neighbors--Syria, Lebanon and Jordan--and with the Palestinians on an interim (autonomy) agreement. The talks were largely the initiative of the United States, the world's only superpower following the breakup of the Soviet Union and the end of the Cold War. The United States had strengthened its position internationally, and particularly in the Middle East, by leading the coalition to victory over Iraq following that country's invasion of Kuwait. Washington now moved to exploit its achievements and dampen the Middle East powder keg.

Israel and Syria entered into negotiations following considerable hesitations. Some of their considerations were peculiar to each country; others were surprisingly similar or even identical. Among the major reasons,[1] the first was that each country continued to perceive the other as aggressive. Further, Syria has always appeared to view Israel as a state whose very existence conflicts with its interests. It views Israel as looking for a suitable opportunity to take over the entire Middle East "from the Nile to the Euphrates." Deep-rooted feelings of enmity and hatred for Israel seem to motivate the Syrian leadership. This attitude was succinctly expressed many years ago by Syrian Defense Minister Mustafa Tlas: "No country is more hostile to Israel than Syria, or hates the Israelis more than our country."[2] Syria views its conflict with Israel and with Zionism as deep and basic--a "fateful struggle"[3] in which the return of the Golan Heights to Syria is but one stage. Meanwhile, in the Israeli view, Damascus has consistently been hostile, refusing to resolve the conflict and make peace.

Accordingly, decades of mutual suspicion and mistrust have marked relations between the two countries. Because of Syria's unremitting militant hostility toward Israel, the latter has doubted whether Syrian policy has reached a turning point which could produce a process of substantial change.

In addition to these general considerations, each state has a central tactical consideration that contributes to its reluctance to negotiate: Israel believes that Syria wants the Golan Heights but is not ready for an agreement that will really remove the threat of war. Syria believes that without military pressure exercised by itself, or political pressure from Washington, Israel will not give up the Golan, and that even if Israel were willing to withdraw from most of the Golan, Syria could not make the kind of peace Israel wants.

One key question is whether there are signs, in Syria and the other neighboring states, of a basic strategic shift regarding Israel. This does not seem to be the case. Note, in this connection, a comment by one of the world's foremost orientalists, the late Eli Kedourie:[4] "In my view, there has been no change" in the Arab world's attitude toward Israel, and Assad "remains the same opportunist he always was." The Syrians, Kedourie added, are champions of pan-Arabism, have ambitions to lead the Arab world, "and it will be difficult to reach a settlement with them." Israel, he emphasized, cannot rely on President Assad or anyone else, only on security arrangements. Western visitors to Damascus report that Syria considers itself to be negotiating with the United States, not with Israel, and indeed, wants to drive a wedge between them. The results of the June 1992 election in Israel made it all the more difficult for Syria to engineer such a break.

What, then, besides the return of the Golan Heights, does President Assad want to achieve in the conflict with Israel? Experts on Syria maintain that it is important for him to conclude his political career as a nationalist Arab leader who did not submit to Israel, and that he wants a settlement in which Syria acquires the status of a powerful and dominant Arab state in the Levant (Syria, Lebanon, Jordan, the Palestinians) as a counterweight to Israel.

Syria seems to have been quick to grasp the significance of the outcome of the Gulf War and the onset of a "new world order." Hence its consent to the US proposal to begin negotiations with Israel on a peace settlement based on UN

Security Council resolutions 242 and 338 (concurrent with negotiations between Israel and other Arab states and the Palestinians). In agreeing to hold talks, Syria abandoned two of its previous basic conditions. The first was its insistence on a prior Israeli commitment that negotiations would lead to a full IDF withdrawal from the Golan Heights. Instead, Syria accepted a US pledge to support a territorial solution based on Resolutions 242 and 338 (without interpreting them). The second condition it abandoned was its longstanding demand that negotiations be held under UN auspices. Instead, Damascus agreed to hold direct talks with Israel.

Besides grasping the lessons of the Gulf War, President Assad also understood early on the change that had occurred in the status of the Soviet Union and, consequently, in its willingness to back Syria and supply it with advanced weapons. The implications were twofold: Syria's prospects of achieving "strategic parity" with Israel were greatly reduced, and the likelihood that Iraq would dispatch large forces to assist Syria in the event of a war with Israel was diminished.

Assad first used the term "strategic parity" during the Rabat summit conference of Arab states in 1974, referring to the need to place the Arabs' military strength on a par with Israel's. At the end of the 1970s, following the signing of the Israeli-Egyptian peace treaty (March 1979), Assad revised the concept, holding that it was up to Syria alone to reach the goal of parity in military might with Israel, in order to cope with Israel by itself and change the status quo.

According to Assad, strategic parity entailed three objectives: First, to enable Syria to withstand an Israeli attack alone. The Syrians believe they attained that goal some years ago. In 1986, Assad stated: "If we are attacked, we have the capacity to defend ourselves."[5] Three years later Vice President Abd al-Halim Khaddam added: "We have reached the point at which Israel will realize that it cannot carry out an adventure without taking Syria's defensive capabilities into consideration."[6]

Second, strategic parity was intended to allow Syria to negotiate from a position of strength that would enable it to achieve a political settlement on its terms. As President Assad put it, "Without parity between us and Israel, it will be difficult to achieve peace."[7] And, again: "Anyone who wants to see a just peace in the region...must have the conviction that a strategic balance must exist in the region."[8] Defense Minister Tlas was blunt: "We must be so strong militarily that when, one day, we talk with the Israelis we will not have to hide the stick behind our back, but lay it on the negotiating table. This is the only language the Zionists understand."[9] Strategic parity was therefore a prior condition for Syria's ability to enter into a political process in which it could hope to make concrete gains.

A third purpose of strategic parity was to provide Syria with an offensive option to liberate by force the Golan Heights and the other territories, in the event that the mere declared existence of strategic parity did not induce Israel to accept Syria's political terms. In the words of Defense Minister Tlas, "Only by violence can the occupied territories be liberated."[10] Syrian Information Minister Ahmad Iskander Ahmad added: "We want Syria to be capable of winning a victory and of liberating the occupied Arab territories."[11]

It was long clear to the Syrians that the attainment of strategic parity depended, above all, on the supply of qualitative weapons from the Soviet Union, and in the quantities required. "Strategic parity with Israel will be achieved by the arming of Syria,"[12] President Assad stated in 1985, and Defense Minister Tlas declared: "As long as...the Soviet Union supplies us with weapons, we shall not relax our war on Israel."[13]

Syria's prolonged effort to achieve strategic parity had a price: growing economic hardship, necessitating even a temporary reduction in the order of battle, in 1987. Nevertheless Damascus persisted, because of the high national importance ascribed to this objective. However, some observers maintain that even before the sea-change in Soviet foreign policy, and before the Soviet Union's decline as a superpower, it was clear to President Assad that strategic parity with Israel was beyond his reach. The reason: Israel received from the United States weapons of a higher quality than those available to Syria. According to this account, Assad contented himself with achieving a deterrent capability vis-a-vis Israel.[14]

Ultimately, the revision in Soviet policy, followed by the breakup of the Soviet Union, reduced the possibility that Syria would be able to launch a war against Israel unaided. This included a new public stand on the idea of Syrian strategic parity. Already in late 1989 the Soviet ambassador to Damascus expressed his country's opposition to the offensive element in the strategic parity concept, as this was no longer compatible with Moscow's foreign policy.[15] Moscow now suggested that Syria work to achieve a "parity of interests" (i.e., a political settlement) with Israel rather than "strategic parity."

Further, Iraq's defeat in the Second Gulf War and the loss of much of its military infrastructure means not only that Iraq is no longer a military threat to Syria. It is also doubtful (at least in the foreseeable future) whether, in the event of a war with Israel, Iraq could substantially reinforce the Syrian armed forces. Thus the threat to Israel's eastern front has been reduced.

For the Syrian leadership, the absence of a military option means the inability to change, at least for the near future, the status quo of Israeli rule on the Golan Heights. Therefore, despite its many drawbacks, the only possibility to get back the Golan is to emulate the route taken by Egyptian President Sadat in the 1970s, namely the way of negotiation.

Yet despite this Syrian assessment, or perhaps because of it, Damascus has engaged in a major military buildup since the Second Gulf War. Taking advantage of the collapse of the Soviet Bloc in Eastern Europe and the thirst for foreign currency shown by its former member-states, the Syrians have been able to purchase, relatively cheaply, large quantities of advanced weaponry. For example, in early 1992 Czechoslovakia began supplying hundreds of high quality T-72 tanks to Syria. The Syrians also added divisions to their ground forces. And the better part of the aid funds Syria received from Saudi Arabia following the Second Gulf War were earmarked not to improve the standard of living in the country or for civilian investments, but for arms acquisitions.

At bottom, then, Syria's basic conception--that the largest and most powerful army possible is required in order to pressure Israel--remains unchanged. Damascus believes it can bring Israel to make concessions in negotiations. It also seeks to limit the freedom of action of Jordan and the Palestinians in the talks, thus preventing Syria's possible isolation.[16] All this, by virtue of the very existence of its large and powerful armed forces. And if absolutely necessary, the Syrians would also be in a position to attempt to use military force in order to achieve their immediate goal of regaining the Golan Heights.

As for the so-called "new world order" that, according to some concepts, has evolved in the aftermath of the Gulf War and the breakup of the Soviet Union, and particularly its effect on the Arab-Israel conflict, we may postulate that, first and foremost, the emergence of the United States as the only superpower translates into greater American influence in the Middle East. The end of the Cold War and consequently of US-Soviet competition, particularly in the Middle East, has produced a more balanced US global policy. To this equation must be added Syria's interest (and that of other Arab states) in fostering good relations with Washington (although not to the point of dependence) and Israel's overriding dependence on the Americans.

Secondly, many states, especially in sensitive regions such as the Middle East, are now less prone to resort to military force for conflict resolution. When military action becomes less likely, priority is given to moderating conflicts globally. This is particularly so in the Middle East, where political solutions are now preferred.

Finally the global, or UN system (with the US at its center), now exercises a powerful regional influence in the Middle East, if only because of its strengthened ability to operate in unison and to impose sanctions in crisis situations.

The foregoing suggests that the difficult process launched in Madrid has a fair prospect for success. This scenario gains credence given the basic US inclination to support the central interest of each party: Washington backs the Syrian demand of territory for peace, but also Israel's insistence on true normalization.

A few words must be devoted to the personality of Syrian President Hafez al-Assad, who dictates his country's position in the negotiations. According to books by British journalist Patrick Seale[17] and Prof. Moshe Maoz of the Hebrew University,[18] Assad is highly intelligent (though he never completed academic studies), has an excellent memory, takes a comprehensive approach and is aware of world politics. He is one of the world's most forceful individual rulers and his regime is extremely personal in character. President Assad is the dominant figure in Syria in foreign relations and in intelligence assessments. He makes his own decisions, although he listens to others' opinions. He does not react quickly, needing time to think and formulate a position. Not being impulsive, he does not make dramatic shifts. He is cautious and has sharp instincts. At bottom, he is neither a strategist nor an ideologue, but a highly capable tactician, a pragmatist who takes a realistic view of a situation and its attendant possibilities, and a master of brinkmanship. He is a virtuoso negotiator, impossible to unnerve, devious and unpredictable. Above all, he plays his cards close to the vest.

Chapter 2. The Palestine-Syria and Israel-Syria Border

General Background

The demarcation of the border between Syria and Israel (before 1948, between Syria and Palestine), certain to be a highly contentious issue in peace talks, was already the subject of negotiations on three earlier occasions:

First, from 1916 to 1926--between France and England, the Mandatory powers in Syria and Palestine, respectively. The talks began before and continued after Turkey's defeat in World War I. They did not always proceed smoothly, but ultimately resulted in an agreement (March 7, 1923) on the location of the international boundary between Syria/Lebanon and Palestine. In 1926 a good-neighbor agreement was signed between the French government in Syria and the British government in Palestine.

Secondly, following the Israeli War of Independence negotiations were held between Syria and Israel on an armistice agreement (March 4-July 20, 1949). These focused on the location of the armistice demarcation line. Israel wanted a line corresponding with the international boundary, whereas Syria sought a line to the west of the international frontier which would reflect, as far as possible, its gains during the war.

Third, from October 9, 1952 until May 27, 1953, Israel and Syria held secret, high-level talks on dividing the Demilitarized Zone (DZ), most of which was situated west of the international boundary. By its very entry into these talks, Israel agreed implicitly that part of the DZ west of the international boundary would become Syrian territory.

Because the basis for the demarcation of the international boundary was, as noted, the Anglo-French agreement of 1923, events connected with that accord will be the main focus in what follows.

International Boundary Between Syria and Palestine[1]
(Map No. 1)

Although there are many differences between British interests after World War I concerning the location of the Syria-Palestine boundary, and Israeli interests today, there are also two important similarities. The first is Britain's desire for exclusive control over three sources of water--the Jordan River, Lake Hula and Lake Tiberias (Lake Kinneret)--and, for security reasons, control of the Golan Heights. The British were concerned primarily about raids by Bedouin. Even though the Turks had moved Circassians to the Golan in order to defend against Bedouin marauders, the British insisted that the boundary follow a line of hills on the Golan Heights, rather than the Jordan River. Incidentally, the Zionist movement tried to have the entire Golan incorporated within Palestine.

The second analogy is that the Golan's northern boundary, from the town of Kuneitra to Mount Hermon, as agreed upon at one stage of French-British negotiations, resembles the borders of the Golan as held by Israel since the Six-Day War, whereas under British rule the southern border was far closer to the Jordan River.

Sykes-Picot Agreement (1916)

Until World War I Palestine was part of the Ottoman Empire, which divided the region into a number of administrative districts. The Golan Heights, known as the Kuneitra Subdistrict, were part of the Damascus District. During World War I the British and French, contemplating the conquest of the Middle East, moved to carve up this and other regimes between them. Negotiations began on October 26, 1915 and concluded on May 16, 1916, when the two countries signed an agreement partitioning the lands of the Ottoman Empire. The Sykes-Picot Agreement (so named for Mark Sykes and Georges F. Picot, the British and French representatives, respectively, who signed the accord) was kept secret until the end of 1917. It divided Palestine into four areas:

1. **Upper Galilee** north of a line connecting the Mediterranean coast (at a point just north of Acre) with the northwest shore of Lake Tiberias would come under French authority.
2. **Haifa Bay and the surrounding area**, including Acre, Haifa and Mount Carmel, would fall under British authority.
3. The **area south of Area 1** (above) and with the exception of Area 2 (above)--i.e., Lower Galilee, Samaria, Judea and the entire area south to the Gaza-Dead Sea line--would become an "Allied Condominium," to be administered under the supervision of France, Britain and Russia.
4. Finally, the **majority of the area of what is today Syria (including the Golan Heights)** was to be transferred to an Arab state under French protection.

France, then, was assured of rule on the Golan Heights and in part of Palestine: the Dan River, Lake Hula, the Banias Springs and part of Lake Tiberias fell within the boundaries of Syria. The chief political officer in the headquarters of the British expeditionary force to Egypt noted that Sykes-Picot was signed before Britain made its pledge to the Zionist movement and that the agreement was not in Palestine's best interests.[2] The upshot was that in later negotiations with France (beginning in 1919), Great Britain worked to secure changes in its favor in the Sykes-Picot Agreement.

British forces captured the Golan area from the Turks in September 1918, and in the following month they created a military administration ("in captured enemy areas") of which the boundaries corresponded in part with Sykes-Picot. The administration was headed by Major General Arthur Money. In a temporary arrangement, the entire area east of the Jordan, including the Golan Heights, and east of the Lebanese Bekaa, was subordinated to an Arab officer in Damascus who, in turn, was accountable to General Edmund Allenby.

Positions Prior to Negotiations on the Region's Future

The Zionists wanted the border to run from the Mediterranean in the west, via the hills of Lebanon, the sources of the Jordan and the peak of Mount Hermon in the north, to the Syrian desert in the east.[3] As early as 1915, Shmuel Tolkovsky submitted to the Zionist Executive in London a document specifying the borders required to defend Palestine. The optimal border in the east, he noted, is "the Hijaz railway line...and the railway line which will connect it with Aqaba."[4] In early 1919 the Zionist Executive asked Aharon Aronson (head of the Nili underground in World War I) to prepare a memorandum on the boundaries of Palestine to serve as a basis for the Zionists' claims at the peace conference. Aronson made two primary assumptions: first, that an area was needed that would be sufficiently large to absorb, within little more than a generation, the majority of the world's 13 million Jews; and secondly, that the decisive criterion for demarcating the borders was not strategic terrain (whose importance varies as strategy develops and weapons improve), but water sources.

Aronson concluded that the peak of Mount Hermon must be inside the northern border of the Land of Israel. He drew the eastern boundary along the Hijaz railway line and from there to the Gulf of Aqaba, to incorporate the western Hauran (a mountainous area on the eastern edge of the Golan).[5]

The Paris peace conference opened on January 18, 1919. Representatives of the Zionist movement appeared before the conference on February 3, 1919. As they considered the Golan Heights to be part of the Land of Israel, they asked that the boundary follow the dividing line between the eastern and western slopes of Mount Hermon, to Mazrat Beit Jann, along the watershed to the Hijaz railway line, and along that line from the Yarmuk River to the Gulf of Aqaba. The rationale for this plan, as presented to the British in a document signed by, among others, Lord Walter Rothschild, Chaim Weizmann and Nahum Sokolow, was Aronson's: Palestine must be large enough to accommodate all of world Jewry, and its economy was inextricably linked to the availability of water. Therefore, it was essential not only to ensure the current supply of water, but to control its sources as well. The Hermon, Palestine's major water source, must be wholly within its boundaries.

Later, the Zionist Organization requested arrangements to facilitate its use of the waters of the Litani and the Yarmuk. Opposition was also expressed to placing the entire Hijaz railway line in Arab hands, on two grounds. One was strategic: the line, it was argued, which ran the entire length of Palestine's eastern boundary, would provide the desert Arabs--who repeatedly launched punishing attacks on Palestine--with a base from which to pose a permanent threat to the country's Jewish population. The second reason was economic. The Zionists argued that to hand over the rail line would cause severe economic damage, as the area east of the Jordan (where Zionism had interests) would lose a means of transportation that was crucial to its rapid development and would be dependent on the good will of the Bedouins. Similarly, the Zionist Organization fiercely objected to placing in Arab hands the sources and headwaters of rivers that were vital for irrigation and for generating power.

Great Britain, too, viewed the Golan Heights as an integral part of Palestine, and sought to alter the terms of the Sykes-Picot Agreement in accordance with the Zionist approach. But there were disagreements between the British Ministry of Defense and the Foreign Office. The former held that the entire area south of Damascus, including the Hermon and the Golan, should be under British control, while the latter agreed (May 1919) to a line crossing the Golan Heights from north to south. The French, for their part, refused to budge from the line stipulated in the Sykes-Picot Agreement.

British-French Negotiations

Formal talks between Britain and France on the region's future got underway in December 1919. The French representative, Philippe Berthelot, put forward a proposal meant as a compromise between the British demand (Litani-Hermon-

Hijaz railway line) and the terms of Sykes-Picot. The Berthelot line traversed the Golan Heights. Britain was inclined to accept this proposal but finally rejected it under Zionist pressure. In March 1920 the French agreed to a line which would cross the Golan at its center, from the peak of Mount Hermon to the Yarmuk at a distance of 6 to 10 km from the Jordan River and Lake Tiberias. Subsequently, the French even agreed to a line which would cross the upper part of the Golan, leaving Kuneitra inside Palestine. This, however, was again rejected by the British and the Zionists because they insisted on getting the entire Golan Heights and all of northern Palestine (the French boundary line crossed the Galilee). In June 1920, following a change of government in Paris, the French backtracked and proposed a line leaving only 5 km of the Golan Heights inside Palestine and annexing part of Lake Tiberias to French territory.

The French capture of Damascus in July 1920 brought to an end the kingdom of Faisal, son of the Sharif Hussein from the Hijaz, who scarcely three months earlier had crowned himself monarch over all Syria. The High Commissioner of Palestine, Herbert Samuel, proposed sending a military force to seize the Golan Heights. Preparations were made, but the Foreign Office blocked the operation in order to avoid becoming involved in an open confrontation with France so soon after the end of the war.

The capture of Damascus opened the way for new French claims regarding the Golan Heights. The line on which they finally insisted, in September 1920, ran from Samakh in the south to Wadi Masudiye (east of the Jordan's entry to Lake Tiberias), leaving the eastern third of Lake Tiberias outside Palestine. From there the boundary ran northeastward toward Kuneitra (up to the edge of Tell abu Neda) and continued to the source of the Banias, which remained in Palestine.

Agreements of December 1920 and March 1923

On December 23, 1920 the Franco-British Convention relating to "Syria, Lebanon, Palestine and Mesopotamia" was signed in Paris. The agreement demarcated the boundary between the territory of the French Mandate in Syria-Lebanon and of the British Mandate in Iraq and Palestine. The boundaries of the Golan Heights and of Palestine were essentially those which had been urged by France the previous September. By the terms of the agreement, the Yarmuk Valley would come under French control. From there the border ran to Samakh, crossed Lake Tiberias to the mouth of Wadi Masudiye (2.5 km from the Jordan's entry to Lake Tiberias), then westward to Kuneitra, from there to the Banias and on to Metulla. Thus the western part of the Golan Heights, north of Lake Tiberias, remained in Palestine, but Syria received one-third of the lake and the entire area to its east, including Ein Gev and al-Hamma. A four-member commission with broad powers was formed to determine and demarcate the boundary. Of the numerous disputes which arose within the Commission--co-chaired by Lieutenant Colonel M. Paulet (France) and Lieutenant Colonel S.F. Newcombe (Britain)--some were resolved on the spot and some under the guidance of the local authorities in Beirut (the French) and in Jerusalem (the British), while differences of principle were referred to Paris and London for high-level decision. The demarcation work went on for months, being concluded in 1922. In March 1923, following the ratification and signing of the Franco-British agreement, the line determined by the committee became the official boundary between Syria, Lebanon and Palestine.

The Commission in fact considerably altered the December 1920 boundary line: France retained the entire Golan Heights while Britain received the whole of Lake Tiberias. In return for territory which the British received south of Lake Tiberias, and exclusive control over the Jordan River and all the waters of Lake Tiberias and the Hula Valley, they ceded the western part of the Golan Heights which had been earmarked for Palestine in September 1920. The British (or, at least, the Foreign Office) did not consider the Golan Heights to be an essential area, but the Yarmuk Valley was crucial for a railway line and an oil pipeline from Iraq to the Mediterranean. The British indeed assured themselves full control of the lower

Yarmuk (in Palestine and Transjordan), as well as rights to a rail line and oil lines in the Syrian areas of the Yarmuk Valley.

Both sides were anxious to resolve the border issue, a vestige of World War I, in a manner that would cause a minimum of disruption to the population in the new border areas. The Commission, in which the main moving force was Lt. Col. Newcombe, followed three guiding principles: to make the border correspond as closely as possible to prominent natural features; not to dislodge villagers from their land (the Commission ignored the fact that 20,000 acres of land on the Golan Heights were owned by PICA, the Palestine Jewish Colonization Association); and not to sever villages from important roads.

The major geographical principles which guided the two sides were, as Lt. Col. Newcombe put it on January 17, 1923: "Road rights for the French and water rights for Palestine."[6] The French took the position that all the water originating in Syria should belong to Syria, while Palestine could receive the runoff from the Yarmuk and from the sources of the Jordan located in Syria. On the other hand, in order to implement a hydroelectric project proposed by the Russian-born engineer Pinhas Rutenberg, the British sought to obtain exclusive control of the entire length of the Jordan, and all of Lake Tiberias and Lake Hula, even if this meant foregoing the Golan Heights.

Thus the British were able to ensure, first of all, that the sources of the Dan River would lie within Palestine. To assure exclusive control of the Jordan River, the British did not designate Tell Dan as the site of a border marker (even though it was a relatively prominent terrain feature). Instead, they situated the border a short distance to the north of Tell Dan (Tell al-Kadi) so that the sources of the Dan River lay inside Palestine. They saw to it that the agreement stated explicitly that "Tel EL Kadi...remains in Palestine."

Secondly, a British demand that the boundary of Palestine incorporate the source of the Banias (Map No. 2) was initially accepted. The French said they were willing to cede the Banias and its source if they could keep Banias village and the road linking it with Suweida and Kleia, along which they wanted to install a telephone line. The British agreed, but the French subsequently reneged. When the British "temporarily" relinquished their request, the border as demarcated left the Banias Springs in Syrian territory. The penultimate paragraph of the Commission's concluding document states that the British reserve the right to raise their demand for a change in the boundary which would place the source of the Banias in Palestine. However, they did not exercise this option during the 30-year Mandate.

Next, it was agreed that along the entire eastern side of the Hula Valley the boundary would be 100m above the level of Lake Hula, thus ensuring that the entire valley, including its water sources, lay inside Palestine. Further, between the Hula and Lake Tiberias the boundary line did not follow the Jordan River but ran a few dozen meters to its east, ensuring that the entire river was incorporated within Palestine. Similarly, the positioning of the border about 10m to the east of the northeastern part of Lake Tiberias was meant to place that entire body of water in Palestine (even though the 1920 Franco-British agreement had given the French one-third of Lake Tiberias, its eastern section and the right to build a dock at Samakh).

To partially compensate the French for shifting the border away from Lake Tiberias and Lake Hula, the agreement granted the Syrians and the Lebanese certain fishing and other rights. Thus, the railway as far as Samakh would remain under Syrian ownership and the inhabitants of Syria and Lebanon were to have the same fishing and navigation rights in the Hula, Lake Tiberias and in the section of the Jordan between the two lakes as the inhabitants of Palestine, though the government in Palestine would be responsible for policing the lakes.

In February 1922 the border Commission submitted to the French and British governments a detailed report, including three maps showing the precise location of the border as it was marked on the ground. The agreement was approved on March 7, 1923 and signed by the French authorities (in Syria and Lebanon) and the British (in Palestine). The line demarcated by the Commission became the official border between Syria and Lebanon, and Palestine.

Years later, on November 12, 1946, the Syrian Foreign Ministry, through the British legation in Damascus, asked the British government to enter into talks on two fundamental claims, with the aim of shifting the boundary westward: (1) In contravention of the agreement of December 23, 1920, the Mandate government (France) had, in Syria's name, ceded Syrian territory; (2) other Syrian territories had been annexed to Palestine (the Syrian prime minister explained orally that the areas in question were located near Lake Hula and Lake Tiberias).

On July 29, 1947 the British legation replied that the border between Syria and Palestine had been approved by the League of Nations in 1935, and that therefore the matter was closed. Britain also rejected Syria's request to discuss other areas, noting that Damascus had not specified which areas it had in mind.[7] The international boundary thus remained intact.

Good-Neighbor Agreement, 1926

Since the border, as demarcated on the ground, failed to resolve several administrative problems, negotiations began in 1923 on a good-neighbor pact to settle the outstanding questions. On February 2, 1926, the British High Commissioner and the French High Commissioner signed, in Jerusalem, a good-neighbor agreement between Palestine and Syria-Lebanon.[8] Under its terms, those residing near the borders were granted certain privileges. Thus Syrians and Lebanese could use freely, without passports, roads and paths which formed part of the boundary line between their countries and Palestine. The same applied to inhabitants of Palestine (Art. I). Moreover, all those with harvest, cultivation or irrigation rights, or who owned land across the border, could continue to exercise their rights as in the past. To accomplish this, they could cross the border back and forth freely, without passports (Art. III).

The agreement also defined the powers vested in the authorities. In cases of military need, the governments of Syria, Lebanon and Palestine were given the right to make use of roads and paths constituting the border in order to move forces. The relevant government was to be informed as soon as possible (Art. II). Further, the local authorities on both sides of the border would make arrangements ensuring close cooperation in order to preserve public safety. A reciprocal agreement between the police forces allowed cross-border pursuit of anyone committing a serious crime (Art. V). Lastly, all disputes on the agreement's implementation which could not be resolved between the local authorities on both sides of the border, would be referred to a joint commission. That body would consist of four representatives (one each from Syria and Lebanon, and two from Palestine) and a chairman to be appointed with the consent of the French and British high commissioners (Art. XII).

This agreement was not implemented during the course of the Israel-Syria armistice regime, as it was intended to serve states that maintained peaceful relations. The armistice agreement, in contrast, bore a military character and barred border crossings in either direction.

Mandatory Border Agreements: Interim Conclusion

The demarcation of the borders in the Middle East after World War I by Britain and France left the Golan Heights outside the boundaries of Mandatory Palestine and outside the State of Israel that succeeded it. This happened in the course of a series of deals made by the British with the French concerning the Syria-Iraq boundary (Syria received access to the Tigris), the Syria-Transjordan border, and Africa (partitioning of Cameroon). The British moves in this period did not satisfy the needs of the Zionist Organization. Nor were the British eager to fight for the Zionists' positions. They did achieve the inclusion in Palestine of the Dan River (the primary source of the Jordan), the Jordan, Lake Hula and Lake Tiberias, but they ceded the Golan Heights and the Banias Springs. The result, then, was that only one of the Jordan's sources was included in Palestine, a situation which in the years ahead would spark a struggle between Israel and Syria over control of water. From the Israeli point of view, then, Britain's achievements on the border question left much to be desired: it ceded the Golan and failed to incorporate all the water sources within the area of Palestine.

The Syrian-Israeli Armistice Line[9] (Map No. 3)

We now move to Syrian-Israeli border negotiations in 1949 and the early 1950s. The discussions on the location of the armistice line--within the framework of the negotiations that led up to the signing of the armistice agreement--began in a meeting with the Syrians held near Mahanayim on April 21, 1949. This key issue would remain a focus of discussion throughout the negotiations. Since the Syrian Army had succeeded during the 1948 war in capturing areas west of the international boundary (notably west of Banat Yaqub Bridge and southeast of Lake Tiberias), Israel found itself in a situation which was the reverse of its experience in earlier armistice talks with Egypt, Lebanon and Jordan. In those cases Israel wanted the armistice lines to reflect the war's military outcome--i.e., the truce lines--as these were more convenient for it than the lines contained in the UN partition plan or than any other line that the Arabs could accept as a basis for negotiations. With Syria, however, Israel sought to invoke a new principle, according to which the armistice line would correspond with the international boundary. Syria's position was that the armistice line should be congruous with the ceasefire line.

The Syrian delegation took an extreme opening stand on other issues as well. According to Henri Vigier, the representative to the talks of UN mediator Ralphe Bunche, the Syrians sought "Jewish withdrawal from western Galilee." They also sought the replacement of the truce lines with armistice lines on the Israeli-Syrian frontier, in order to consolidate the status quo of their conquest. If accepted, this situation would have perpetuated the Syrian forces' advance in the Banias area and left Mishmar Hayarden on the Syrian side; the Jordan River would become the armistice line between Lake Hula and Lake Tiberias, which would have been "halved by north-south." According to Syrian Foreign Minister Emir Aadel Arsalan, "Fawzi Selo, head of the Syrian delegation to the negotiations, wanted to secure conditions even better than those over which [Syrian ruler Hosni] Zaim was ready to compromise."[10] It is, accordingly, possible that some of these demands were initiated by the Syrian representative to the talks and were not dictated by the political level.

The Israeli delegation stated its final position from the outset. After the third meeting, the delegation received clear orders from which it was not permitted to budge: "The only demarcation line which is to be inserted into an armistice agreement is the international frontier." It was emphasized strongly that "this is not a position for bargaining, it is the last word of the Israeli delegation."[11]

The differences between the two sides over the demarcation line were well understood by Vigier. His assessment as the talks began was that the "Syrian position is first in series of positions for bargaining while Israeli position may as they stated be final."[12] Both countries wanted to extract optimal territorial gains from the demarcation lines while creating a convenient point of departure for possible future political negotiations (the assumption was that peace talks between Israel and the Arab states would commence within six months).

Israel was in a stronger position in the talks, its other neighbors having already forsaken the military option as part of the armistice agreements. Damascus was concerned that Israel would renew the fighting now that Syria was the sole remaining adversary. In fact, Israel was not thinking in those terms, its national priority then being the absorption of new immigrants.

Under the compromise that was eventually reached, Syria was to withdraw from all the territory it had captured in the war west of the international boundary. That land, together with other areas (such as Ein Gev), would be demilitarized. The two countries were unable to reach agreement on the question of sovereignty in the Demilitarized Zone (DZ) and preferred to leave the issue unresolved rather than risk renewed hostilities. This impasse set in motion a struggle which initially--in the first years of the armistice regime--was played out cautiously, through the use of passive means (purchase of land, etc.), but later turned violent. The armistice line in the DZ, where it did not correspond with the international boundary, passed between the Israeli and Syrian ceasefire lines. As a result, the armistice line declined in importance in the DZ and in effect two lines were created: an eastern line, corresponding with the international boundary and serving as both the border of Syria and the eastern boundary of the DZ; and a western line which demarcated the DZ on the Israeli side but which Israel treated, to all intents and purposes, as though it were nonexistent, other than observing the prohibition on military forces crossing the line.

Negotiations on Partitioning the Demilitarized Zone[13]

In May 1951 a serious confrontation erupted between Syria and Israel (against the backdrop of Israel's Hula drainage project) during which the DZ was partitioned de facto along the following lines:

* **Southern sector**: Al-Hamma, Hirbet Tawfiq, Nuqeib and the ascent to the Golan Heights were under Syrian control; the rest was in Israeli hands.
* **Central sector**: The area east of the Jordan and the triangle west of the Jordan and north of the Jordan's entry to Lake Tiberias were under Syrian control; the area west of the Jordan was Israeli-controlled.
* **Northern sector**: The majority was under Syrian control.

Neither side was interested in further violence. The time had come to reach an understanding, perhaps even a compromise, on the cause of the conflict, namely the DZ. The initiative to hold talks was apparently Syria's, beginning in February 1951. The initial proposal, adduced by the Syrian prime minister, was to arrive at a modus vivendi according to which Syria would administer those areas that were populated by Arabs, with the rest under Israeli administration. Subsequently, the Syrians expressed readiness to discuss the dissolution of the DZ and its partition between the two states.

Following months of prior discussion in informal meetings between the sides' senior representatives to the Mixed Armistice Commission, the first high-level official meeting was held on October 9, 1953. All told, ten such meetings took place during a seven-month period; the final session was held on May 27, 1953.

In these secret negotiations, nearly all of which took the form of direct but informal meetings, with minimal UN intervention, the two states tried to reach a settlement despite the tense situation which by then prevailed between Israel and other Arab states. Agreement was indeed reached on the issues of greatest concern to Israel, namely the location of the new boundary line, which left Israel with the water sources of the Jordan, Hula and Tiberias, and Israel's execution of a project to divert the waters of the Jordan. But the sides were unable to agree on partitioning the DZ because neither leadership was willing to make the necessary concessions. Israel would not give up territory it considered its own (the area of the DZ west of the international boundary) without a quid pro quo in the form of a revision in the status of its relations with Syria--in other words, a transition from armistice to peace. Syria, for its part, believed that a territorial settlement with Israel (leaving the majority of the DZ in the latter's hands), which might pacify the Syrian-Israeli border, would constitute a deviation from the collective stand of the Arab states, i.e., continuation of the state of war.

Conclusion

One lesson derived from the experience of the armistice regime is that an Israel-Syria peace treaty must not leave crucial issues open and undefined, as this can lead to conflict instead of conciliation. In effect, between 1948 and the Six-Day War of 1967 no clearly defined border existed between Israel and Syria. In certain sections the line corresponded with the international boundary, while elsewhere--in areas where a demilitarized zone was supposed to be established under the terms of the 1949 armistice agreement--the border reflected the de facto partition of the area between Israel and Syria, with the bulk of the territory under Israeli control. Generally speaking, in the 18-year period between the start of the armistice regime and the 1967 war, Israel sought to have the border correspond with the international boundary, whereas Syria opposed this and tried to acquire status and influence in the area of the DZ to the west of the international boundary.

The international boundary between Syria and Palestine was decided by France and Great Britain, following protracted negotiations. Although there is nothing sacred about this line--indeed, the Syrians later (1946) raised certain objections to it--it remains a recognized international boundary. It is to this line that Syria has demanded, and will continue to demand, that Israel pull back from the Golan Heights.

Syrian maps demarcate this international boundary. Conceivably, however, in peace negotiations Syria would demand not only Israeli withdrawal from the Golan and Syrian sovereignty there, but also control over areas just west of the international boundary which were formerly in its control, such as al-Hamma.

Chapter 3. Lessons from Agreements and Negotiations

In the period between the 1948 Israeli War of Independence and the Madrid conference in 1991, Israel and Syria engaged in four rounds of negotiations, which produced two agreements: the General Armistice Agreement of 20 July 1949, which existed de jure until the Six-Day War of 1967 but was maintained de facto only until 1954; and the Disengagement Agreement, which was signed in May 1974 and remains in effect as of this writing (early 1994) and is therefore dealt with in some depth in this chapter.

The four negotiating rounds had little in common; indeed, there were substantial differences among them. Despite this, and despite the fact that considerable changes have since taken place in both Syria and Israel, it is useful to glance at these earlier talks and try to glean from them lessons which may be applicable to the 1990s.

The first negotiations (April 5-July 20, 1949) produced the armistice agreement, as described above. Israel had previously concluded armistice accords with Egypt, Jordan and Lebanon; Syria was the last Arab state that entered into negotiations on this issue.

A number of factors in this round of negotiations are worthy of note. First, when the talks began the two sides displayed polarized approaches over an issue that each regarded as crucial:[1] Syria wanted the armistice line to reflect its military gains west of the international boundary, while Israel insisted that Syrian forces withdraw to that boundary. In the course of the talks, Syria gradually backtracked from its opening position.

Secondly, in this period the UN had a prominent standing in the Middle East, where it exercised greater influence than the Great Powers (the US, Soviet Union, Britain and France). The UN was directly involved in the negotiations from the outset, its representative serving as an active mediator. Although fear of the war's renewal contributed heavily in convincing the Arabs to agree to an armistice, it is very doubtful whether agreement would have been reached without UN mediation.

Finally, in these negotiations military officers from the two sides, who were not previously acquainted, held several secret and informal meetings in an effort to surmount difficulties which were immediately apparent and to prevent a possible renewal of hostilities. The purpose of these meetings was to overcome the major obstacle of demarcating the armistice line. Three such encounters took place without a UN or other external presence,[2] beginning on April 15, ten days after the start of the formal negotiations. Although this direct dialogue did not produce the hoped-for results, it did reflect the awareness by both sides, at this very early stage, of the need for informal, private talks to supplement the formal framework. Syrian ruler Hosni al-Zaim even proposed a meeting with the Israeli prime minister in order to discuss the armistice line and a separate peace between the two countries. The meeting was never held.

The second round of negotiations began on July 25, 1949 and continued until the end of 1953. These "continuing" talks were held by representatives of the two states to the Mixed Armistice Commission (which oversaw the agreement's implementation). Their goal was to moderate border relations and solve ongoing problems. The distinctive fact about these negotiations was that prior to May 28, 1951[3] they consisted of formal and informal meetings alike. Beginning in November 1951 only informal meetings were held, during which the sides gradually moved farther apart, and tension on the borders increased.

For nearly two years, then, until May 28, 1951, the Mixed Armistice Commission (MAC) met about once a week in order to consider complaints raised by the sides. Informal, personal conversations were also held on these occasions and it was through these, rather than in the formal contacts, that agreements were reached. The venue alternated between the Customs House on the Syrian side of the border, and the Shulamit Hotel in Rosh Pinna, on the Israeli side.

On May 28, 1951 the regular meetings of the MAC were suspended. The reason was Israel's objection to the commission serving as a platform for Syria to air complaints about matters relating to the Demilitarized Zone. Syria, however, was adamant on this point. Since neither country wanted a deterioration along the borders, two ways were found to circumvent the deadlock. In cases of serious incidents, the commission convened in emergency session, while to deal with ongoing problems unofficial meetings were held between the heads of the two delegations. These meetings, which in some cases took place in the presence of the UN chairman, continued until nearly the end of 1954. The first unofficial meeting in the series took place on November 13, 1951, following which 18 meetings were held in 1952, three in 1953 and two in 1954.

In the informal meetings the delegation heads discussed matters of interest to both states, although not the DZ. If the UN representative was not present, he was later briefed jointly by the two delegation heads. During this period the two states conducted a pragmatic border policy; by meeting informally over a period of three years they were able to reduce and sometimes prevent tensions, maintain quiet along the border and resolve current problems.[4] Thus, for example, Syria was the first Arab state to sign (January 19, 1952) a mutual agreement with Israel for returning ships which, for reasons beyond their control, such as inclement weather, had strayed into the other state's territorial waters.[5] The informal meetings also allowed the sides to develop the understanding necessary for the opening of high-level, secret negotiations on partitioning the DZ (see below). In most cases the two countries took a practical approach. The agreements that were reached were always honored--with a single exception, when the Syrians reneged on an agreement, reached July 31, 1952, on dividing the waters of the Doufeila Spring, near Kibbutz Shamir.

Concurrently, Syria and the United States were engaged in secret negotiations to improve their relations. During those talks, Syrian ruler Adib Shishaqli expressed readiness to reach a "nonbelligerency" settlement with Israel. The Syrian-American negotiations ended without an agreement being reached.

The third round of negotiations, which began on October 9, 1952 and lasted until May 27, 1953, centered on partitioning the DZ, the bulk of which lay west of the international boundary. By the very fact of entering into these talks, Israel signaled its readiness to transfer part of the DZ to Syrian control.[6] Ten meetings were held within this framework, in most of which the Israeli delegation was headed by Major General Moshe Dayan and the Syrian delegation by Colonel Ghassan Jdid.

The singular aspect of these negotiations was that they were unofficial, were conducted by high-ranking personalities, and third-party (i.e., UN) involvement was minimal. Indeed, no compromise proposals were put forward by a third party throughout the talks. Through direct contact the sides arrived at compromises and agreements, e.g., regarding demarcation of the new boundary line along most of the front. Although both sides ultimately drew back from an agreement to partition the DZ, the negotiations were conducted in a manner radically different from those that preceded the signing of the armistice agreement in 1949. By now the two sides no longer required the assistance of a mediator and were able to make mutual concessions and compromises on their own.

As for the fourth round of negotiations, it produced the Disengagement Agreement on the Golan Heights, which was concluded in 1974--in the aftermath of the Yom Kippur War the previous October--and was still in effect as this book went to press, in 1994. The negotiations began against the backdrop of a recent precedent: on January 18, 1974 the chiefs of staff of Egypt and Israel signed a disengagement agreement relating to the Sinai Peninsula. Virtually the entire talks were conducted by US Secretary of State Henry Kissinger,[7] who negotiated with each side separately. Kissinger's shuttle diplomacy between Jerusalem (23 talks with the Israeli team of ministers) and Damascus (14 talks with President Assad),[8] which had been planned to take one week, lasted 32 days.

The two countries were at cross-purposes. Syria wanted to set in motion a process that would bring about Israel's withdrawal from the Golan Heights, whereas Israel viewed the negotiations as an instrument to secure quiet and to strengthen its hold on the Golan Heights.[9] Israel and Syria were invited to send delegations to a conference in Geneva only after Kissinger was able, through his marathon shuttle, to effect a compromise between the positions of the two states on the Disengagement Agreement. The disengagement lines were agreed upon during these negotiations, but the final evacuation stages had yet to be concluded and a precise summation was required concerning the location of the lines in a number of places.

The Israeli side, seeking to confer upon the Geneva Conference political significance, included senior civilian officials in its delegation (Mordechai Gazit and Shabtai Rosenne from the Foreign Ministry). The Syrian team consisted of officers and one civilian. The officers in both delegations appeared in uniform. The conference went on for one week. Major General Ensio Siilasvuo, commander of the UN Emergency Force, sat at the head of the table with the delegations on either side. The Syrian representatives displayed a businesslike attitude; they had authority and they kept their word.

However, there was no contact between the Israeli and Syrian negotiators. Indeed, the Syrians came to Geneva not as a separate delegation but as part of the Egyptian military working group. In the meetings, the Syrians addressed only the UN chairman, never the Israelis. They did not talk to the Israelis, did not shake hands with them and kept their distance from them. Nor were there any informal contacts with the Syrians.[10] In other words, there were no direct negotiations between Israel and Syria.

Two agreements were signed at Geneva. The Disengagement Agreement, signed on May 31, 1974, was based on the summations which Kissinger worked out with the two sides (see Appendix 1). The second agreement (June 5) detailed the military limitations imposed on both sides and the role of the UN. Neither side signed this agreement. It was incorporated in a statement by General Siilasvuo which asserted that the two sides agreed to it (see Appendix 2).

The Disengagement Agreement (see Map no. 4) brought to an end the war of attrition which Syria had waged against Israel since the end of the Yom Kippur War. Its main points[11] were:

A. Israel and Syria undertook to "scrupulously observe the ceasefire on land, sea and air," and to "refrain from all military actions against each other."

B. The IDF would withdraw from the territory it had captured in the Yom Kippur War, as well as from the town of Kuneitra and the village of Rafid as far as Line A, which would now become the Israeli forces' forward line. The Syrians' forward line would be Line B.

C. The entire area east of Line A would come "under Syrian administration, and Syrian civilians will return to this territory."

D. An "area of separation" would be created between Israeli and Syrian forces by means of a narrow demilitarized zone between Line A and Line B. A United Nations Disengagement Observer Force (UNDOF), numbering 1,250 personnel, would be stationed in that area.

E. An area of 20 sq km on each side of the separation (demilitarization) zone would be divided equally into two strips, in which forces and weapons would be limited:

(1) In an area extending 10 km east of the Syrian line (Line B) and 10 km west of the Israeli line (Line A), each side could maintain a military force no larger than two brigades, to include: 6,000 soldiers, 75 tanks and 36 122 mm short-range howitzers (or the equivalent).

(2) In the second strip, beginning 10 km from each line of separation and extending a further 10 km, each side could maintain 162 guns with a range not exceeding 20 km (such that the forward forces of each side would be outside the other's artillery range) and 450 tanks of all types. Surface-to-air missiles were not to be deployed closer than 25 km from both sides of the lines of separation.

F. Each side's air force could operate as far as its line of separation "without interference from the other side."

G. The function of UNDOF would be to maintain the ceasefire and ensure its strict observance. The UN force was to supervise the agreement's implementation by carrying out inspections at least once every 15 days, and when requested by either side, and report the results to both parties. It would be equipped with "personal weapons of a defensive character," which would be used only in self-defense. The troops were to be selected by the UN Secretary General from UN member-states that were not permanent members of the Security Council.

The Disengagement Agreement on the Golan Heights has been upheld successfully since 1974, for a number of reasons. First, from the outset, expectations from the agreement by both sides, and Israel in particular, were far lower than those which they entertained regarding the earlier armistice agreement. Whereas the 1974 agreement was intended only to prevent the use of force, the armistice accord had been meant explicitly to constitute a transition stage from a ceasefire, which was already in effect, to a peace treaty.

Secondly, the Disengagement Agreement is relatively simple in character. The boundary (i.e., the separation-of-forces line) is clearly defined and contains no problematic loopholes such as a demilitarized zone in an area which both sides consider sensitive and in which sovereignty or authority is undefined. Because it contains no vaguely worded clauses on crucial issues, the Disengagement Agreement offers little cause for the two sides to become involved in a struggle. A less positive element is the absence of a joint mechanism, such as a mixed commission of Israeli and Syrian officers. Still, the agreement has been maintained, with the aid of UNDOF, without contact between the sides. Indeed, as neither Syria nor Israel regards a change in the status quo on the Golan Heights as urgent, both can continue to live with the May 1974 agreement.

But the main reason for the agreement's observance is that since 1949 the experience of both sides is that violence may begin on a limited scale, but it ultimately evolves into a large-scale war. Syria has learned that there are no "small" wars, and that if it launches limited hostilities it must be ready for total war. Since Syria is not prepared for a conflict on that scale, its current interest is to maintain quiet on the border, including the prevention of terrorist raids from its territory into the Israeli-held Golan Heights. In Lebanon, too, the Syrians are careful not to cross tacitly agreed "red lines" in order to avoid a premature confrontation with the IDF. Yet this passive, pragmatic policy clearly does not reflect Syria's basic goal, which is to bring about a change in the status quo, whether by force or by political pressure, without becoming involved in a war before it wishes to.

In view of the longevity of the Disengagement Agreement, we should look also at UNDOF's contribution. This will help determine how useful a similar presence might be as part of the security arrangements in a future political agreement. An objective and thorough analysis of UNDOF was published in 1987.[12] It may be summed up as follows:

UNDOF bears no responsibility for making peace between Israel and Syria. Its success stems from the desire of the parties not to cause problems on the Golan Heights. It enjoys optimal conditions at the local level; in both Syria and Israel the armed forces are under political control with respect to major decisions; both governments are interested in preserving quiet on the Golan Heights; and the quarter-of-a-million Palestinians residing in the Damascus area are prohibited from conducting an independent policy. Were they given free rein, and were they to shell Israeli forces west of the separation line, UNDOF could do nothing.

Although the UN force cannot create the conditions to ensure its success, it also contributes to maintaining quiet. UNDOF prevents incidents stemming from supervision of the demilitarization accord. The mutual suspicion held by Syria and Israel toward one another make supervision by an objective third party important. UNDOF also reduces suspicions and tension on both sides, even if only by means of regular inspections which show that there has been no increase of forces in the areas of limitation. If such an increase does occur on one side, UNDOF can warn the other state. Finally, UNDOF is able to mitigate crises, but only if the sides wish to cooperate.

To sum up this point, UNDOF contributes, albeit in a limited manner, to the preservation of the Israeli-Syrian Disengagement Agreement. The agreement, and UNDOF's mediation, are viable because both states have an interest in them. The deployment of each army enables it to defend against and repulse a surprise attack by the other side. In other words, Israel's defense of the Golan Heights and Syria's defense of Damascus are based on each country's armed strength, and the presence of UNDOF in the demilitarized zone between the sides can contribute as long as the two countries wish to preserve the status quo.

Conclusion

On the basis of past experience, the success of negotiations with the Syrians would appear to depend on the following elements:

* The IDF's deterrent capability.
* The similarity of the goals pursued by each side.
* The degree of readiness for compromise on disparate issues.
* A mutual determination to overcome mistrust and suspicion.

From the perspective of the current talks, the principal lesson to be drawn from past negotiations is that a lengthy period of peace negotiations between Israel and Syria would be marked by fierce and acrimonious discussions. Neither country would budge from its opening positions. During this lengthy period, a third party (the US) would undoubtedly have to intervene and put forward compromise proposals which take into account the interests of the two states. Only after this, when the two sides have embarked on the road of mutual concessions, could negotiations conceivably be based on mutual compromise. It is most improbable that Syria would be willing to conduct substantive secret talks with Israel, at least as long as Israel is unwilling to agree to withdraw from the Golan Heights. The stability of the Disengagement Agreement shows, further, that Syria is capable of fulfilling and maintaining an agreement.

Chapter 4. Security Relations, 1949-1955[1]

Before analyzing possible security risks and problems that Israel will face as the result of a political settlement with Syria, it is useful to survey the security relations between the two states that prevailed during the armistice regime. During part of that period the border was quiet and the two sides cooperated to preserve that situation.

The armistice regime between Israel and Syria (and between Israel and its other neighbors) was intended to serve as a brief transition stage leading to peace. Instead, it took on a permanent status. Despite proposals by two Syrian leaders, Zaim and Shishaqli, to embark on a process leading to a peace treaty, and despite Israel's desire for peace, the two sides did not move in that direction. The principal problem lay in their inability to overcome their basic differences over the Demilitarized Zone (DZ), which were already apparent in the negotiations on the armistice agreement. Because of that impasse, the sovereignty and political status of the DZ were left undefined and hence were open to conflicting interpretations. This key issue was to become a serious obstacle in the implementation of the armistice agreement.

In any event, in Israeli-Syrian border relations, what was supposed to be a provisional phase hardened into a permanent situation. The two sides were faced with the choice of either adapting their policy to the new situation and trying to strengthen the armistice regime, or undermining and eventually abrogating it. In reality, they assayed both options. At times a policy of force determined border relations; at other times confrontation was avoided, direct negotiations were conducted and agreement was reached on certain arrangements. As Table 1 shows, relations between the two states fluctuated between pragmatism and power plays.

For much of this period, then (July 1949-April 1951, July 1951-early 1954), Israeli-Syrian border relations were relatively calm, in contrast to the tension that prevailed at the time between Israel and the other border states (with the exception of Lebanon).

This fact contradicts the prevailing picture--in the diplomatic community, in scholarly research and among Israeli and world public opinion--of Syria as always having been the most extreme and most violent Arab state vis-a-vis Israel.

A second conclusion to be drawn from the period of the armistice regime is that--again, contrary to the prevailing Israeli view--both countries, and not only Syria, were to blame for the tension and violent clashes. Israel was not always the innocent lamb and Syria not always the wolf. In the first years of the armistice regime it was Israel that tried unilaterally to effect changes in the status quo in the DZ. Syria responded violently, because at the time its interest was to preserve the status quo.

The existence of the Mixed Armistice Commission (MAC) frequently helped the two countries to pursue a pragmatic policy. This was reflected in contacts between the delegations and their joint handling of current border problems. These moves, however, were motivated not by a common aspiration for peace but by a desire to avert a slide into violence and, finally, war. Until mid-1954, even when the sides opted to use force, at times quite intensely, they always sought to control it and steer clear of a broad collision. Indeed, the outcome of that policy spurred both Syria and Israel to return to a cautious and pragmatic relationship. Following this period, border relations began to deteriorate, the Armistice Commission ceased to meet even on an informal basis, and pragmatism was gradually superseded by an approach based on use of force.

The Israeli-Syrian armistice regime lasted until the June 1967 war, but years earlier, in late 1954 and early 1955, it had already reached a watershed. Contact and cooperation between representatives of the two countries ended, the MAC virtually ceased to function, and border relations were exacerbated. In contrast, the earlier period from 1949 to 1953 witnessed not only struggles and clashes but also settlements and compromises, with both sides displaying considerable pragmatism. The armistice agreements that Israel signed with Egypt, Jordan and Syria did not

Table I. Syrian-Israeli Relations, 1949-1967

Period	*Description*	*Content*
April-July 1949	Limited pragmatism along with confrontation	Armistice negotiations, including proposal for Zaim-Ben-Gurion meeting to discuss peace; Syrian readiness to absorb 300,000 Palestinian refugees.
August 1949	Limited, non-violent confrontation	First crisis portending possible collapse of agreement, over Israel's right to establish new settlements in DZ and, later, status of the police there. Change in UN interpretation provides way out: new settlements could be created, but with chairman's consent; no Syrian regional police force to be set up in DZ.
September 1949-February 1951	Pragmatism and limited confrontation	Calm during first 18 months, both sides wishing to avoid renewed military clash and give priority to alternative national goals. Period typified by: cautious security policy, close contact by two states' representatives, search for understanding, and compromise rather than extreme positions.
February-March 1951	Between pragmatism and confrontation	Beginning of conflict over Israel's Hula drainage project. Negotiations include meeting of two sides' deputy chiefs-of-staff, in search of a compromise. Sporadic Syrian light-arms fire directed at Israel's heavy earthmoving equipment.
April 1951	Violent confrontation	Violent clashes over Hula drainage project, no meetings between sides. Seven members of Israeli police patrol to al-Hamma killed by a Syrian outpost. Israel retaliates with aerial bombing; Tel al-Mutila clashes. De facto partitioning of DZ.

Late 1951-August 1953	Advanced pragmatism	Violent clashes had shown that use of power could not solve problems and that moderation and calm were required. Period of reduced violence and greater pragmatism ensues. In formal contacts: during Syria-US talks, Shishaqli expresses readiness to improve relations with Israel by signing non-belligerency agreement, absorbing several hundred thousand refugees. Talks and agreement on ad hoc problems: e.g., commercial vessels entering other side's waters in storm would be released, talks on dividing Doufeila waters, abortive secret talks on partitioning DZ.
September 1953-early 1954	Confrontation and limited pragmatism	Conflict over Jordan diversion is political, non-violent. Syria objects to Israeli works in DZ aimed at diverting Jordan waters into Lake Tiberias (Kinneret). But Syrians do not initiate hostilities; pragmatism still carries a certain weight in Israeli-Syrian relations.
March 1954-June 1967 war	Violent clashes, little pragmatism	Conflict over northeast area of Lake Tiberias. Return to period of violent confrontation, though not on full scale. Reliance on force, but also on political efforts such as Armistice Commission and emergency sessions, with both sides trying to win political support from the Commission for their claims.

eliminate violent confrontation between them. But a survey of relations between Syria and Israel shows that the two states often opted for mutual accommodation on issues of principle.

Pragmatism in relations between the two countries took two forms. There was "passive pragmatism," with both sides pursuing a cautious policy and avoiding violence; while the more advanced form was an "active pragmatism," in which the two countries cooperated in trying to resolve routine border problems by mutual consent. This second form of pragmatism was basically tactical in character, but there were cases when it took on strategic ramifications. For example, the agreement with Syria on returning errant commercial vessels, which was implemented in practice for several years, was undoubtedly a deviation from the armistice agreement in the direction of peaceful relations. Then too, the very fact that secret negotiations on partitioning the DZ were conducted in a period when the other Arab states rejected any new agreements with Israel, reflected the strength of the relations that had developed between the sides (even if these negotiations produced no results).

Finally, there were the proposals put forward by two Syrian leaders, Zaim in 1949 and Shishaqli in 1952, to enhance Israeli-Syrian relations and ultimately make peace, with Syria ready to absorb a large number of Palestinian refugees. These showed that the Damascus leadership (particularly Shishaqli) believed that improved relations would ameliorate Syria's domestic situation, and that it was willing to go far beyond the rest of the Arab world at that time.

Several factors aggravated border relations, while others helped moderate them. Among the primary causes of exacerbation was the fact that the Syrian territory in this sector, which was heavily fortified along its entire length, was some 500m above the Israeli area (with the exception of a narrow strip at the Jordan's entry into Lake Tiberias, where Israel had the topographical advantage). Superior terrain gave the Syrians a tactical advantage which enabled them to disrupt life in Israeli settlements in the Jordan Valley and in the Hula Valley even with light-arms fire.[2] In contrast, to silence the Syrians Israel had to launch an extensive military operation.

Secondly, because the compromise on the creation of a demilitarized zone (nearly all of it west of the international boundary) did not include agreement on sovereignty or responsibility for civil administration and control in the DZ, a struggle gradually evolved between the two countries over the future of the zone. Syria was ready to accept the DZ's undefined status, but Israel initiated activity on the ground to change the status quo in its favor and secure full control of the area.[3] Many of the ensuing incidents were triggered by Israel's attempts to extend the areas under cultivation on Arab-owned land in the DZ, with the Syrians opening fire in response. A large-scale military confrontation during the period March-May 1951, sparked by Syrian opposition to Israel's Lake Hula drainage project, developed into a violent struggle for control of the entire DZ.[4]

Further, following early years in which they adopted a pragmatic approach toward Israel, the Arab states gradually changed their attitude for the worse. Readiness to preserve the status quo created by the armistice agreements was supplanted by an anti-Israel stance. Limited hostilities erupted, followed by fierce Israeli reprisal raids. As a result, security relations between the sides deteriorated and the countdown began to the Sinai Campaign of October 1956. Then too, the acute polarization between Israel's water needs and Syrian interests, a situation compounded by the fact that the sources of Israel's running water lay either near or across the border, was a major source of tension between the countries (see Ch. 17). Finally, a central element of Syrian nationalism, which had burgeoned even before the Ba'th Party assumed power in 1963, was opposition to Israel.

But there were also moderating factors in the relationship. One was the aforementioned pragmatic policy conducted by Syria and the Arab states in the first years following the signing of the armistice agreements, in the aftermath of their failure in the 1948 war. Note, for example, a document written by Moshe Dayan in October 1949, in the wake of a dispute with the Syrians over the establishment of Jewish settlements in the DZ, in which he states that the Syrians "intended [originally] to fulfill the [armistice] agreement sincerely according to their interpretation."[5] In the same vein, one may speculate that the Arab states may have been willing to sign a peace treaty with Israel if the latter had been ready to forego the territory it had captured beyond the 1947 partition lines and to absorb all the refugees who had abandoned their homes during the war. The US government supported both conditions.[6]

Indeed, at least until the end of 1963, the two states did not want to go to war. It was only at a meeting of Arab chiefs of staff, held in December of that year, that Syria urged a war (in order to prevent Israel's diversion of the Jordan waters). This was rejected at the time by the other Arab states. In this context we note that, until the Six-Day War, Syria was cautious about utilizing its topographic advantage at the western extremity of the Golan Heights to disrupt life in the Israeli settlements below on a continuous basis. The Syrian leadership evidently understood that Israel would find this an intolerable situation and a casus belli. The total control exercised by the Syrian military over troops and civilians in the border area meant that no locally initiated incidents developed there, in contrast to Israel's other borders.

It is extremely difficult, perhaps impossible, to draw direct lessons from the security relations between Syria and Israel in the early 1950s and apply them to the peace process of the early 1990s. Syria has undergone vast changes in the intervening four decades (the Ba'th Party has ruled there for nearly 30 years), as has Israel and indeed the entire Middle East. Still, it is a reasonable assumption that the latest peace negotiations between Syria and Israel have been prompted by the concern of both countries that the persistence of the status quo could lead to a devastating war from which neither side would benefit. Certainly this points to a foundation of continuity in Syrian-Israeli relations since the early 1950s.

Chapter 5. Israel's 1967 Proposal and 1970 Plan

More than a quarter of a century has passed since Syria (and Egypt) rejected a peace proposal put forward by the Israeli government in June 1967, based on the principle of "territory for peace." An entire generation, filled with dramatic developments in the global and Middle Eastern arenas, passed before Syria, in the 1990s, adopted the approach it had once spurned. By then, however, Israel had its own reservations about the original principle. Indeed, an Israeli peace plan from late 1970 left two-thirds of the Golan Heights within Israel's boundaries.

The Peace Proposal of June 1967

Israel's peace proposal of June 19, 1967 contained a major security element regarding the Golan Heights--one that has remained a constant ever since: complete demilitarization. While the Six-Day War still raged, Israeli Prime Minister Levy Eshkol asked Cabinet ministers to work out their stands on the Arab-Israel conflict in the light of the emerging Israeli victory. Among the subjects to be addressed were: future relations with Egypt; the status of the Sinai Peninsula, the Gaza Strip, the West Bank, the Old City of Jerusalem and the formerly demilitarized areas in the north; and the water issue (sources of the Jordan).[1] Eshkol's questionnaire, to which ministers were asked to respond in Cabinet meetings, came in response to a memorandum from Defense Minister Moshe Dayan which, among other points, urged the prime minister to set policy goals.[2]

What induced the Israeli government to make decisions of principle on the territorial issue so soon after the war? Part of the reason probably lay in the precedent of 1957. At that time, following the Sinai Campaign, Israel was forced to pull back to the Green Line without receiving a political quid pro quo. This was due at least in part to Israel's failure to grasp that a basic change had occurred,[3] and its belief that the United States would not demand a pullback. During and immediately following the

1967 war there was also a flood of queries from the world press about Israel's policy on the newly captured territories. Finally, on June 14, 1967, Abba Eban and Gideon Raphael reported to Eshkol that the situation at the UN required Israel to make certain decisions, and a series of discussions was held on the subject.[4]

The Cabinet and the Ministerial Committee on Security deliberated the new policy from June 15 to June 19, but already at the conclusion of the first day's discussion a draft document was drawn up. This stated, with respect to Syria, that a peace treaty would be based on the international boundary, and that until such a treaty was signed, Israel would retain the territories it had captured. The terms of a peace treaty were, first, absolute demilitarization of the Golan Heights, the details to be determined in the treaty; and secondly, an ironclad guarantee of Syrian noninterference with the flow of water from the sources of the Jordan to Israel, whether by means of a border adjustment or through an agreement between the two countries which would secure the water sources.[5]

Few disagreements arose in the Cabinet discussions about the terms of a peace settlement with Syria. Herut (later Likud) leader Menachem Begin, who had joined the government a few days before the start of the war, consented to the above formula, stating at the June 15 meeting: "Israel will remain on the Golan Heights until Syria signs a peace treaty, and when Syria agrees, even then [Israel] will not return the area before Syria agrees to the terms of the Golan Heights' demilitarization."

Other ministers also spoke out. Yigal Allon proposed that in a peace treaty with Syria both the demilitarization of the Golan Heights and border adjustments were essential, as was an Israeli presence at the Banias (a source of the Jordan) to prevent its diversion. Abba Eban argued, in contrast, that it would suffice for the peace treaty to include a clause prohibiting Syrian diversion of the Jordan's sources. As for Defense Minister Dayan, he thought that, practically speaking, there was no prospect that Egypt and Syria would sign peace treaties with Israel. Still, Dayan proposed that Israel consent to sign such treaties on the basis of the international boundary, without further elaboration of terms. A different approach was taken by Eliahu Sasson, who said that peace treaties should be signed only after the Arab states agreed to conditions that Israel considered *sine qua non* for peace, such as demilitarization and freedom of navigation, and also implemented them in practice. Prime Minister Eshkol's view was that Israel should spell out in advance its terms for signing peace treaties. In the case of Syria, he thought that the international boundary should become the official border. Eshkol did not mention any other conditions.[6]

On June 19 the government decided to adopt the June 15 proposal of the Ministerial Committee on Security on the conditions for making peace with Syria (and with Egypt). The section of the resolution referring to a settlement with Syria stated:

> Israel proposes making a treaty of peace with Syria on the basis of the international boundary and the security needs of Israel.
>
> The peace treaty will necessitate:
> 1. Demilitarization of the Syrian plateau now held by the IDF;
> 2. Absolute assurance of [Syrian] noninterference with the flow of water from the sources of the Jordan to Israel.
>
> Until the signing of the peace treaty with Syria, Israel will continue to hold the territories which it holds at this time.

Even a perfunctory reading of this Israeli stand indicates that border adjustments with Syria were not deemed a strategic necessity. As part of a peace treaty--Israel's political demand--the entire Golan Heights could be demilitarized and returned. The clear priority was for a settlement based on peace for territory. Israel's water rights would have to be guaranteed.

The government's decision was kept secret--perhaps even from the General Staff.[7] On June 19 a special session of the UN General Assembly was scheduled at the initiative of the Soviet Union. The government instructed Foreign Minister Eban to apprise the US administration of its practical proposals for a peace settlement and to request Washington to convey them to Egypt and Syria. Eban duly met with Secretary of State Dean Rusk and with ambassador to the UN Arthur Goldberg and delivered the message. A few days later, the Department of State passed on to Israel the replies it had received from the two Arab states. According to Eban, the responses were unequivocally negative. The Arab states demanded an unconditional Israeli withdrawal without any quid pro quo or change in previous territorial and statutory relationships.[8] The Arabs' public response to Israel's June 19 resolution was delivered at a summit conference of Arab states held in Khartoum, Sudan, at the beginning of September. Here the Arabs articulated their position in terms of three "noes" vis-a-vis Israel: no negotiations, no recognition, no peace. Syria, indeed, called for the continuation of the armed struggle.

Earlier, on July 16, 1967, Yigal Allon had submitted to the Cabinet a map of proposed peace boundaries. The "Allon Plan," as it came to be known, addressed the borders in both the east (including the border with Syria) and the west. However, the Cabinet decided not to discuss the plan.

Against this backdrop of political impasse and the growing recognition that peace with Egypt and Syria was not imminent, the government turned its attention to Israel's strategic situation. In the Cabinet meeting of December 26, 1967, Defense Minister Dayan took the position that the IDF should remain on the Golan Heights ceasefire line indefinitely and that the idea of demilitarization should be abandoned (in Sinai as well). Speaking in a Cabinet session five days later, Minister Without Portfolio Israel Galili stated: "All the members of the Cabinet have reached the conclusion that we will not be able to return the Golan Heights to Syrian rule and that the international boundary cannot be the peace border." Galili added: "I want us to release ourselves from the June 19 resolution regarding Egypt and Syria." Prime Minister Eshkol: "On Syria--our stand is changed."[9]

The Cabinet's deliberations in December were summed up in guidelines drawn up for the prime minister's visit to the United States. The document played down the question of peace. It made no direct reference to any Arab state and contained none of the details about commitments which were included in the June 19 resolution. Instead, there were two brief, general statements: "Israel [will be willing] to enter into negotiations with every Arab state that is prepared to do so. At a future date the government will discuss and decide upon the basis for an agreement."[10] Where Syria was concerned, this meant the revocation of the June 19 resolution for a territorial settlement as part of a peace treaty.

Israel's generous offer to Egypt and Syria of "territory for peace" was rejected by both states and was effectively superseded by the Cabinet resolution of December 1967. In the peace negotiations between Israel and Egypt which culminated in a treaty 12 years later, Egyptian President Sadat fought for the principle of territory for peace. Syria insisted on the same principle in the negotiations which began at the end of 1991.

The Israeli Peace Plan of 1970[11]

In late 1970 senior members of Prime Minister Golda Meir's government formulated a secret plan, complete with detailed maps, depicting the boundaries and the maximum concessions to which Israel would agree. A year earlier, in October 1969, US Secretary of State William Rogers had put forward a plan centering on Israel's withdrawal to the 1967 lines, with minor border adjustments. When he presented the plan, Rogers indicated to his Israeli interlocutors that even though the plan bore his own name, President Richard Nixon himself was behind it.

Now, with the prime minister about to visit Washington, she feared that in a face-to-face meeting with the president she would not be able to reject once again the underlying concepts of the Rogers Plan. It was therefore imperative that Israel come up with an alternative plan of its own. In great secrecy Mrs. Meir asked Yigal Allon to draw up such a plan. Meeting with Allon on September 14, 1970, on the eve of her visit to Washington, she explained that in her view Israel had no choice but to present to the president and his advisers maps highlighting, with red lines, those parts of the Territories captured in 1967 which Israel would never relinquish. Golda Meir asked Allon to prepare a map for each of the three sectors: Sinai, Gaza/West Bank, and the Golan.

The fact that the prime minister entrusted Allon with this task was of considerable political significance. In the aftermath of the Six-Day War Allon, the deputy prime minister, was the only policymaker who had drawn up a plan for political agreements that addressed the problem of the Territories and their inhabitants at the strategic level.

On the day after his meeting with the prime minister, Allon gave her three maps marked with red lines beyond which, in his view, Israel could not withdraw under any circumstances. The maps were accompanied by explanations in Hebrew and in English regarding the plan's rationale. Everything was done in the greatest secrecy: only Prime Minister Meir was privy to the material prepared by Allon. Meir was ready to adopt the Allon proposal as the Israeli government's binding policy and present it to the Americans without revealing her intentions to the government.

"For the most part," Allon wrote in his proposal, "the proposed boundary lines constitute the red lines beyond which there must be no concessions, and I regard them as the only alternative to the Rogers Plan. It is possible that for bargaining purposes, more extensive territorial claims will have to be advanced so that our final proposal will be accepted as a compromise." As for the importance of the maps in describing future Israeli policy to the US president, Allon stated: "If it were possible to obtain American understanding for the principles of the plan, this would be a major achievement." However, he added, "I doubt whether conditions are ripe for this at the present stage."

The borders of the "future map of Israel," Allon noted, "should be founded on four principles:" they must be strategically defensible; they must be grounded in the moral right of the people of Israel to the Land of Israel; they must ensure the Jewish character of the State of Israel; and they must be politically realistic.

The borders, Allon wrote, "must be based on a topographic system that will constitute a natural obstacle in defensive deployment against mechanized land forces, while also constituting a basis for our forces to deploy in a counter-offensive. [The borders] must afford the state reasonable strategic depth and ensure the best possible early warning system in the face of enemy aircraft approaching from far way. In addition, the possible development of guerrilla warfare, terrorism and sabotage must be taken into account."

As for the Syrian sector: "Our permanent hold on the Golan Heights is a security necessity. It is not only that Upper Galilee, Lower Galilee and the Jordan Valley, which are threatened by Syria, form a considerable part of the State of Israel and are entitled to full protection. This area contains our primary water sources, which also supply water for the south of the country." Allon added: "The border proposal marked on the attached map is one that Israel cannot forego, a line based on topographical strongholds which blocks axes of advance toward Israeli territory, affords cover for offensive deployment if required, and enables early warning of approaching enemy aircraft from great distances.... The proposed border is for the most part not congruous with the ceasefire line and allows for one-third of the territory we are holding to be transferred to Syria within the framework of a peace treaty."

Furnished with Allon's maps--Israel's political alternative to the Rogers Plan--Golda Meir left for Washington on September 16, 1970, for what was expected to be a fateful meeting with President Nixon. Evidently, Meir intended to present the maps to senior officials of the US administration and thus launch a new era in Israeli policy on the Territories.

In the event, Allon's maps were never unpacked in Washington; the territorial issue was almost completely avoided in Prime Minister Meir's talks. One reason for this was the activity of the Egyptians in the Suez Canal sector. In breach of the agreement that had led to a ceasefire ending the War of Attrition, the Egyptians, with Soviet assistance, had begun moving surface-to-air missile batteries eastward and were building a dense air defense system close to the canal. Israel's requests to the United States to put a stop to these developments and restore the status quo ante had gone unfulfilled. Golda Meir told her American hosts that as long as the Russian missiles that had been moved into the weapons-free zone in violation of the ceasefire agreement were not removed, Israel would not return to the talks being conducted by the UN's special envoy to the Middle East, Gunnar Jarring. This stand by the prime minister, which the Americans could not claim was without justification, effectively weighed against possible talks on the territorial issue.

The second reason was the situation in Jordan: it was in "Black September" 1970 that Syrian troops invaded northern Jordan while the Jordanian army was trying to quell an insurrection by Palestinian groups. In the September 18 meeting between Prime Minister Meir and President Nixon, both sides acknowledged that as long as King Hussein's political future was unclear, little purpose would be served by discussing the territorial issue. Far from raising the question of Israeli concessions in the West Bank, Nixon focused on finding solutions to save King Hussein. The result was that the potential shift in Israeli policy was stymied even before it was discussed.

On September 22, the day after her return from the United States, Golda Meir convened the Cabinet to discuss the events in Jordan and to brief the ministers on her talks in Washington. The prime minister said nothing about Allon's maps or about a change in policy regarding the Territories. As the ministers knew nothing in the first place about the maps and the red lines, they did not raise the question either. Thus the maps that might have changed the course of events in the Middle East, had they been shown to President Nixon, were without further ado filed away in the Prime Minister's Office. They are still there.

Conclusion

Two Israeli peace plans were drawn up by the country's political leadership in the first years after the 1967 war. There is no indication that later plans were prepared. Both plans presupposed that peace with Syria would entail considerable territorial concessions on the Golan Heights. The first plan (June 1967) ceded the entire Golan Heights, while the second (September 1970) proposed an Israeli withdrawal from about one-third of the area, in the eastern sector. It is noteworthy that both plans were drawn up primarily because of political constraints relating to the United States. In 1970 in particular, American involvement in the region and various plans put forward by Washington obligated Israel to submit an alternative of its own.

Conceivably, then, the Americans' direct involvement in the peace negotiations which began in 1991 could have the effect, perhaps even more intensively than in the past, of forcing Israel to come up with a clearly defined concept relating to the future of the Golan Heights--one involving territorial concessions, which would in effect be negotiated with both Syria and the United States.

Part II

Major Obstacles in Peace Negotiations

Syria and Israel have certain overlapping interests that could positively affect serious peace negotiations between them. One major interest is to avoid a war which both sides know will be bloody and disastrous. Another is to improve relations with the United States and with the countries of Western Europe. This means that neither side can permit itself to be blamed for torpedoing political negotiations.

However, as the two countries also have conflicting interests on several basic questions, negotiations will be difficult, complex and lengthy. The major areas of dispute are the territorial issue, the substance of peace, the future of the Jewish settlements on the Golan Heights, the fact that Israeli law has been applied on the Golan Heights, the linkage between Israeli-Syrian negotiations and Israel's negotiations with Lebanon and with the Palestinians, and the status of the Druze population on the Golan Heights.

No one can say whether the considerations that guide Syria and Israel will induce them to make major concessions during negotiations, or whether the talks will collapse. Both leaderships are liable to face difficulties and internal pressures against making the mutual concessions needed to produce an agreement. The Ba'th Party and nationalist groups would almost certainly object to concessions, while in Israel the same attitude would be taken by the inhabitants of the Territories and right-wing parties.

Still, if President Assad could regain full Syrian sovereignty over the Golan Heights in return for making peace with Israel according to the Israeli-Egyptian model, he would probably have sufficient freedom of maneuver to reach a settlement. Syrians and western experts on Syria with whom the author consulted believe that in order to sign a treaty with Israel, Assad would need the assent of his senior officer corps, which should not prove difficult. According to this assessment, the strength of the Ba'th Party (and of nationalist elements) has been greatly reduced and would not impede Assad--if only because the

Syrian public wants the state of war with Israel resolved. Ba'thist ideology, then, would not affect the conflict with Israel.

The content of the peace and the territorial question are the main stumbling blocks in Israeli-Syrian negotiations. Both issues would affect the future of the Jewish settlers on the Golan Heights, since it stands to reason that the settlements would be removed from every part of the Golan transferred to Syria. Similarly, they would determine the future of the application of Israeli law on the Heights, as that status would be revoked (if only for internal Israeli reasons) from any territory transferred to Syrian sovereignty.

Within the Syrian-Israeli context, Syria's prime objective for many years has been to regain the Golan Heights and reassert its sovereignty there. For some years Damascus has understood that this cannot be done by military means. Syria joined the negotiations that began with the Madrid Conference in October 1991, in order to achieve this objective by political means. For Syria, peace is primarily a payment (the smaller the better) that has to be made to regain its territory, as it was for Egypt at the start of Israel's contacts with that country.

Israel's aim, in contrast, has been to obtain security by achieving peace and normalization with Syria and with the other Arab states. In Israel there are two fundamental perceptions of the equation of peace with Syria. One advocates "peace for peace," i.e., no territorial concessions, while the other speaks of a territorial compromise, i.e., readiness to cede part of the Golan Heights in return for full peace. The Syrians, it should be emphasized, accept neither approach. They want the entire Golan Heights.

Chapter 6. The Territorial Question and the Content of Peace

The Territorial Issue

Despite pronouncements by President Assad and other leading Syrian personalities to the effect that the West Bank issue is more urgent or important than the Golan Heights,[1] in reality the return of every inch of the Golan Heights is of crucial importance to Damascus, not least because of the precedent of Israel's return of Sinai to Egypt.[2] Indeed, getting back the entire Golan Heights is a Syrian condition for making peace with Israel. An Israeli refusal to agree to renewed Syrian sovereignty will be construed by Syria to mean that peace talks are unproductive. Yet even under such conditions, Syria would probably want negotiations to continue in the hope of improving its relations with the United States and Western Europe.

Syria would try to avoid becoming isolated in the negotiations, as this would undermine its ability to prevent progress in talks between Israel and other Arab elements. But Syria has additional important interests that affect its approach on the territorial question. Damascus has long regarded itself as the spearhead of Arab nationalism. This, together with its central interest (greater than recovering the Golan Heights per se) in achieving hegemony in the Levant, or at least in Lebanon, and preventing the emergence of an Israeli-Jordanian-Palestinian axis, are at the foundation of Syria's broad conception relating to the Arab-Israel conflict.

Syria, according to its foreign minister, Farouq al-Shara, seeks more than Israeli withdrawal from the Golan Heights: "Every inch of Arab land which was occupied by Israel in war and by force--the Golan, the West Bank, Jerusalem and the Gaza Strip--must be restored in full to its legitimate owners."[3] In the direct negotiations with Israel, Syria has insisted on an Israeli withdrawal, within the framework of peace treaties, from all the territories it captured in the Six-Day War and from southern

Lebanon. This is no mere opening position; it reflects a fundamental Syrian stand deriving from Syria's nationalist posture and its thrust for regional hegemony. It is for much the same reasons that President Assad opposes separate agreements between the Arab states and Israel: individual treaties are seen as reinforcing Israeli supremacy. Thus, Arab states are seen to have two options if they wish to protect their interests: either make all-encompassing peace with Israel, or forego peace.

Syrian leaders continually assert that the operative element in Security Council Resolution 242 is full Israeli withdrawal from the Territories it captured in the Six-Day War. Nothing remains to be discussed; the resolution must be fulfilled. In return, Syria is prepared to annul the state of war with Israel.[4] Genuine reconciliation with Israel and elimination of the sources of conflict may be more than Syria is willing to give, even for the Golan Heights.

In Israel there is a range of views concerning the territorial aspect of an Israeli-Syrian peace treaty. The position of the government that held power in Israel when peace talks began in late 1991 was expressed by Prime Minister Yitzhak Shamir, who said that neither concessions nor territorial compromise were conceivable on the Golan Heights. No country on earth was willing to give up part of its territory, Shamir said, and Israel was no exception. Asked by a reporter what, then, Israel would negotiate, Shamir replied: "We will negotiate peace, the conditions of peace, and cooperation in various spheres, like the economy and tourism."[5] The status of the Golan Heights, Shamir stated, was no different from that of Judea and Samaria: "The [Jordan] Rift Valley, like Judea, Samaria, Gaza and the Golan, will forever be the ancestral patrimony, under Israeli sovereignty."[6]

Around the same time Rafael Eitan, a former chief of staff who was then minister of agriculture, asserted: "We must not forego the Golan Heights, even if this means that no formal peace agreement is signed with Syria."[7] Yitzhak Hofi, a former head of the Mossad, agreed: "I am ready to forego peace if the quid pro quo must be to return the Golan Heights, because peace is a relative situation and could change."[8]

Opinion within the Labor Party is divided between those who oppose any concession whatsoever on the Golan Heights,[9] and advocates of territorial compromise.[10] Speaking at the Labor Party convention in late December 1991, Yitzhak Rabin declared that it would be impossible to make peace with the Syrians based on "peace for peace."[11] It would be better, he said, to discuss the Golan Heights in terms of a territorial compromise rather than in terms of peace for territory.[12]

In 1990-1991 even some in the Likud, then in power, argued that if a peace treaty with Syria were to include positive elements not contained in the treaty with Egypt (e.g., a reduction in military forces), then "the entire Golan Heights, to the last meter, is not essential from the military point of view."[13] Similarly: "Will we be able to say...once the Syrians talk peace, that the Golan Heights is amenable to bargaining? I say yes."[14]

Still, Israel and Syria remain at odds on the territorial question. Probably not even the Rabin government's tendency toward a territorial compromise on the Golan Heights would satisfy the Syrians as a basis for negotiations. "Whoever thinks that Syria would relinquish a grain of occupied Arab soil is mistaken,"[15] noted the Syrian information minister in late 1991, quoting President Assad. He, too, added that Syria would insist on the return of the entire Golan Heights. Because this is not an urgent Syrian goal, and because there is no chance that Syria would be willing to divide the area with Israel, the latter will ultimately be called upon to make considerable territorial concessions, while the Syrian quid pro quo will be expressed on non-territorial issues.

Evidently the United States has not yet determined its stand on the territorial question; its current position is that the sides should negotiate this topic. Washington will probably lean more toward the Syrian position. If so, the stand expressed by President Gerald Ford in his 1975 letter to Prime Minister Rabin will no longer be binding. Ford wrote that the United States has no final position concerning the disposition of the Israeli-Syrian border within the framework of a peace treaty between the two countries, but that when Washington does formulate a stand, "it will give great weight to Israel's position that any peace agreement with Syria must be predicated on Israel remaining on the Golan Heights."[16]

Content of the Peace

Here again, the two states are very far apart. Within Israel, however--in contrast to the territorial question--both government and opposition, and indeed the majority of the public, agree that peace must include real normalization. But Syria may have some freedom of maneuver here.

Although peace negotiations between Syria and Israel began in late 1991, as of early 1994 Syria had yet to recognize Israel's existence. Its leaders, including President Assad, continued to repeat that Syria could not be compelled to recognize Israel,[17] and that this was a subject for negotiations.[18] Nor had the Syrian delegation to the peace talks replied affirmatively when asked by their Israeli interlocutors whether Syria was ready to recognize Israel's existence.

This divide reflects the two states' conflicting interests regarding the content of the peace. Its key elements in the Syrians' perception, as expressed by Assad as far back as 1977, are: "withdrawal from the territories it occupied in 1967 [in the Six-Day War], the rights of the Palestinian people [to self-determination, to its own state and to the right of return] and the termination of the state of war."[19] As for the content of the peace, Assad said that "when the Arabs agree to end the state of war, this means they agree to peace."[20] In this sense, even if the Arab states were able to bring about Israel's total withdrawal from the Territories and the establishment of a Palestinian state, the Syrian leadership would still find it very difficult, perhaps impossible, to make peace as that concept is normally understood. Still, the stands put forward by a state before and during negotiations need not be identical with its final position. For example, President Sadat said in an interview to the *New York Times* in late 1970 that even if Israel were to withdraw to the lines it held before June 5, 1967, Egypt "will never"[21] establish diplomatic relations with it. Nine years later, Sadat signed a peace treaty that established precisely such relations between the two states.

Israel, unlike Syria, requires a peace (in the form of a contractual agreement on the Egyptian model) that constitutes the foundation for a new relationship with the Arab states; a peace that would greatly reduce, or even prevent, the danger of an Arab attack on Israel. Moreover, because the Golan Heights provides only tactical depth, the potential military dangers posed by Syria are far greater than in the Egyptian case. Therefore, the peace with Syria must be broader and more comprehensive than the one with Egypt.

Conclusion

Syria and Israel will be able to conclude a peace treaty and reduce the risk of war if they can overcome their differences on two fundamental issues: the territorial question and the content of the peace. It is difficult to determine whether, in order to realize their goals--Syria, to regain the Golan Heights, Israel to achieve peace and normalization--the two states will be able and disposed to compromise at the expense of crucial interests. In any event, this is the only route by which they can bring their relationship to a peaceful resolution.

Chapter 7. The Jewish Settlements on the Golan Heights

The future of the Jewish settlements on the Golan Heights will no doubt be one of the obstacles in peace negotiations with Syria. This issue is clearly connected with, and indeed stems from, the question of an Israeli withdrawal from the Golan Heights. Syria will insist on total evacuation of the Jewish settlements, while in Israel the subject will spark tremendous controversy. Israel's propensity to display relative flexibility on a withdrawal from the Golan Heights, in particular on the removal of the Jewish settlements there, will increase to the degree that the peace with Syria is more comprehensive and provides Israel genuine security.

It will be useful to preface an analysis of the subject with background information about the Jewish population on the Golan Heights and the viewpoint of its leaders. There were 32 Jewish settlements on the Golan Heights in early 1994 (Map 5 and Appendix 3). The first of them (Merom Golan) was established in late 1967. It was followed by three more settlements in 1968, one in 1969, two in 1970, and so forth. The peak year was in 1978, when four new settlements were established. This very slow pace is accounted for by scarce natural resources, notably water and land suitable for agriculture. Indeed, farming will not draw additional settlers to the Golan Heights. However, key personalities there believe that it is possible to attract new settlers who will find employment in tourism and in industries in which the Golan has an advantage (as the wineries there have shown). Thought has also been devoted to the idea of establishing a university in Northern Galilee which could be a magnet for employment.[1]

The small Jewish population on the Golan Heights--in early 1994 it stood at about 13,000--is only about one-tenth of the Jewish population in Judea-Samaria and is less than the Druze population on the Heights (about 16,000). According to the same personalities quoted above, the growth potential of the Jewish community on the Golan Heights is limited for several reasons. One is distance from the center of the country: far fewer Israelis are willing to settle on the Golan Heights than in Judea-Samaria, which is close to the center. Significant growth of the Jewish population on the Golan Heights therefore depends to some extent on new immigrants being settled there. A second reason involves prospects for employment: this is a severe problem on the Golan Heights, as in many parts of Israel. Between 1992 and 1994 a chocolate plant and a spectacle frame factory were established, and existing mineral water and wine industries were expanded.

These problems do not affect the tremendous public and political support in Israel for the Golan Heights as a crucial element in Israel's security, necessitating a permanent Israeli presence and continuing Jewish settlement there. Public pressure on the government not to cede the Golan Heights and not to remove Jewish settlements could have a decisive impact. Opponents of withdrawal view the Jewish settlements on the Golan and the 1981 Golan Heights Law--which applied Israeli law, jurisdiction and administration to the area--as powerful constraints on any government that might decide to return the territory to Syria.

Naturally, the political future of the Golan Heights preoccupies the area's residents. They know that in the event of a Syrian attack the Golan Heights will be the main theater of battle. But to those for whom the Golan Heights is also home, the greatest fear is that Israel will forego the area in political negotiations and dismantle the settlements there, just like in Sinai, following the signing of the peace treaty with Egypt. There is also a small minority of settlers who see a possibility of compromise in which, even if Israel cedes the Golan Heights, the Jewish settlers would be able to remain there and live under Syrian rule.[2]

We turn now to a brief presentation of the approach espoused by the leaders of the Jewish population on the Golan Heights. Although opinion is divided as to what should be done if the government decides on withdrawal, there is a broad consensus regarding the territorial issue. This approach argues that the Golan is an integral part of Israel, and is no different from any other area in the country. It holds that there is nothing sacred about the international boundary, which was determined arbitrarily by the French and British Mandatory powers without taking into account all the needs of Palestine. It contends that Israel's presence on the Golan Heights is the realization of Zionism; in this sense the settlers are not there merely to afford physical security to Israel and the inhabitants of the Jordan Valley. Israel transformed the territory from a military zone--its status under Syrian rule--into a fertile, developing area. It should not be a subject for negotiation.

The Golan Heights have no Syrian Arab residents; some 70,000 people, who had resided in 35 villages, fled the area in 1967. Again, according to the Israeli settler leadership, the 16,000 Druze on the Golan Heights want to remain under Israeli rule and not become Syrian subjects again--though they admit this only in private conversations, fearing for the fate of their families in Syria. Their stand cannot, therefore, be utilized by Israel for political purposes, but the very fact that there is no Druze political and propaganda activity in favor of Syrian rule on the Golan[3] is significant. Clearly, there is no basis for comparison between the Golan Heights and Judea-Samaria, not least because there is no intifada on the Golan. In time, the Golan settler-leaders argue, the world will accept Israeli rule on the Golan Heights, as this does not entail ruling another people.

In the author's view, in contrast, if and when the 16,000 Golan Druze are asked officially and publicly whose rule they prefer, they will probably opt for Syria. This is not only because Syria can put pressure on them through their families, but also because they still feel a part of the Arab world, even though Israel has ruled on the Golan Heights for more than a quarter of a century. While the non-Jewish population on the Golan consists primarily of Druze, and therefore control is more easily achieved than in Judea-Samaria and Gaza, this is not likely to persuade the international community to accept permanent Israeli rule on the Golan Heights.

Although Syria has declared that it will not make peace if Israel refuses to leave the Golan, that position, state the Golan settlement leaders, may change. In relation to Syria, the Golan Heights is a very small area. It is of no inherent importance to Syria, and therefore if Syria were willing to accept Israel's existence, it would also be ready to cede the Golan Heights. The author's view, as explained in Chapter 6, above, is that Syria cannot be expected to forego the Golan Heights--an area which, it should be recalled, is very close to Damascus.

The leaders of the Israeli settlers on the Golan Heights argue that precisely because an Israeli-Syrian peace made now would entail the IDF's withdrawal from the Golan, this is not the time to make peace with Syria. Indeed, the Israeli presence on the Golan Heights should be strengthened and the government pressured to avoid concessions and defer negotiations with Syria until that country is ready to end the conflict without recovering the Golan. But these same leaders are also aware that the meager Jewish population on the Golan will not increase significantly and that developing global processes, which affect the Middle East as well, diminish their ability to influence events. Overall, then, the Jewish population on the Golan Heights is very concerned about the future, even as it maintains its daily routine and continues to develop the area.

In contrast to the settlers, the Israeli political leadership sees the Golan's importance primarily in terms of security needs. What, then, is the security contribution of Jewish settlements in general, and particularly those on the Golan Heights?

The establishment of Jewish settlements reflects a general security doctrine holding that the regional defense system is an element of military strength. In the special conditions of Judea-Samaria and the Golan Heights, and given that Israel's regular force is limited, Jewish settlements acquire a certain defensive importance. Not all settlements are of equal security importance, however. Some were deliberately established at sites where constraints and restrictions of various kinds prevailed (such as problems of land ownership); security was not always the primary reason. Still, as long as the IDF is in the area, a few hundred inhabitants can contribute to the forward defensive deployment in case of a surprise attack, and beef up regular forces until reserves can be mobilized. Settlements can also assist with routine security, such as by preventing terrorist infiltrations. Some settlements are small, and their contribution in a war would be limited--indeed, they might become a burden, if the women and children had to be evacuated--but the more they grow, the more likely they are to become a security asset.

If the IDF pulls back during a period of transition while the Jewish settlements remain, their security value will be greatly reduced, even if they have weapons for self-defense. Settlements located a few dozen kilometers from Israel's forward troops would be unable to withstand an attack. In fact, they could well become the target of an enemy offensive, which only the IDF's presence nearby could prevent. The settlements' security importance would increase if they were integrated into the army's defensive alignment, but even if not, Israel should not forego them too quickly. Their very existence on the Golan after withdrawal could deter the enemy from sending forces into the Golan, as this would compel Israel to send in troops to defend its citizens.

In looking at the views of the political and security establishment on this issue, we note first a number of fairly characteristic statements about the Jewish settlements: Yitzhak Rabin, when he served as minister of defense in the "national unity government" in 1987, said:[4]

* As weapons become more sophisticated and military might increases, the relative importance of the regional defense system declines and the burden devolves ever more on the IDF.
* The answer to the Arab armies that threaten Israel lies in the IDF, not in settlement, and "in the face of a possible offensive tomorrow on the Golan Heights, Jewish settlement is not important."
* Settlement derives its value primarily because it is an act of striking roots in the land. In other words, "it becomes

increasingly political settlement and less security-oriented."

* At the same time, the very existence of the settlements along the "confrontation line" and their ability to deploy defensively if they are properly armed and fortified, is a "contribution to security in the event that we are taken by surprise and do not manage to mobilize the entire IDF on time."

Prof. Yehezkel Dror agrees that the settlements are primarily of political importance because they "can enhance the Israeli government's freedom of action in peace negotiations or even for an interim settlement."[5]

According to Maj.Gen.(res.) Yisrael Tal, regional defense is a major contribution if one's goal is static defense. However, the limitation of this form of defense is that it is committed to territory. Settlements enhance routine security, but despite the measures taken to strengthen them since the Yom Kippur War, they are also a burden.[6] Another retired major general, Moshe Peled, argues that "from the purely security aspect, given the same monetary investment, the army will do things better than all the settlements combined." But this, he says, is not the relevant question. Peled believes that where there is no moshavnik [cooperative farmer], there will soon be no State of Israel, either.[7]

We see in these statements the outline of two major schools of thought about the security importance of the Jewish settlements on the Golan Heights. One argues that they are of very limited value, as the task of fighting a war would fall on the IDF and the settlements are likely to be a burden. The other view is that territory (the Golan Heights) is of innate security value and the existence of settlements both ensures that the territory will not be ceded and contributes to its defense.

Advocates of the first view--those who argue that the settlements have little security value--argue, first, that if there were sufficient advance warning of an imminent Syrian attack, then the addition of a few hundred soldiers in the settlements would be of no significance, as the IDF would have time to mobilize and deploy in large numbers. Moreover, in the event of a complete surprise attack, it would be very difficult for the IDF to evacuate the women and children from the settlements, as its major task would be to stop the advancing Syrian Army.[8] A precedent exists: in the Yom Kippur War, which caught Israel by surprise, the entire population of the settlements was evacuated, the women and children on the first day and the men the day after. The settlements hindered rather than contributed to the Israeli war effort.

Even Shimon Sheves, in 1987 the defense minister's adviser on settlement in the Territories and an ardent supporter of Jewish settlement on the Golan Heights (and in 1994 director-general of the Prime Minister's Office), pointed to the problems. According to Sheves,[9] even though the settlements are equipped and organized for a war situation, the small population presents a basic problem: the number of potential soldiers is not thousands but hundreds. The settlements could be attrited in a war.

Secondly, the Syrians have apparently concluded that in the 1973 war they made a mistake in not attacking the Jewish settlements on the Golan Heights. It must be assumed that in a future war the Syrians would target settlements, particularly those in the breakthrough sectors.[10] Settlements there might endure heavy artillery shelling and suffer tremendous devastation. Another possibility is that the Syrians would try to seize several settlements right away and hold them as a very strong bargaining card against Israel.[11]

Proponents of the second view maintain that, although the settlements were established basically for political rather than security reasons, the addition of combat-ready personnel anywhere on the Golan Heights contributes to security. Though many of the settlements are very small, even 20 or 30 defenders at a crucial road junction might hold up a Syrian advance long enough for the IDF to arrive. This advantage outweighs the principal drawback of the settlements, namely the need to evacuate the women and children in the face of a Syrian offensive. The latter is a problem one has to live with: male-only civilian settlements are not a viable option.[12]

As an immediate lesson of the Yom Kippur War, a drive began to fortify all the settlements on the Golan Heights. Today every settlement is integrated with a system of nearby outposts, and constitutes a true obstacle with the ability to provide local defense. Militarily, it is preferable to situate settlements in backup, rather than primary areas, so that with modern weaponry, such as anti-tank weapons and artillery, they can become a security asset. The Golan settlers share this view, arguing that if the combatants among them are well-trained and supplied with advanced weapons, they could contribute more meaningfully to defense.[13] This approach holds that in a future war the settlements will not be evacuated, and their hundreds of combatants will man outposts and "hedgehogs" in the first hours of the fighting.[14]

These combatants, note the settlers, could be deployed rapidly (within two hours of call-up)[15] and thus make a major contribution in the event of a Syrian surprise attack.[16] The Syrians, they say, view every settlement as a force with defensive capability. And of course only women and children, and not combatant males, would be evacuated in a war situation.[17]

Proponents of this viewpoint also argue that the existence of the settlements helps motivate IDF soldiers to fight and has a positive psychological value.[18] The settlements give the Jewish residents confidence that the IDF will put up a stubborn fight for the Golan Heights.[19]

In the early years of Israeli settlement on the Golan, the tendency was to defend the territory of Israel west of the international boundary. Nowadays the settlers consider themselves an integral part of Israel, no different from any other residents. Their main goal, then, is to defend not the settlements close to the Green Line, but themselves.[20] In line with their purpose of preventing the return of any part of the Golan Heights to Syria, they have followed the "tower and stockade" model of the pre-state period and established settlements as close as possible to the ceasefire line. In contrast, most of the generals who have headed

Northern Command over the years argued that settlements should not be established closer than five kilometers from the Israeli-Syrian boundary line, and that they should be situated behind hills to prevent exposure to Syrian observation posts. This approach holds that the settlements should base themselves on nearby industry and agriculture, while pasture (which does not require a constant presence in the fields) could extend right up to the border. However, this concept was vetoed for political reasons.[21] In practice, about one-third of the Golan Heights settlements (ten out of 32) are located less than five km from the border.

In 1991 one-quarter of the settlements had fewer than 30 families each. In Natur, for example, there were seven families, 25 in Hadnes, 19 in Kanaf, 22 in Odem and in Alonei Habashan, 30 in Geshur and 19 in Kela, while in Metzar all the settlers were unmarried (see Appendix 3). Clearly, the number of potential combat soldiers in such settlements is too small to constitute a fighting force of tactical significance. There are few settlements with more than 70 families, out of which a platoon or more could be formed from the males. These include one town (Katzrin, with about 1,000 families), two regional centers (Bnei Yehuda with 116 families and Hispin with 75), two moshavim (Ramot with 70 families, Ramat Magshimim with 74), and three kibbutzim (Afik, 86 families; Mevo Hama, 80; and Merom Golan, 75).

In the author's assessment, three elements must be present for a settlement to be of tactical security value: location on (or near) dominant terrain, advanced weaponry, and combat-trained personnel comprising at least a platoon. The final criterion alone would probably rule out two-thirds of the settlements. It is the deployment of the IDF on the Golan Heights, and not the existence of Jewish settlements, which is the direct reason for the confidence of the Upper Galilee agricultural settlements that the Syrian army will leave them in peace.

Politically, the Syrians take a far graver view of the Jewish settlements on the Golan Heights than they do of the IDF's presence. As they see it, the danger of the settlements is that they are furthering, indeed determining, Israeli sovereignty, whereas the IDF's presence (which the Syrians hardly welcome) could be temporary and hence less of a risk. It stands to reason that in peace negotiations the Syrians would insist on the removal of the Golan settlements. They would also probably insist that the Syrian citizens who resided on the Golan Heights until 1967 be allowed to return and that a Syrian civil administration be established there, in order to entrench Syria's sovereign status.

It is unlikely that any of those involved--the Jewish inhabitants on the Golan Heights, the Israeli government, or Syria--would agree to Jewish settlements existing under Syrian sovereignty. The struggle between Syria and Israel over the settlements will be part of the larger contest over the political future of the Golan Heights, which indeed will determine the fate of the settlements. Both sides are aware that this issue will constitute a major stumbling block: if Syria is called on to make concessions regarding the content of the peace, Israel will be called on to reciprocate on the territorial question and on the Jewish settlements. If Israel were to recognize in principle Syrian sovereignty on the Golan Heights, and if Syria were to agree to defer the application of that sovereignty for a long period of years, it might be possible to work out an arrangement regarding the settlements for a specified period.

The majority of the settlers on the Golan say that they have struck roots, that the Golan Heights is their home and is essential for Israeli security, and that a territorial compromise and removal of settlements from the Golan is out of the question, because the watershed line is Israel's security border.[22] Others say they would leave, albeit reluctantly, in return for peace,[23] because "peace is what we need most."

It is too early to say how the Jewish population on the Golan Heights would react if the government decided on the removal of the settlements in a peace treaty with Syria. This subject preoccupies the settlers and there is a wide range of opinion. Some are loath to comment, saying it is too soon and that they are busy trying to preempt precisely such a decision. They believe that Israel may not have to give up the Golan. Others say that if peace were made with Syria, in return for Israeli withdrawal from the Golan, they would find themselves caught between a rock and a hard place, torn between two fundamental elements of Zionism: peace vs. giving up part of the Land of Israel. In the event, if the peace truly ended the Israeli-Syrian conflict and the security arrangements on the Golan Heights were perceived in Israel as being effective, the majority of Golan settlers would probably not seek recourse to violent action against withdrawal.

Conversations with government officials involved with the Golan Heights, and with some leaders of the Jewish community there, suggest that in practice the majority of the settlers (from the kibbutzim and some of the moshavim) will oppose evacuation with all the legal means at their disposal (passive resistance), but will finally accept the decision and leave. However, some of the settlers (from the religious moshavim and from the Herut-Beitar movement) could prove more obstinate. Many will be unwilling to cede the Golan even in return for a full peace with Syria. Conceivably they will wage a far fiercer struggle than was the case during the evacuation of Yamit and the settlements in Northern Sinai.[24]

The settlers in Judea-Samaria and Gaza will view an evacuation of settlements on the Golan Heights as an ominous development. From their point of view, this second evacuation (after Yamit) of a relatively large Jewish population, and despite the application on the Golan of Israeli law, will be a very grave event. The settlers in Judea-Samaria and Gaza can therefore be expected to spearhead the struggle against withdrawal from the Golan Heights.

Conclusion

Following the 1973 Yom Kippur War, the security of the Jewish settlements on the Golan Heights was considerably improved. The settlements were fortified and supplied with weapons that afford them limited local defensive capability. As a result, they could have a certain security significance in a war, although the need to evacuate the women and children in the event of a Syrian surprise attack would be an arduous task for the IDF, and would place the families in jeopardy. In the author's assessment, on balance the importance of the Jewish settlements is primarily political, with their security contribution less significant.

Any Israeli government will find it difficult to decide on the removal of the settlements. Although the Jewish population on the Golan Heights is relatively small (about 13,000) and less able to exert pressure than the settlers in Judea-Samaria (where the Jewish population is ten times as large), two central factors help offset this. The first is the broad consensus in the country that the Golan Heights is crucial for the defense of northern Israel and its water sources, and therefore the IDF--and the settlements--must remain there. The second is the problem the Labor Party will face in supporting a withdrawal when most of the population involved comes from Labor's own land-settlement movement.

While the Israeli government will not easily agree to uproot settlements on the Golan Heights and to accept Syrian sovereignty there, the Syrians, for their part, will almost certainly not agree to make peace with Israel as long as settlements under Israeli sovereignty continue to exist on the Golan.

Chapter 8. Israeli Law on the Golan Heights

On December 14, 1981, the Knesset enacted legislation applying Israeli law on the Golan Heights. The Golan Heights Law is one of two laws in the history of Israel that were passed in a single day. It was indeed a speedy affair. In the morning the Cabinet unanimously accepted Prime Minister Menachem Begin's proposal to enact the law, at 4 p.m. the bill was presented to the Knesset, and before the day was out it had been given the three required readings.

The final vote was 63-21 in favor. Besides the Likud and the National Religious Party, eight members of the Labor Alignment voted for the law. Nay votes were cast by Hadash (Communists), Shinui, Telem and 13 members of the Alignment. The split vote in Labor reflects the strong support in the party for Jewish settlement on the Golan Heights, an enterprise that was initiated by Labor. Indeed, Labor has consistently enjoyed the electoral support of the majority of the Golan settlers.

The Golan Heights Law states, in its entirety:

1. The law, jurisdiction and administration of the state [of Israel] will apply in the territory of the Golan Heights as described in the Appendix [a map of the boundaries of the Golan Heights].
2. This law goes into effect on the day it is approved by the Knesset. The Interior Minister is in charge of executing the law.[1]

Prime Minister Begin cited the following grounds for submitting the bill:

Historical. According to Begin, historically the Golan Heights had been and would be "an inseparable part of this Land [of Israel]," notwithstanding the boundary determined by two colonial Powers (Britain and France) after World War I.

Security. Here the reference was to the security of the Israeli population residing proximate to the international boundary.

Since Israel's establishment, Begin said, "the Syrians turned the lives of thousands of those people [Israelis residing in the vale], into hell." There was, he said, a national consensus that "Israel would not be able to step down from the Golan Heights or hand it over to the Syrians."[2] Moshe Arens, then chairman of the Knesset Foreign and Security Affairs Committee, added that the Golan's strategic importance was not only to residents of the north, but that "the security of the entire State depends on continued Israeli rule on the Golan Heights."[3]

Political. Several times Israel had urged the Syrians to enter into talks on a peace treaty, but "the Syrians rejected the hand we stretched out to them by totally negating our right to exist, our very existence as the Jewish state."[4] Begin said that the government had submitted the bill to the Knesset following explicit statements by Syria's president and its foreign minister that "Syria will not recognize the State of Israel even if the Palestinians do."[5]

As MK Benny Shalita (Likud) stated in the debate, the purpose of the law was to ensure that "no future government, of whatever stripe, will be able to allow itself to ignore the Knesset's decision on this day."[6] The Druze MK Amal Nasser al-Din (Likud) added that it was a great day for the Jewish people and that the law would produce a feeling of "inner assurance among the Jewish, Druze and Alawite residents on the Golan Heights."[7] Years later the defense minister's adviser on settlement in the territories, Shimon Sheves, noted that the law provided the Jewish settlements on the Golan with a political anchor, even if negotiations were to be held with the Syrians and an agreement reached.[8]

During the debate, the government made the "reassuring" declaration that the application of Israeli law on the Golan Heights would not prevent future negotiations with Syria. Thus Moshe Arens stated: "I am convinced that this particular move will not prevent negotiations [between the Syrians and] whichever government will then be in power."[9] Arens cited historical precedents in which territory was transferred from one sovereign power to another after negotiations. Prime Minister Begin declared: "The moment that the president of Syria says that he is ready to conduct negotiations with Israel on a peace treaty, at that moment the negotiations on a peace treaty with Israel will commence, and nothing will stand in our way."[10] Israel's senior representative at the United Nations reiterated this position in a letter of December 29, 1981, to the UN secretary-general: "Israel wishes to reiterate that it is willing to negotiate unconditionally with Syria, as with its other neighbors for a lasting peace. The Golan Heights Law does not preclude or impair such negotiations."[11] Indeed, the Golan Heights Law did not prevent the start of political negotiations between Syria and Israel in 1991.

Like the Golan Heights Law, the law that was passed on June 27, 1967 regarding East Jerusalem also applied the "law, jurisdiction and administration" of the State of Israel, without mentioning annexation. A brief comparison may be relevant. Two leading Israeli experts on international law differed at the time as to the law's interpretation. One argued that the law should not be construed as annexation, since "annexation of the territory of a foreign state as a result of war is possible--according to international law--only when the foreign state (whose territory is being annexed) has disintegrated completely, i.e., has ceased to exist."[12] He added that the ideal juridical solution for East Jerusalem was an agreed arrangement between Israel and the Arab states which would transfer to Israel part of the occupied territories.[13] In contrast, the other jurist maintained that it was indeed misguided to speak about "annexation," because "Israel does not annex territories which until 1948 were part of Mandatory Palestine,"[14] and Israel does not regard its status in them as that of an occupying state. This expert concluded that the law regarding East Jerusalem meant the application of Israeli sovereignty there. By inference, we may conclude that the Golan Heights Law is indeed problematic from an international jurisprudential standpoint.

Syria reacted furiously to the passage of the Golan Heights Law. For example, the Speaker of the Syrian parliament stated in a meeting of that body held on December 16, 1981: "The meaning of Israel's decisions is the annexation of Syrian-occupied territory, a declaration of war on Syria and the abolition of the ceasefire."[15]

Already on December 14, the day the law was enacted, Syria formally asked for an urgent meeting of the UN Security Council, in order to discuss "the decision of the Israeli Government to apply Israeli laws to the occupied Golan Heights."[16] On December 17 the Security Council adopted a unanimous resolution stating that it:

> 1. Decides that the Israeli decision to impose its laws, jurisdiction and administration in the occupied Syrian Golan Heights is null and void and without international legal effect;
> 2. Demands that Israel, the occupying Power, should rescind its decision forthwith.[17]

The General Assembly also condemned the law sharply, and on January 20, 1982 the Security Council voted on a draft resolution submitted by Jordan calling for sanctions against Israel. The resolution stated that the "continued occupation of the Syrian Golan Heights since June 1967 and its annexation by Israel on 14 December 1981 constitute a continuing threat to international peace and security." Therefore, the Israeli government's decision of December 14 was an act of aggression, and all member-states of the United Nations should consider "applying concrete and effective measures in order to nullify the Israel annexation of the Syrian Golan Heights and to refrain from providing any assistance or aid to and cooperation with Israel in DZ fields in order to deter Israel."[18] This resolution had the support of nine states, while five abstained (including Great Britain, France and Ireland), but it was vetoed by the United States. Because of the impasse in the Security Council, the subject was referred back to the General Assembly, where on February 5, 1982, 86 states voted to impose sanctions, 21 voted against (among them the United States, Great Britain, Canada, France, Netherlands, Sweden, Germany, Denmark and Portugal), and 34 abstained. This resolution called on the member-states "to refrain from supplying Israel with weapons, related equipment and military assistance, refrain from acquiring weapons or military equipment from Israel; suspend economic, financial and technological assistance and cooperation, sever diplomatic, trade and coastal relations...in order totally to isolate it...."[19]

Because of American opposition to sanctions, which meant that the Security Council would not be able to pass an operative resolution (the General Assembly's vote was nonbinding), the issue lost its urgency on the world political agenda. At the same time, Syria apparently realized that the application of Israeli law on the Golan Heights did not constitute a fundamental change in either the current situation or Syria's future options. President Assad, addressing the Druze residents of the Golan, said in early 1986: "You may rest easy: your homeland is in a good situation. There is nothing to worry about regarding the Golan, because 12 million Syrian citizens can regain the Golan.... And if the Israelis are working to include the Golan within their borders, then we shall work so that the Golan will be in the center of Syria, and not on its border."[20]

If for political reasons an Israeli government should wish to annul the Golan Heights Law, new legislation would be required. According to legal experts, previous Knesset legislation cannot be abrogated by a decree, but only by new legislation.[21] A Likud government would in any event not try to have the law abolished, as it has been shown in practice that its existence is not an obstacle to political negotiations with Syria. As for the present (early-1994) Labor government, which espouses a different policy, it too could probably not bring about the repeal of the Golan Heights Law prior to the signing of a peace treaty with Syria. Any such attempt would have to overcome broad support for the law and for Jewish settlement on the Golan--based on a perception of the area's security importance--that crosses party lines and includes factions of the Labor Party.

The law's repeal is thus not an immediate concern. Its existence could become a problem if Israel and Syria were to sign a political agreement establishing formal relations between them (contractual peace) and if Israel were forced (or agreed) to cede all or most of the Golan Heights. Jewish settlers on the Golan believe that the Knesset could sidestep the law, albeit with great difficulty. In their view, if Israel is forced to withdraw, it will do so in spite of the 1981 law. In any event, it is improbable that Israel would agree (or be forced) to repeal the Golan Heights Law other than as part of a peace treaty.

Conclusion

Notably, the application of Israeli law on the Golan Heights should not be construed as the area's annexation. The fact is that Israel and Syria were able to begin peace negotiations. Repeal of the law will become a practical issue only if a political settlement includes full peace and involves an Israeli withdrawal from all or most of the Golan Heights, particularly if it entails the removal of Jewish settlements. Indeed, an Israeli government will probably find it more difficult to dismantle settlements and cede territory than to repeal the 1981 law. Without Israel's consent to transfer all or large parts of the Golan to Syrian sovereignty and to evacuate Jewish settlements, the question of repealing the Golan Heights Law will not become relevant. If during the negotiations Israel should decide to withdraw from the Golan, Syria might forego the law's repeal, as it would no longer have practical significance. Probably, though, the government would ask the Knesset to annul the law, a move which would almost certainly generate considerable parliamentary opposition.

The Sinai precedent shows that if the government submits to the Knesset a package in which territory is ceded as the quid pro quo for a peace treaty, the law will probably be repealed. This assessment is offered despite two major differences between the agreement with Egypt and a possible agreement with Syria. First, Israeli law was never applied to Sinai. And secondly, the opposition at the time of the peace treaty with Egypt (the Labor Alignment) supported the government's stand, whereas the present opposition (Likud) will almost certainly oppose a similar treaty, involving the return of land to Syria, worked out by a Labor government.

Chapter 9. Linkage With Additional Agreements

Although the negotiations which began at Madrid in late 1991 are being conducted separately with Syria, Lebanon, Jordan and the PLO, both Israel and Syria consider the four sets of talks to be interconnected. For example, Israel will seek (from Syria) the removal of Syrian forces from Lebanon, the cessation of terrorist raids across the Lebanon border and the reduction of the Syrian threat to Israel via Lebanon. In addition, Israel might make the execution of a peace treaty with Syria, particularly withdrawal from the Golan Heights, conditional on the Palestinian refugees being rehabilitated in the Arab states and the removal of this Arab-nationalist element from Syrian-Israeli relations. Syria might wish to weaken Israel's capacity to launch a thrust into Syria via the Bekaa Valley, and to bring about the elimination of the Israeli enclave in southern Lebanon. Furthermore, Syria might refuse to sign an agreement with Israel until the Palestinian problem is resolved and Israel agrees to a complete withdrawal from Judea-Samaria and Gaza.

In pursuit of its policy to bring other Arab states, and the Palestinians in particular, into its sphere of influence, Syria is endeavoring to coordinate negotiating positions with the other delegations and place them under its auspices. It is unlikely that Syria would be willing to sign a completely separate agreement with Israel.

The Lebanese Context

Syria has long sought to achieve hegemony in the Fertile Crescent, and in particular to impose its will on Lebanon, an ambition guided by an array of security, economic and political interests. It is important for Damascus to dictate Lebanon's international and inter-Arab policy, especially with respect to the Arab-Israel conflict, and to ensure that Beirut does not again become a center of organization and activity for Syrian dissidents. In addition, Syria seeks legitimization for continuing to deploy troops in the Lebanese Bekaa, for both defensive and, if necessary, offensive purposes against Israel.

One idea raised in Israel in the past was to cut a deal with Syria whereby Israel would accept Syrian freedom of action in Lebanon, and in return Syria would agree to leave the Golan Heights under Israeli control. Conceivably, 15 or more years ago (after Syria began moving forces into Lebanon, in May 1976) Syria may have been interested in obtaining Israel's consent for a takeover of Lebanon. But in the intervening years Damascus has been able to create a strong power base there. The main stages in this development were the Ta'if Agreement (October 22, 1989), which affirmed the principle of "preferential relations" between Beirut and Damascus; the ouster of General Michel Aoun, a Lebanese Christian, by a Syrian commando force; and the entrenchment of Lebanon's dependence on Syria by means of a friendship, cooperation and coordination agreement signed by the presidents of the two countries in Damascus on May 22, 1991. That agreement, with its generalized phraseology, stipulated the creation of joint committees to cement its terms. It legitimized a long-term Syrian military presence in Lebanon and granted Syria senior status in security, political and economic affairs. Only extreme circumstances, such as a war with Israel in which Syria is outflanked, or the collapse of the Ba'th regime, are likely to reduce Syrian influence in Lebanon.

At present, in view of Syria's deep influence in Lebanon and Israel's inability to jeopardize it, Israel has little to offer Syria at the political level regarding Lebanon. Nor does Syria need to negotiate with Israel over Lebanon. Syria may carry less weight with Jordan and the Palestinians in their talks with Israel, but it can dictate to Lebanon.

What is at stake, from the Syrian viewpoint, is Israel's control of southern Lebanon. Syria's interest is to bring about Israel's withdrawal and the end of Israeli influence there, while extending its own sphere of influence to that region. Southern Lebanon is a thorn in the Syrians' side, one they cannot ignore. Indeed, since the Lebanese Army seems incapable of preventing Hizballah terrorist attacks on Israel through southern Lebanon, the

Syrians may have to fulfill that mission in an agreement. However, even though the Syrians would like to see Israel leave southern Lebanon, this is not an urgent matter on their agenda and does not justify making major concessions to Israel on the Golan Heights. Israel, though, might be able to use its presence in southern Lebanon as a lever to extract from the Syrians less vital concessions.

Although Lebanon is not a primary Israeli bargaining card, and will not generate concessions of principle from Syria on the Golan Heights, Syria would probably not sign a peace agreement with Israel unless and until its interests were assured in the negotiations between Israel and Lebanon. Israel would want to ensure that a peace agreement with Lebanon (or with Syria and Lebanon) greatly reduced Syria's security involvement in Lebanon, including the removal of Syrian troops from Lebanon, and that Syria undertook not to support terrorist activity against Israel from inside Lebanon. If Israel and Syria could resolve their own differences, the question of Lebanon would not constitute a major obstacle.

The Palestinian Context

The Syrian leadership, including President Assad, has long asserted that the problem of Palestine is Syria's problem.[1] "The Palestinian cause is the basis of our struggle"[2] and the "axis of the Arab struggle,"[3] Assad has declared. Indeed, "we actually want Palestine and only afterward the Golan."[4] Other Syrian leaders have reiterated that the priority is "Palestine" and that "it [the Golan] cannot be traded for Palestine."[5]

This explains at least part of Syria's reaction of anger and dismay when Israel and the PLO unveiled the Oslo Agreement in August-September 1993: a separate deal between Israel and the Palestinians was antithetical to Syria's comprehensive approach, and to its concept that the Palestinian issue must be solved under its own tutelage. An additional aspect of that reaction was Assad's antipathy for Chairman Arafat and the mainstream PLO, and his scepticism regarding Arafat's viability as a partner in an Israel-Arab settlement.

But the Syrians understand that the Israeli-Palestinian equation involves far more than "Gaza-Jericho first." Hence their certain ongoing involvement in the Palestinian issue. From the Syrian point of view, there are two main elements in the Palestine question: territory and full rights. As for territory, since the 1967 war the Syrian leadership has consistently insisted on an Israeli withdrawal from all Arab territories which were captured in that war, including, of course, Judea-Samaria and Gaza.

The question of full national rights for the Palestinians has various component elements. First, even though Syria, in common with most of the Arab world, opposes the establishment of a Palestinian state not under its own aegis, for public consumption Damascus states that such a state should be created in Palestine within borders to be agreed on by the Palestine Liberation Organization (PLO). Apparently the only instance in which President Assad deviated from this position was his 1979 statement to a journalist: "We agree to the establishment [of a Palestinian state] on the soil of Palestine between the Jordan River and the Mediterranean Sea"[6]--that is, in place of Israel.

Secondly, Syria supports realization of the "right of self-determination" which, in the PLO's definition, means the "complete liberation of the homeland and the establishment in it of the Palestinian national state."[7] This would seem to involve the right to decide on three fundamental questions: who are the Palestinians (Arabs residing in Palestine, including those who resided there until 1947 and their descendants); the type of regime in the future state; and relations with the Arab states.

Third, Syria insists at least rhetorically on the "right of return" to the homes, property and areas of residence of Palestinian refugees who left the country during the 1948 war. Israel argues that fulfillment of this "right" would mean its destruction from within. Israel does, however, have an interest that the Palestinian refugee problem be resolved as part of the peace process. Here, as we shall see, Syria does have a role to play.

Besides Syria's consistent opposition to a separate settlement of its own (and by any other Arab actor) with Israel, the Palestinian question, in addition to the inherent obstacles which it poses, serves as a Syrian bargaining card on three key issues: first, a resolution of the Palestinian problem on the Palestinians' terms will weaken Israel and work to Syria's advantage; secondly, continued support for the Palestinians is mandated by the Syrians' longtime Arab nationalist line, and any retreat from that position will weaken Syria's inter-Arab status; and third, if Syria wishes to achieve dominance in the Levant--i.e., vis-a-vis Palestine as well--it must work to further a Palestinian solution within a Syrian-led inter-Arab framework.

Some experts assess that in return for the entire Golan Heights, Syria might agree to a separate nonbelligerency treaty with Israel, even if the Palestinian problem is at that stage unresolved.[8] However, it is most improbable that Israel would be willing to cede all or even most of the Golan without a comprehensive peace; nor does it appear likely that the present Syrian leader, or his successor, will make a separate peace agreement with Israel while the Palestinian question remains unresolved.

To a very large degree, then, the Israeli-Syrian and Israeli-Palestinian negotiations remain linked. Syria is concerned that the more rapid progress made in 1993 in the Israeli-Palestinian talks, might compel Damascus to make concessions. In any event, Syria will try to keep the two negotiations tightly linked so that it can exert influence on the Palestinians. And Syria may not agree to a full peace settlement with Israel even when the Palestinian question successfully enters the transition stage of an autonomy regime.

In the author's view, Israel, too, should consider the negotiations with Syria and the solution of the Palestinian problem to be interconnected. This problem is one of the roots of the Arab-Israel conflict; the larger conflict will not be terminated until it is resolved. Therefore, even though an existential strategic threat to Israel is posed by the military might of Syria and the other Arab states, the risk of war will be greater as long as no solution is found for the Palestinian problem, and particularly for the rehabilitation of the refugees outside Israel. Thus Israel should seek to ensure that, in conjunction with the transition toward a full peace with Syria and the transfer of sovereignty over most of the Golan Heights to Syria (accompanied by the implementation of agreed security arrangements), the Palestinian refugees are rehabilitated in the Arab states. Syria's direct role should be in rehabilitating the 300,000 or so Palestinian refugees on its soil.

Conclusion

It is unlikely that either the Palestinians or Lebanon will become subjects for direct bilateral negotiation between Israel and Syria. Israeli acceptance of Syria as the representative of either or both would needlessly strengthen Damascus' position in the Levant. Moreover, this would be contrary to Israel's traditional and current policy. Israel will negotiate separately with every party on the questions of relevance to each.

Given the potential threat posed by the large Syrian forces in Lebanon, some of them deployed on the Bekaa axis between Damascus and the Israel-Lebanon border, it is difficult to envisage an Israeli-Syrian peace agreement that does not incorporate a solution for this situation and for southern Lebanon. Thus, from the security standpoint, a direct connection exists between Israel's negotiations with Syria and with Lebanon.

In addition, both Israel and Syria perceive the talks to be linked with the Palestinian question. Syria not only rejects a separate agreement with Israel but will almost certainly not sign a peace treaty before agreement has been reached on resolving the Palestinian question, or at least before Israel has agreed to withdraw from Judea-Samaria and Gaza. Israel, for its part, should insist, at the least, on synchronization between the rehabilitation of the Palestinian refugees in Syria and the other Arab states and the signing of a peace treaty with Syria.

Chapter 10. The Druze Population on the Golan Heights

As already noted, the Druze population on the Golan Heights (See Map No. 5) outnumbers the Jewish settlers, and the question that arises is whether the Druze will constitute an obstacle in Israeli-Syrian negotiations.

In the 1967 war the majority of the Syrians on the Golan Heights, who had resided in some 35 villages, fled the area. Until then, in addition to Druze and Alawites, the population also included Circassians (in 12 locales, of which the largest were Kuneitra and Hushniyah); Mugrabis (four villages in the southeastern Golan); Turkmens (a semi-nomadic tribe based in Kafr Naffah on the road between Banat Yaqub Bridge and Kuneitra); and Bedouin (one tribe in the northern Golan and two in the southern section).

After the war only Druze and a few Alawites remained. Since then the Druze population has almost doubled itself by natural increase. In 1994[1] there were 17,000 Druze living on the Golan Heights. The Druze reside in four villages in the northern Golan, of which the largest, with 8,000 inhabitants, is Majdal Shams. The three other villages are Buk'ata (4,000), Mas'ade (3,000) and Ain Qinia (2,000). The majority of the area's 1,500 Alawites reside in the village of Ghajar.

The agriculture-based economy of the Golan Druze has grown tremendously since 1967. With the exception of the younger generation, the majority appears to prefer Israeli rule over Syrian.[2] The younger generation, which never lived under Syrian rule and who will set the tone in the future, are incited by Radio Damascus and by events in the Territories. They are the nucleus of resistance to Israel.

In 1977 and 1978 the Golan Druze experienced a crisis when, for the first time, their confidence about the region's political future was shaken. The cause was the visit to Israel of Egyptian President Anwar al-Sadat and the subsequent Camp

David accords. Suddenly the possibility loomed that a similar pattern would be followed between Israel and Syria, leading to a restoration of Syrian sovereignty on the Golan. A small minority of Druze tried to convince Israel to annex the area. The majority objected. They insisted that the status quo not be altered and that they continue to be regarded as Syrian nationals until the area's future was decided. There were four main reasons for this stand: genuine fear of severe suffering under the Syrians if the area were to be returned; concern for the fate of relatives in Syria; concern for the disposition of property in Syria owned by Druze on the Golan; and heavy pressure exerted by the Syrians on the Druze in Lebanon.[3]

Two laws enacted by the Knesset in 1980-1981 generated powerful shock waves in the relationship between Israel and the Golan Druze. The first was an amendment to the Law of Citizenship, passed on August 18, 1980, following more than a year and a half of comprehensive deliberations at the political level and intensive lobbying by MKs and others. The amendment, dubbed the "Druze law," enabled the Druze to receive an Israeli ID card, provided they first accepted Israeli citizenship.

The Druze took a very grave view of this legislation, as it would effectively revoke their Syrian citizenship and make them full-fledged Israeli citizens, albeit at their request. Acceptance of Israeli citizenship meant burning all bridges with Syria. Besides fearing for their own fate if the Syrians should ever return, the Druze were concerned about their families across the border: 93 percent have relatives in Syria, of whom 43 percent are first-degree relations.[4] Under Syrian law, a Syrian citizen who voluntarily accepts foreign citizenship loses his Syrian citizenship and forfeits all his and his family's property in Syria.[5]

With passions running high, extremists among Syrian sympathizers on the Golan launched a campaign of terrorism and intimidation against acceptance of Israeli citizenship. Balking at nothing, they sent murder notes, stoned those who opted for citizenship, sullied their honor and beat their children. Recipients of Israeli citizenship were excommunicated and ostracized. This pressure, and the Israeli authorities' inability to formulate a suitable response to the agitators, placed those who accepted citizenship in a precarious situation. Most of them quickly returned their papers.

The second act of legislation was, of course, the December 1981 Golan Heights Law, which applied Israeli law, jurisdiction and administration to the area. This law had little practical impact on the status of the Druze, as already in 1970 the Golan Heights had effectively undergone "Israelization" in virtually all spheres. Moreover, the 1981 law was a fait accompli, its implementation not dependent on the will or choice of the Druze. Enactment of the law sparked no protests, as the new ID cards the Druze had to accept (in place of those distributed by the military government in 1967) did not confer Israeli citizenship, but signified only residence on the Golan Heights.

Still, 1981 witnessed the beginnings of conflict between the Druze and Israel, revolving around three principal issues. First, recipients of Israeli citizenship were excommunicated by the religious elders of Majdal Shams, following an upsurge in the number of those seeking Israeli ID cards. The excommunication decision was made public on March 25, 1981, in a document called the "National Charter," the sharpest anti-Israel document published on the Golan Heights.

In turn, acute countermeasures were taken by the Israeli authorities, including a closure placed on the Druze villages. Finally, a strike by the Golan Druze began on the day Israeli law was applied. It ended eight months later, on July 22, 1982, after gradually petering out. The conflict ended with all the residents receiving Israeli ID cards and with Israeli law being applied in full on the Golan Heights.[6]

Conclusion

The growing uncertainty about the political future of the Golan Heights is causing disquiet in the area and preventing full cooperation by the residents with the Israeli authorities. The

Golan Druze still suffer from a national identity problem and from conflicting messages about the future of the area.

The Druze on the Golan Heights enjoy absolute religious-social autonomy and a liberal democratic regime which is responsive to their needs in a way that the Syrians never were. Nevertheless, the application of Israeli law on the Golan and the authorities' efforts to make the region Israeli in every way have not persuaded the majority of the Druze there to view the area as anything other than Israeli-occupied Syrian territory--and themselves as living under occupation.[7]

When negotiations with Syria enter a decisive stage, the Druze may face a serious internal conflict. But they will not--at least not publicly--be able to oppose the return of the area to Syria.[8] The Golan Druze will have no influence on the terms of a political solution between Israel and Syria. Although there may be some minor troubles during the negotiations, the Druze will not constitute a serious obstacle in the negotiations. Syria will not be satisfied with a territorial arrangement that returns only the Druze villages, although it may agree to such an interim settlement for a specified period, to be followed by total Israeli withdrawal. In the final analysis, the Druze will accept whatever agreement Syria and Israel reach.

Part III

Topography and the Balance of Forces

Chapter 11. Topography and Security[1]

Topography

The Golan Heights is the western area of the Bashan Region (Hauran in Arabic), which extends eastward as far as Jebel Druze (Mountain of the Druze). It comprises one of the world's largest continuous expanses of basalt. The area of the Bashan (Hauran) is approximately 35,000 sq km.

The area's boundaries are for the most part natural. The eastern boundary of the Golan follows the watershed between the streams which descend directly into the Jordan or into Lake Tiberias (Lake Kinneret), and between those flowing into the Yarmuk. The watershed, which is not a prominent feature of the landscape, is approximately contiguous with the ceasefire line.

The Golan's border (see Map No. 6) is contiguous in the north with the southern slopes of Mount Hermon and more precisely with the valley of Sahar stream, the eastern tributary of the Hermon (Banias) River; in the south, with the Yarmuk Valley; in the west, with the steep descent to the Hula Valley, Lake Tiberias and the Jordan Valley; and in the east, with two other streams, Roqad and Allan. The Golan is difficult to access from the north, west and south; only from the east is access comparatively unproblematic.

Israel holds 1,050 sq km of the Golan's total area, or 1,190 sq km if the Hermon and the Buteiha Valley are included. The length of the Golan and the southern Hermon ridge is about 62 km as the crow flies.

Terrain has rendered the Golan Heights narrow in the north and south and broader in the center (Map No. 7). Its width in the north, in the area extending to the foot of Mount Hermon, is 12 km. From there it becomes increasingly wider until the Butmiye area where, at the intersection of the Rafid-Sheikh Miskin road with the Roqad stream, it achieves its greatest width, 25 km. From here, as it extends southward, the Golan becomes increasingly narrow.

The Hermon is a mountainous ridge lying north of the Golan and rising to a height of 2,814m above sea level. Rectangular in shape, its area is about 1,000 sq km, and its longitudinal axis runs from south-southwest to north-northeast. It ranges in width from 17 to 23 km and is 50 km long, to which must be added a long, narrow extension of 30 km running northward along the axis. Since the 1967 war, about nine percent of the Hermon (approx. 90 sq km) has been under Israeli control, with the rest divided equally between Syria and Lebanon. The mountain's western and southern extensions, which are in Israeli hands, are 2,224m above sea level.

The Hermon is composed of hard limestone which is highly soluble. The heavy rains (annual average: 1,500mm) and the melting snows which penetrate deep into the rock are a major Israeli water source and a partial source for Syria and Lebanon.

The Golan descends gradually from northeast to southwest. The difference in elevation between its extremities is about 900m (from 1,220m to 300m). The elevation difference to Lake Tiberias is 1,400m (900m and an additional drop from +300m to -209m). The northern section drops, along 12 km as the crow flies, from 1,200m to 200m. The same differential is found in the central section along 16 km, near Banat Yaqub Bridge, while in the southern section the drop in the course of 23 km as the crow flies is from 930m (Tell Fares) to -209m (Lake Tiberias).

From north to south, the Golan Heights may be divided into two main areas of terrain: Upper Golan and Lower Golan. These are demarcated by a line running from Rafid junction in the east to Zavitan stream in the west. This line lies at the same latitude as the line that divides Upper Galilee (in the north) from Lower Galilee (in the south).

Northern Golan. The highest part of the Golan Heights (1,220m) is also distinguished by its rocky terrain and heavy precipitation. In its eastern area volcanic hills and mounds rise 150m to 300m above their surroundings. The streams fall steeply westward and run into the Hula Valley. Because of the boulder-strewn terrain, agriculture is possible only in valleys in the volcanic areas. The elevation difference between the foot of the Golan in the west and the crest of the hills, over a distance of between 10 and 15 km, is about 800m. The Upper Golan descends westward from a height of about 1,000m to the Hula Valley depression.

The northern Golan may be subdivided as follows:

* Shamir-Mount Hermonit line to the Golan's northern extremity. Here, ascent from the west is relatively moderate and there are limited possibilities for the movement of armored fighting vehicles (AFVs) from west to east (and vice versa). The continuation eastward, via the moderate ascent, is a steady slope until the high mounds, and traffic is confined to the existing axes.
* Shamir-Mount Hermonit line until Zavitan Stream. Here the ascent is steep, subsequently becoming moderate until the line of the mounds, where traffic is not confined to the axes.

Southern Golan. The southern Golan extends from Zavitan Stream until the southern extremity of the plateau. This area is lower than the northern section. The covering of lava rock gradually disappears, to be replaced by a rich, dark brown lava which is well suited for agriculture.

The southern Golan can be divided into two sections:

* The cleft area in the west, which is a remnant of the original basalt plateau. The slope, which is moderate in the northern section of the Golan, becomes extremely steep toward the Jordan Valley. The slopes are a wall-like cliff, rising 400 to 500m above Lake Tiberias. The terrain here, then, is highly bisected and rich with cliffs and escarpments. The ascent to the Golan Heights in this region, and traffic from north to south, is possible only on the existing axes.
* The uncleft plateau in the east is level, almost completely devoid of volcanic mounds, and has little rocky terrain.

This area is mainly flat plateau, with sections of fertile soil. Movement is not difficult, but is limited by the line of waterfalls in the cleft plateau in the north and by Roqad canyon in the east. Movement in winter is problematic owing to mud. With the exception of Mount Fares, there are no high volcanic mounds on the southern Golan. Only a few small volcanic mounds punctuate the plain: Tell Jokhadar, Tell al-Siqi, Natur, Skofiyah and Rajam Zaki.

From west to east, the Golan Heights, including the passage from the Golan to the Bashan, may be divided into four strips:

Ascent to the Golan. This area is steep and is cut by narrow, deep canyons. The slope becomes steeper and more escarped toward the Jordan Valley, where sheer wall-like cliffs of between 400 and 500m rise above Lake Tiberias. Here the ascent to the Heights is possible only on the existing routes. Adding to the difficulty is the boulder-strewn terrain in the area's northwest. However, from Lake Tiberias to Mount Hermon there are three approaches which are traversable, albeit not easily, by AFVs even off the axes. These are:

* The northern approach from the slopes of Hermon to the Shamir area. The gradient here is less steep than to the south (an incline of 10° vs 40° between Shamir and Banat Yaqub Bridge), with an elevation difference of 300m over a distance of 3 km. Movement of AFVs is difficult but possible from west to east (and vice versa).
* The central approach in the area of Banat Yaqub Bridge from the Jalabina River to 2 km south of the bridge. The gradient here is less steep. The difference in elevation over a distance of 1 or 2 km is between 150 and 200m.
* The approach where the Jordan enters Lake Tiberias, which runs northeast by northwest because of the directions of the streams and canyons. The gradient is moderate, and outcropped with boulders, though armored

vehicles can move between them. Muddy ground in the lower section makes passage there difficult.

Moderate ascent. Relatively broad, this strip is 5 km wide in the north and 18 km in the center. The rise toward the east is moderate. The area is covered with basaltic rock. This strip can be divided as follows:

* The northern sector from the area of the Customs House-Kuneitra road until the Hermon slopes and west of the watershed line. The terrain descends westward moderately, but there are no dominant areas toward the east. From Tell al-Sheban (height: 876m) some control can be exercised toward the east. From southeast of Tell al-Sheban (at a distance of 15 km) there are three rises which afford some control toward the east: the Dalwa area, Mount Shifon (977m) and Mount Yosifon (981m). These can be regarded as a second western line of hills, though it is lower than the eastern line.
* The sector of the brooks and the Customs House-Kuneitra area, as far as El Al in the south. The brooks and canyons run north to south and northeast to southwest. As they do not permit north-south movement (or vice versa), offensive (or defensive) efforts cannot be mounted in this sector. There are no lateral axes, other than the road along Lake Tiberias which runs east of the road from Ramat Magshimim to Aleiqa.
* From east of the brooks and to their south until Roqad there is a level rise which is easily ascended. Movement in this area is more convenient than in the other sectors. The northern section is broader, the southern section narrow. The latter has flat surfaces with two narrows, Fiq (Afik) and El Al, which can serve as defensive lines vis-a-vis the east as well. The Rapid approach is located on the eastern extremity. The watershed line is composed of a system of high mounds and ridges from the slopes of Hermon in the north to Mount Fares or Tell Jokhadar

(Orha Hill) in the south (see Appendix 4). The volcanic mounds were created by occasional buildups of lava; most of them are cratered. They have very steep gradients, reaching an incline of up to 40°. Although they lie well above sea level, they are not themselves high, rising to a height of 100 to 200m above their surroundings.

The **watershed line** connects a series of mounds near the Israeli separation-of-forces line, from the foot of Hermon to Mount Fares. In the northern section, as far as Kuneitra, the mounds are just west of the line (up to 5 km), while south of Kuneitra until Mount Fares they are even closer to the line and at some points contiguous with it. In the northern section there is a second line of more westerly mounds, between 2 and 5 km from the first line. Most of these are west of the Mas'ade-Kuneitra road. The second-line mounds are generally lower than and dominated by the first line of mounds.

Determining whether a mound is on the eastern or the western line may not be simple, depending on the criteria being employed. If the criterion is the location of the mounds in relation to the Mas'ade-Kuneitra road, or their distance from the ceasefire line, then Mount Odem and Mount Baron, for example, will be on the western line, as will Mount Bental and Mount Avital. However, if the criterion is that the more forward mounds in the sector are considered to be on the eastern line, then Bental and Avital will be part of that line. The division here is made according to the second criterion.

The two highest elevations in the entire sector are on the first line of the northern section: Mount Varda (Tell Varda), at 1,226m, and Mount Hermonit (Tell al-Sheikha), at 1,211m. Some of the mounds rise high above their surroundings. The mounds are about 500m long, although some of the larger ones, such as Avital and Bental, are 2 km long.

The mounds on the eastern line create a field of vision of several dozen km toward the east, encompassing, for example, the Dar'a-Damascus road. Electronic control can also be exercised from these elevations. Good observation posts are offered by

Mount Bental (Map No. 8), Mount Fares (Map No. 9), Mount Hermonit, Mount Avital (Figure No. 1), and the Hermon. The Hermon affords long-range observation--it is the only point from which Damascus itself is visible. The steepness of most of the mounds makes them obstacles to movement, although some are relatively flat and hence negotiable, such as Odem (Tell al-Ahmar) and Hermonit (Tell a-Sheikha). Observation from the western line of mounds is limited by the eastern line. On the western line, only Mount Shifon is useful for observation and electronic control, and only for a small sector, south of Kuneitra.

Passage to the Bashan. Between the Golan and the Bashan there are two approaches, Kuneitra and Rafid, where an offensive effort is possible. Problems of trafficability to the north and the south mean that movement which is part of a major effort will be limited almost entirely to these two openings.

The Kuneitra approach is about 10 km wide and runs from the Mount Odem-Mount Varda line in the north as far as Ein Zivan-Mount Avital in the south. It lies east of the eastern line of mounds and an eastward thrust can be mounted through it. In contrast, a westward thrust could be limited if the defender holds the area's dominant mounds.

The Rafid approach is 12 km wide and runs from the cliffs of the Roqad in the south to Tell al-Shu'af Sindin in the north. Most of it lies south of Mount Fares; its section north of Fares can be regarded as the Kudna approach. In the north the approach borders on a fairly dense series of mounds, beginning at Tell al-Shu'af Sindin (height: 993m), which forms a barrier.

To the east of the watershed line and the line of mounds on the Golan Heights the terrain slopes gradually downward. With the exception of the Kudna approach, the highest area is the line of mounds west of the Israeli separation-of-forces line; between Mount Fares and Tell al-Shu'af Sindin (to its north) the Syrians command the high ground.

The northern section of the plateau contains a line of mounds lying between two and four km from the Syrian and Israeli disengagement line. There are five major mounds here (Tell al-Ahmar, 1,200m; Tell al-Daoud, 1,100m; Tell al-Hawah,

1,079m; Tell al-Keva, 1,029m; Tell al-Karoum, 1,011m). In the southern section of the plateau there are two mounds northeast of Mount Fares: Tell al-Kudna, 661m, and Tell al-Ahmar, 877m.

The Bashan consists of primarily level terrain, descending from north to south. At a distance of between eight and 15 km from the Syrian disengagement line, between longitude 238 and 242, the terrain rises again, with a row of mounds--slightly lower than those west of the separation-of-forces line--running as far as Tell Hara in the south. These are: Tell al-Shams, 1,012m; Tell al-Shaar, 1,137m; Tell al-Mal, 1,002m, rising 130m above the surroundings; Tell al-Hara, 1,096m, rising 250m above the surroundings; Tell al-Jabiye, 708m; and Tell al-Jamua, 637m. Further south is another group of mounds.

To the east of Tell al-Mal, as far as Tell al-Shams, there is a large number of mounds of increasingly diminishing height, with level areas between them, until an almost continuous row of mounds at longitude 268 which are 800m or more high. The area is more open in the southern section, where there are very few mounds.

East of the Bashan lies Greater Laja, and north of it, Lesser Laja. Between them, the Bashan links up with Damascus via a broad, passable area. This passage can accommodate the movement of large forces, which can make use of the few axes on Lesser Laja.

Main Axes

A key element of the terrain are the axes of approach leading from the Damascus-Dar'a area (in Syria) to the Jordan Rift Valley. Because any serious east-west offensive or defense against the east is conditional on these roads, they bear closer scrutiny.

Main axes of advance (east to west):

* Sasa - Mazrat Beit Jann - Mas'ade - Banias
* Damascus - Khan Arnabah - Kuneitra. From Kuneitra a westward advance is possible on two roads. The

northerly: Merom Golan - Wasit - Gonen; the southerly: Kuneitra - Banat Yaqub Bridge. These two roads can be considered two axes.

* Dar'a - Kudna - Khushniye - Katzrin junction - Yehodiya junction. From there via either the westerly road--Arik Bridge toward Tiberias--or the southerly: along Lake Tiberias to Ein Gev.
* Sheikh Miskin - Rafid junction - Givat Orha - Afik, from where one of three roads can be taken: northwesterly--Givat Yoav toward al-Kursi; westerly--toward Ein Gev; or southerly--toward al-Hamma, and from there westward toward Samakh and Kibbutz Deganya.

Main connecting axes (north-south):

* East of the Israeli disengagement line, east and west of the Syrian disengagement line, from Hader in the north -Tell al-Ahmar - Khan Arnaba - Jeba, Kudna - Rafid junction.
* Mas'ade - Buk'ata - Mansura - Kuneitra - Khushniye - Jokhadar.
* Mas'ade - Wasit - Kafr Naffah - Khushniye.
* The oil route from Jordan and the south, leading to Naffah and passing near Givat Orha. From Naffah it is the most westerly latitudinal route in the northern Golan. This route continues toward the northwest until the Merom Golan-Gonen road, and north until west of Zaura.
* The cliffs in the southern part of the plateau (east of Lake Tiberias) rule out the possibility of latitudinal axes there. The closest connecting axis is to their east, from Ramat Magshimim via Katzrin junction until the Kuneitra-Banat Yaqub Bridge road.
* From the Syrian Customs House--near the point where the Jordan enters Lake Tiberias--along the eastern shore of Lake Tiberias up to Ma'agan.

To sum up: five systems of axes of advance (each made up of a road and several dirt trails) lead from Syria to the Golan and traverse it, two in the southern Golan and three in the northern Golan. Syria can mount a simultaneous attack of five divisions on these axes--one division per axis.

Possible Defense Systems Toward the East

The size of the Golan Heights, its topography and its five axes of advance limit the size of the forces that can be committed there for either offense or defense. In 1973, for example, the Syrians attacked with three divisions in the first wave. Since then, their forces have increased considerably; today they could mount an attack of five divisions. To withstand this, the defensive system must be arrayed at a certain depth and based on two lines; one is insufficient. The possible systems are:

1. A main line of defense on the watershed line from the Hermon via Mount Ram - Mount Varda - Mount Hermonit -Mount Bental - Mount Avital - Hazaka Ridge - Mount Fares.

   Advantages:

   - A strong barrier, the line blocks almost physically the passage from Syria to the Golan Heights, enables a good hold on the ground and a basis for fire control, and is difficult to circumvent.
   - Its location on the watershed line and its elevation afford good observation and control deep into Syria (several dozen km). This is the only line that enables spotting by electronic means and by observation of Syrian offensive preparations at the tactical level and probably also at the operational level. A pullback to the west of this line would place Israel at a topographical disadvantage and deprive it of good observation and fire control toward the east.
   - As an important component of the IDF's current deployment on the Golan Heights, the area is well

prepared for defense, containing fortifications, minefields and other obstacles.

- The terrain enables a rear defense stop line[2] to be established a few km to the west, from Zavitan Stream until the foot of the Hermon in the north (see below).
- By holding this line, which is only 60 km from Damascus, the IDF can more convincingly deter Syria from launching a war.

Disadvantages:

- The line's proximity to the Israeli separation-of-forces line, particularly southward from Kuneitra until Mount Fares, in an area where the distance between the Israeli and Syrian lines is no more than one km, poses a certain risk to the defender. The danger arises from the fact that the main line is also the forward line, situated close to the Syrian separation line. The IDF's forward deployment means that the Syrian army can attack from its fortified alignment without the need to execute standard pre-offensive moves. Thus, in an offensive, Syria, in a single tactical thrust, could attack the IDF's main defensive line. The situation could be aggravated if the offensive were launched by surprise, i.e., without Israel spotting Syria's final preparations for the attack.
- Another significant risk stems from the fact that the defender's main line of defense is under observation from the western mounds in Syria and is within range of a massive Syrian artillery barrage (Syria has 2,300 guns in its order of battle).
- Some experts believe that the killing areas should be in the center of the Golan Heights and not on the forward line.[3]

- The fact that the IDF is poised 60 km from Damascus could induce Syria to launch a war in order to reduce the threat to its capital.

2. A defense line on the western mounds of the Golan Heights, from the Hermon via Mount Odem - Tell Sheban - the two Dalwa mounds - Mount Shifon - Mount Yosifon - Givat Pazra - Givat Tal - Givat Orha (Tell al-Jokhadar).

Advantages:

- Even if the first line cannot be manned (because of political constraints), it will not be easy for the Syrians to attack this more western line with total surprise because of its distance (5-10 km) from the separation-of-forces line.
- The line is not under Syrian observation.
- Although the mounds here are lower than those of the first line, they afford control toward the east ranging from 2 to 5 km, and therefore offer a certain defensive capability, albeit more limited than on the eastern line.

Disadvantages:

- This line is lower by at least 100m than the first line, and therefore its observation possibilities toward the east, beyond the first line of mounds, are limited (with the exception of a few breaches). It would be impossible to spot Syrian preparations for an offensive and consequently to make advance preparations and take measures to disrupt the Syrians' advance to the eastern line of mounds. In addition, the ability to defend from this line against a full-scale offensive would be limited.
- The mounds on this line are scattered and up to 10 km apart. As a result, they can be by-passed,

and cannot block a Syrian thrust. Nor does this line extend until the southern Golan Heights.

- Because of its proximity to the eastern line of mounds, it is doubtful whether this line can be seen as a rear defense stop line. There are some who believe that the strategic rear defense line should be contiguous with the Jordan.[4]

3. A defense line in the southern section, based on narrow points of control (El Al, Golan Stream, Natur hill, Daliot junction) and on dominant areas in their vicinity (including Natur hill and Bezek hill). This line can be integrated with the western line of mounds:

Advantage:

- With a depth of 10 km and more to the west, this is the last line on the Golan from which Lake Tiberias and the Jordan Valley can be defended.

Disadvantages:

- Although this line contains good natural obstacles (cliffs) and has few roads, it does not contain terrain that is dominant toward the east. Furthermore, the natural obstacles provide dominance only for short ranges (with the exception of Natur hill, from which dominance can be achieved for several km in all directions).

4. A protective line at the extremity of the strip of steep ascent, from the Hula Valley and the Jordan Valley to the Golan, for a distance of 4 km east of the international boundary:

Advantage:

- In the event of a surprise attack on the Golan, the Israeli forces rushed there to wage mobile warfare along five difficult axes would be relatively secure.

Disadvantage:

- This is not a line of defense.

Conclusion

From the strategic point of view, it is instructive to ask which is more important for Israel's security: Judea-Samaria or the Golan Heights? In terms of geographical location, the temporary loss of the Golan Heights, which lies at an extremity of the state, would not jeopardize any Israeli strategic target. In contrast, loss of the West Bank (particularly of Samaria), which borders the vital coastal plain, would pose an existential threat to Israel.

The western part of the Golan Heights is 300 to 500m above the Hula Valley, Lake Tiberias and the area between them (with the exception of the sector in which the Jordan enters Lake Tiberias, where the Israeli side is higher and dominant). As long as the risk of war exists, it is vital for the IDF at least to hold the protective line of this area, for two reasons. First, it hampers Syria's exploitation of its height and terrain advantage, protects the Israeli settlements in the Hula Valley and the Jordan Rift against attacks and terrorist raids, and ensures quiet in the region. And secondly, it secures the IDF's ascent to the Golan along the five difficult axes should the risk arise of a Syrian thrust at the Golan. This is equally relevant if the IDF is deployed toward the east on a topographically suitable defense line on the Golan Heights.

In the author's view, the area's topography calls for the main line of defense to be based along the eastern row of mounds, and for a second line based on the western line of mounds in the center of the Golan. Because of the proximity of the eastern mounds to Damascus (60 km), deployment there also serves to deter Syria from launching hostilities.

Here, however, we must note--even before the political aspect of the problem is examined (see below)--that it is extremely improbable that Syria will agree to the permanent deployment of Israeli forces on the eastern Golan Heights or anywhere else on them: Syria, as already noted, perceives this as a serious threat. Thus, whatever advantages Israel may believe inhere in the defense lines described above, political considerations will ultimately take them out of Israeli hands.

Chapter 12. The Balance of Forces

In the Israeli War of Independence (1948-1949) Syria's ground forces totaled three brigades,[1] while the IDF fielded 11 brigades[2] (on all fronts). In other words, Israel's ground forces were nearly four times as large as Syria's. Since then both sides (and the other Arab states) have steadily increased the size of their ground forces, but this growth has been considerably greater on the Syrian side. In 1973 Israel's ground forces were less than twice as large as Syria's (11 vs. six divisions),[3] in 1989 Israel had 1.6 as many divisions (16 vs. ten)[4] and by 1993 this had declined to 1.3 (16 vs. 12). Over the years, then, the Syrian buildup has gradually closed the quantitative gap with the IDF's fully mobilized ground forces (see Table II).

Current Balance of Forces

We find the same pattern in terms of quality. The Syrian Army has acquired 600 advanced top-of-the-line T-72 tanks, self-propelled guns--in the past it had only towed guns--and long-range (500 km) surface-to-surface Scud C missiles. Syria has made efforts to acquire advanced aircraft (MiG-29, Sukhoi 24) and SA-10 surface-to-air missiles, the Russian equivalent of the American Patriot.[5] By 1992 Syria had 12 operational divisions in two corps, some 5,000 tanks[6] and hundreds of Scud missiles, some armed with a chemical warhead.[7] In a surprise attack the Syrian Army could achieve numerical superiority against the IDF. (While the IDF is still larger when fully mobilized, it requires time to call up its reserves, some of which would almost certainly be deployed on other fronts.) Nevertheless, one cannot ignore the IDF's high qualitative advantage.

Table II. Syria-Israel--Comparative Armed Forces, 1992*

	Syria	*Israel*
Ground Forces		
Personnel		
Regular	306,000	134,000
Reserve	100,000	365,000
Divisions		
Armor	7	12
Mechanized	3	0
Infantry	1	4
Major Arms		
Tanks	4,800	3,850
APCs	4,980	8,100
Guns & Mortars	2,400	1,300
SSM Launchers	60	12
Air Forces		
Combat Aircraft	530	694
Military Airfields	21	11
Helicopters		
Attack	100	91
Transport	185	133
Long Range SAM Batteries	108	unknown

----

* Source: Shlomo Gazit, ed., with Zeev Eytan and Amos Gilboa, *The Middle East Military Balance 1992-1993* (Jerusalem: Jerusalem Post and Boulder: Westview Press, 1993).

Regular Ground Forces

The author's assumption, based on the lesson of the Yom Kippur War, is that Syria would try to achieve surprise if it decided to attack Israel. To cope with a worst-case scenario--i.e., Syrian success in this endeavor--Israel must maximize its regular forces on the Syrian front. Here Israel finds itself in an adverse situation, as the number of troops it can commit to this front, given its security needs elsewhere, is far smaller than the Syrian ground force.

The ratio of regular ground forces between Israel and the Arab confrontation states alone (including Egypt) is 1:5, and in absolute numbers 706,000 Arab soldiers (Egypt 320,000, Syria 306,000, Jordan 80,000) vs. Israel's 133,000.[8] Against Syria alone, Israel is also at a sharp numerical disadvantage (see Table II).[9]

In the author's assessment, only about one-quarter of the IDF's ground divisions are part of the regular army, with the rest belonging to the reserve forces.[10] This estimate can also be arrived at by examining the ratio between the number of soldiers in compulsory service and the total number (including reservists) in the ground army: nearly 1:4 (133,000 regular troops vs. a total of 498,000). Since there are 16 ground divisions, it follows that there are four regular divisions, as compared with the Syrians' 12.

It is no secret that Israel's regular army must be deployed permanently on more than one border. The author's assessment is that, under normal circumstances, Israel has to station one division on the Egyptian front, another on the Jordanian front, and a reduced division on the border with Lebanon. This leaves one division, reinforced by reservists, to confront Syria's 12 divisions.

Operationally, though, the balance of regular forces is less serious than the numbers suggest, since the entire Syrian regular army is not deployed permanently against Israel. Syria maintains a force numbering about two divisions in Lebanon. True, in a war, Syria might well commit all its ground forces against Israel, even if this meant leaving its other borders exposed (as in 1973, when even the Republican Guard, which is responsible for the regime's security, was dispatched to the front). But this will not be the opening situation. In a surprise attack, Syria will effect no changes in its normal deployment, and least of all will it move up forces. The attack would almost certainly be based on Syria's fixed deployment of five or six divisions stationed between Damascus and the Golan. This Syrian corps, deployed opposite the Golan Heights, comprises two mechanized divisions, one armored division and a division-size infantry force; to this must be added a reserve force of at least two armored divisions in the area of Damascus. In other words, in the first stage of the fighting a single Israeli regular division will find itself facing five or six Syrian regular divisions, an opening advantage for Syria of at least 5:1 in the operational balance of forces.

Iraqi Expeditionary Force

Iraq has sent an expeditionary force to the front in every one of the Arab-Israeli wars (with the exception of the 1956 Sinai Campaign). Were an eastern front to be established to attack Israel, such a force could augment the independent strength of Syria and Jordan. This is not immediately likely--the Iraqi Army is still recovering from the drubbing it took in the 1991 Gulf War--but must be taken into account a few years hence. How large is such a force likely to be, and how long would it take it to reach the Golan front?

In 1948 the Iraqis sent two infantry brigades (from a total order of battle of two divisions) which operated from Jordanian territory. In 1967 a supradivisional force of four brigades (out of a total of four divisions) entered Jordan; it remained there until 1970. In the 1973 war, despite an absence of prior coordination between Syria and Iraq, and indeed despite the tense relations between them at the time,[11] Iraq sent two and a half divisions (out of a total of between six and seven divisions) to the Syrians' aid.

The Iraqis have thus constantly upgraded their expeditionary force as their order of battle has multiplied: from seven divisions in 1973, the Iraqi Army numbered 12 divisions in 1980,[12] but by 1989, with the stimulus provided by the Iraq-Iran War, it comprised 50 divisions and 6,000 tanks.[13] In a war against Israel on the eastern front, or even a war limited to Israel and Syria, Iraqi troops would probably take part in the fighting. Possibly the Iraqi force would be split between Jordan and Syria. It is likely that at least five or six divisions would be sent to Syria and an equal or smaller number to Jordan. But given the Syrian order of battle and Syria's aim of achieving a strategic surprise, it is very probable that an Iraqi force will arrive only after the start of the offensive. In any event, Syria may not require an immediate major addition of troops, given its own sizable ground forces. One way or another, the first Iraqi division would not reach the Damascus area less than 36 hours after hostilities began.

Operational Significance

The Syrian force which is permanently deployed between Damascus and the Golan Heights (five to six divisions), comprising about half the total number of Syrian divisions, is large enough to mount a surprise attack. This assessment is based on the size of the regular force which the IDF can station permanently opposite Syria (one division), the area of the Golan Heights and the number of its axes of advance (five), enabling an offensive by five divisions.

The numerical inferiority of the Israeli forces stationed permanently in the Golan theater requires that they be able to rely on terrain which will allow them to mount an effective defense and contain a surprise attack, until IDF reserves are mobilized. The combination of a large disparity in regular forces and the topography of the Golan Heights means that as long as the danger of a Syrian (and Arab) attack on Israel exists, the IDF must be able to deploy on a relatively convenient line of defense--in this case, the eastern line of mounds on the Golan Heights.

Conclusion

The topography of the Golan Heights and the Syrian-Israeli balance of forces there will be cause for concern for a long time. The risk of war will still exist even if Israel and Syria sign a peace treaty, unless Syria agrees to a considerable reduction of its active ground forces. The underlying assumption here is that a peace treaty will involve the demilitarization of the Golan Heights for a lengthy period, during which the danger of war will still exist.

Because the area on the Golan from which a defense can be mounted against a possible attack from the east (i.e., from Syria) is the eastern line of mounds, it is on that line that Israeli forces must be deployed. During a lengthy transition period, when the risk of a Syrian (or Arab) war against Israel remains viable, the terrain permits no other possibility. The ratio of regular forces between Syria and Israel, which places Israel in an adverse situation, especially in a surprise attack, aggravates the topographical problems. The combination of the two factors involves a series of potential risks for Israel, which are examined in the next section.

MAP NO. 1
STAGES IN THE FRANCO-BRITISH NEGOTIATIONS OVER THE SYRIAN-PALESTINIAN INTERNATIONAL BORDER

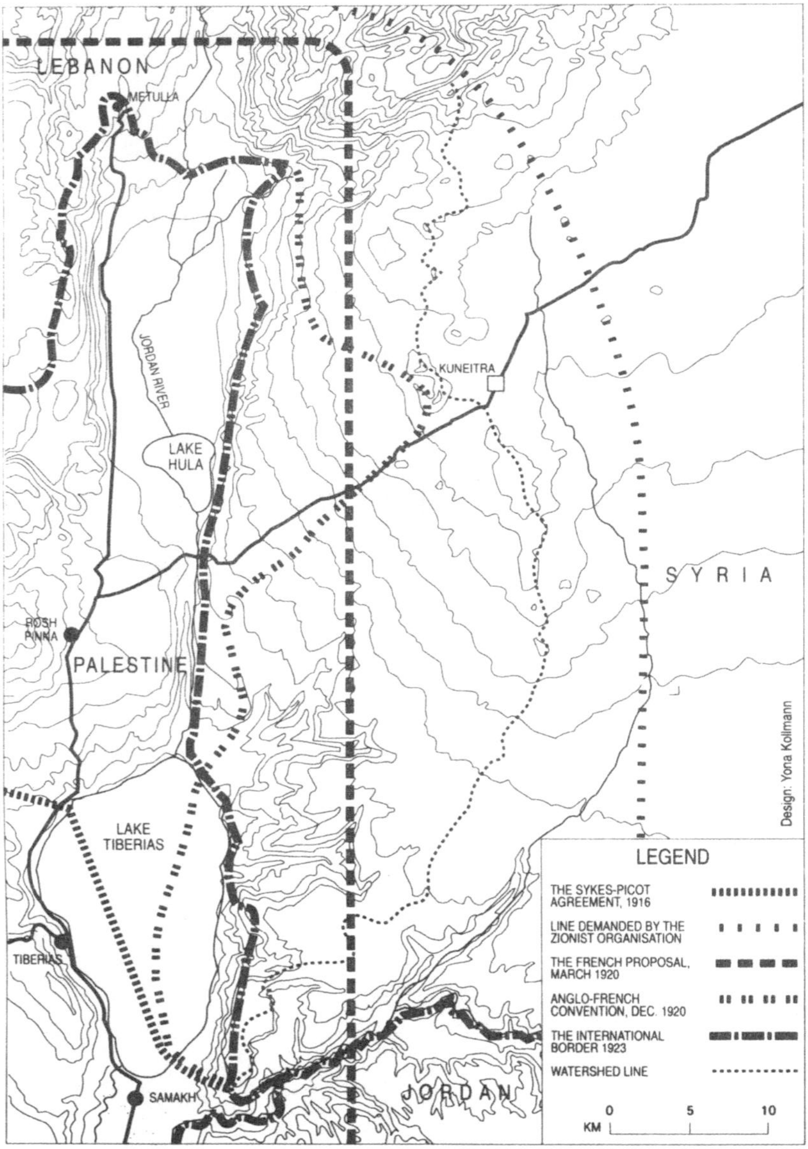

MAP NO. 2
THE SYRIA-PALESTINE BORDER IN THE BANIAS AREA

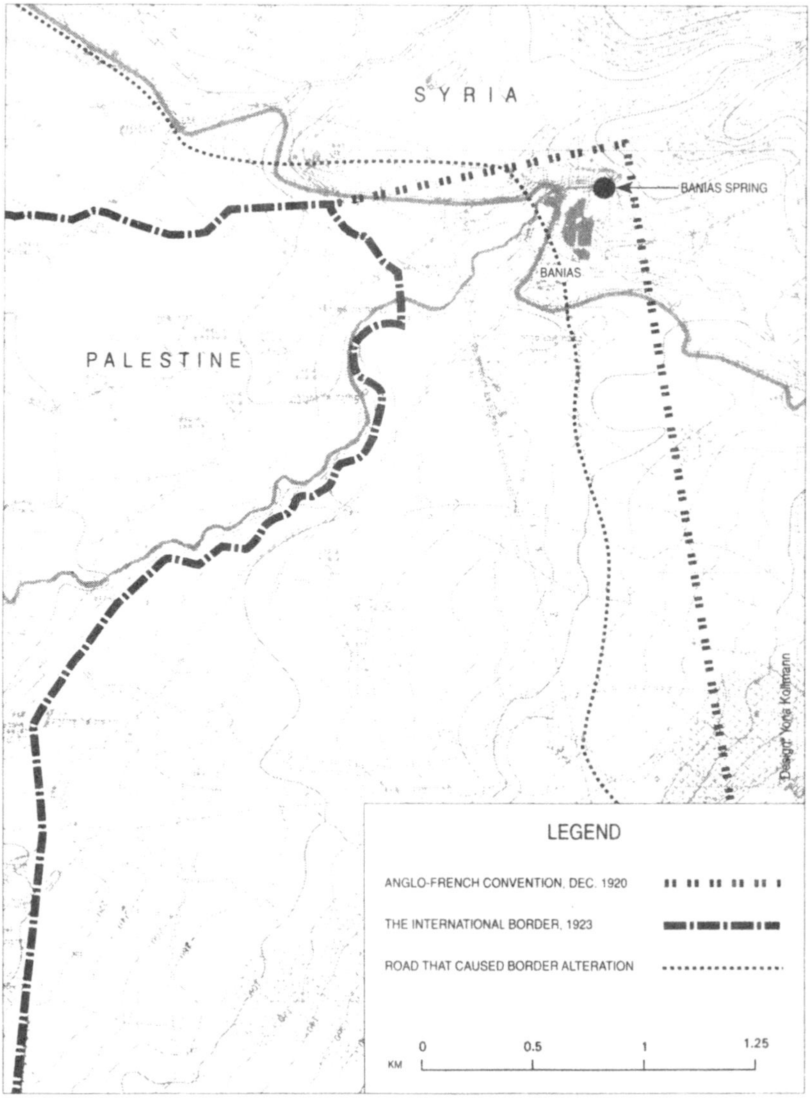

MAP NO. 3
ISRAELI-SYRIAN ARMISTICE AGREEMENT 20 JULY 1949

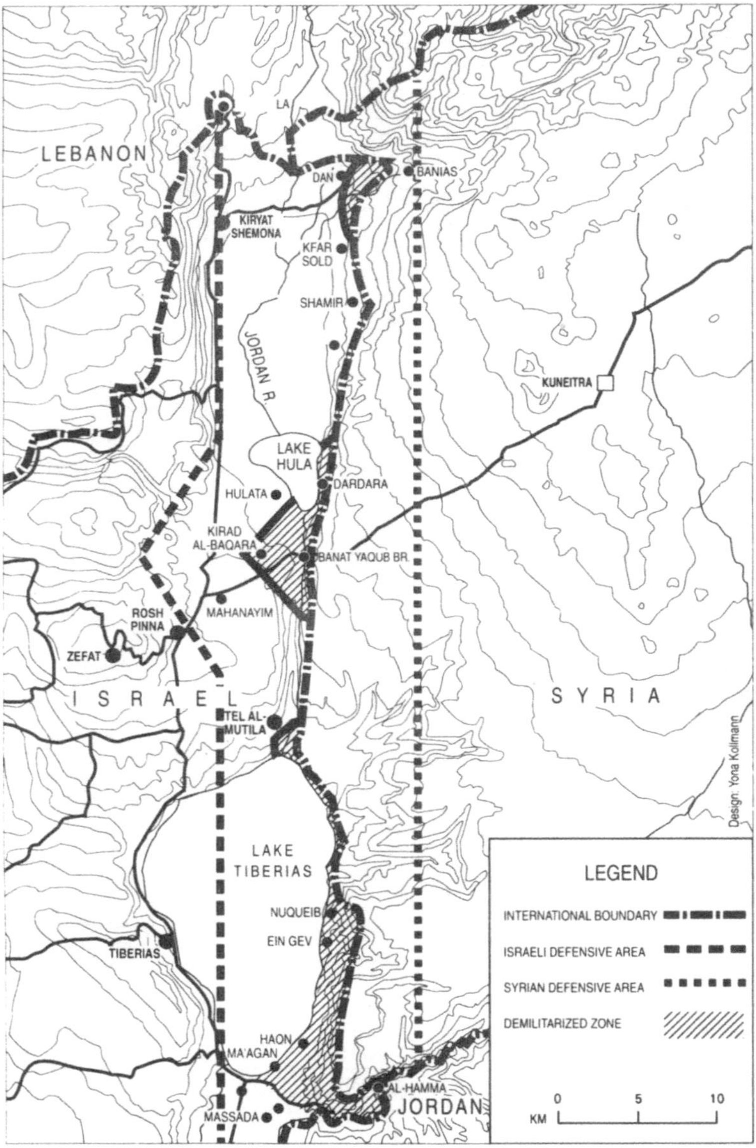

MAP NO. 4
ISRAELI-SYRIAN DISENGAGEMENT AGREEMENT MAY 31 1974

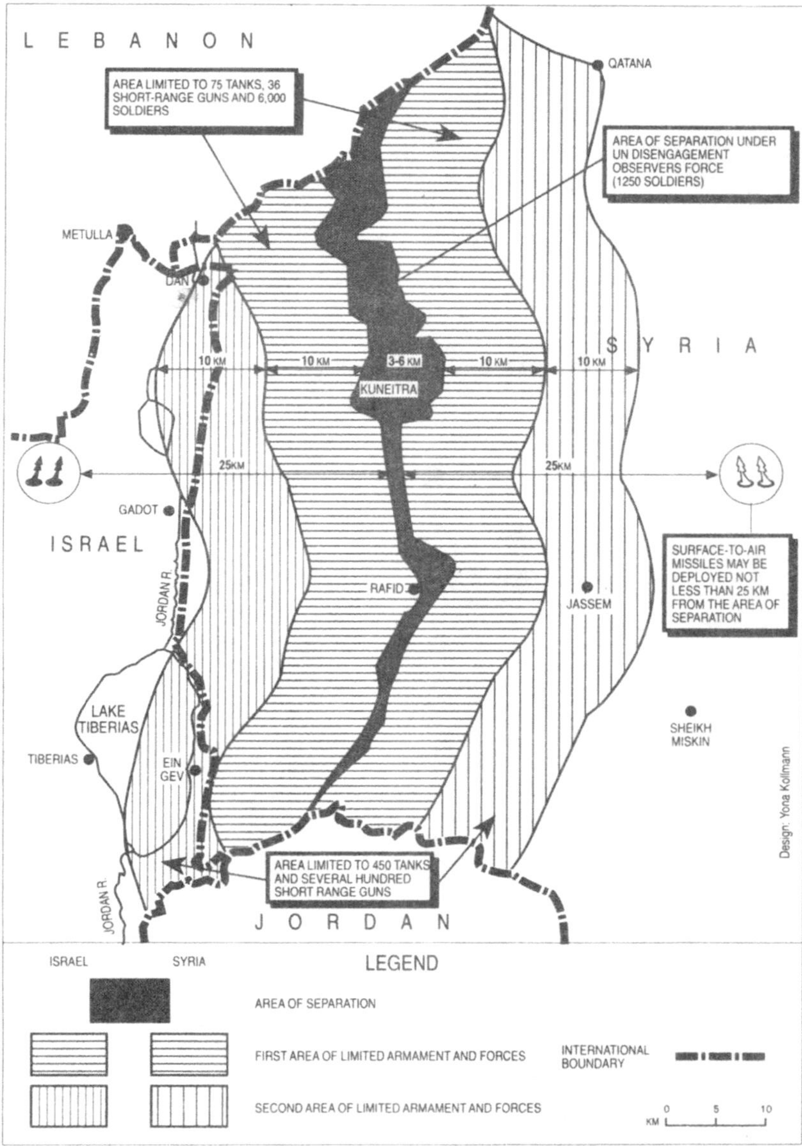

MAP NO. 5
JEWISH AND DRUZE VILLAGES ON THE GOLAN HEIGHTS 1993

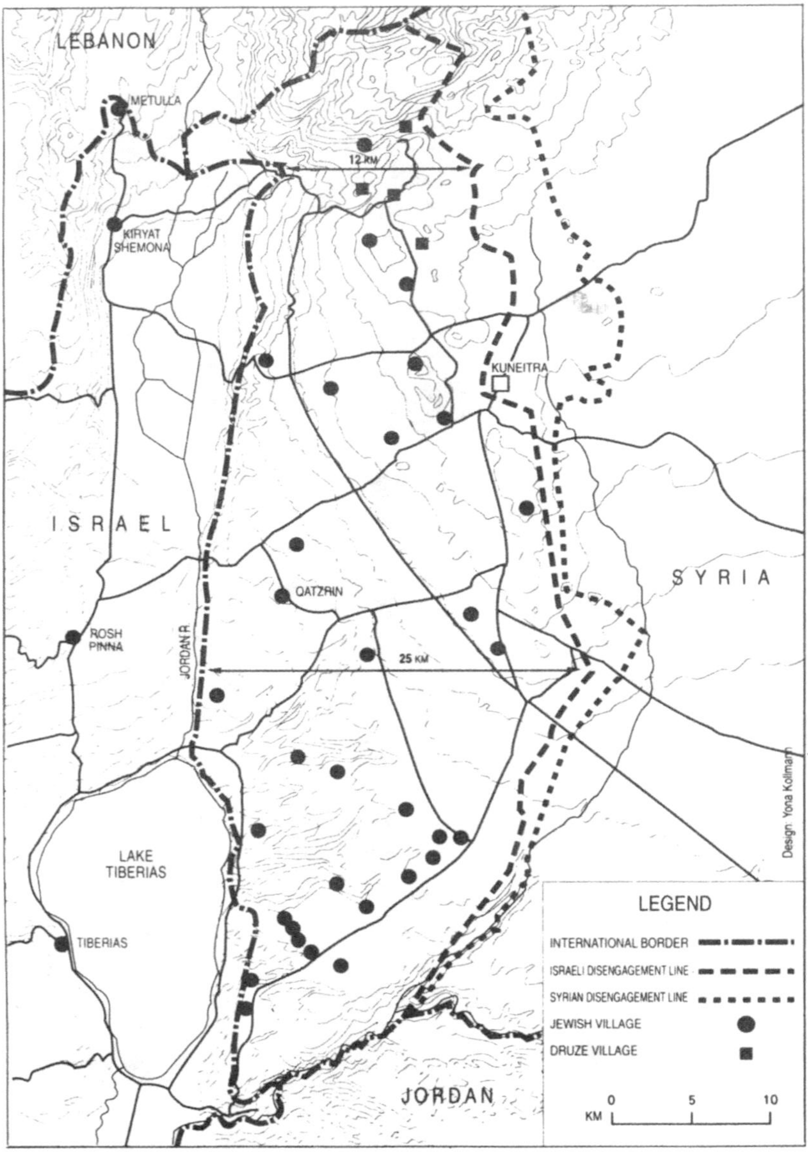

MAP NO. 6 THE GOLAN BETWEEN HAIFA AND DAMASCUS

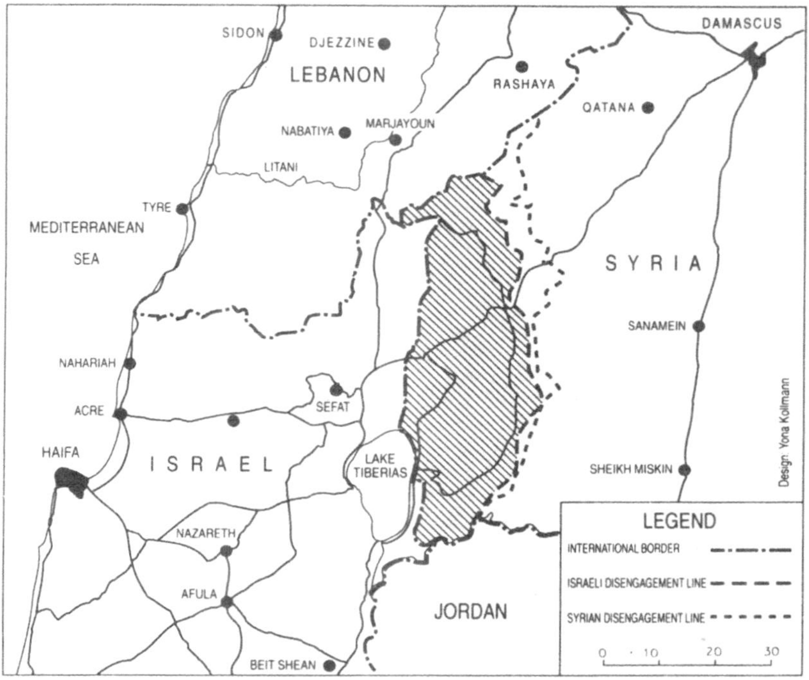

MAP NO. 7
GOLAN HEIGHTS: MAIN TOPOGRAPHICAL FEATURES

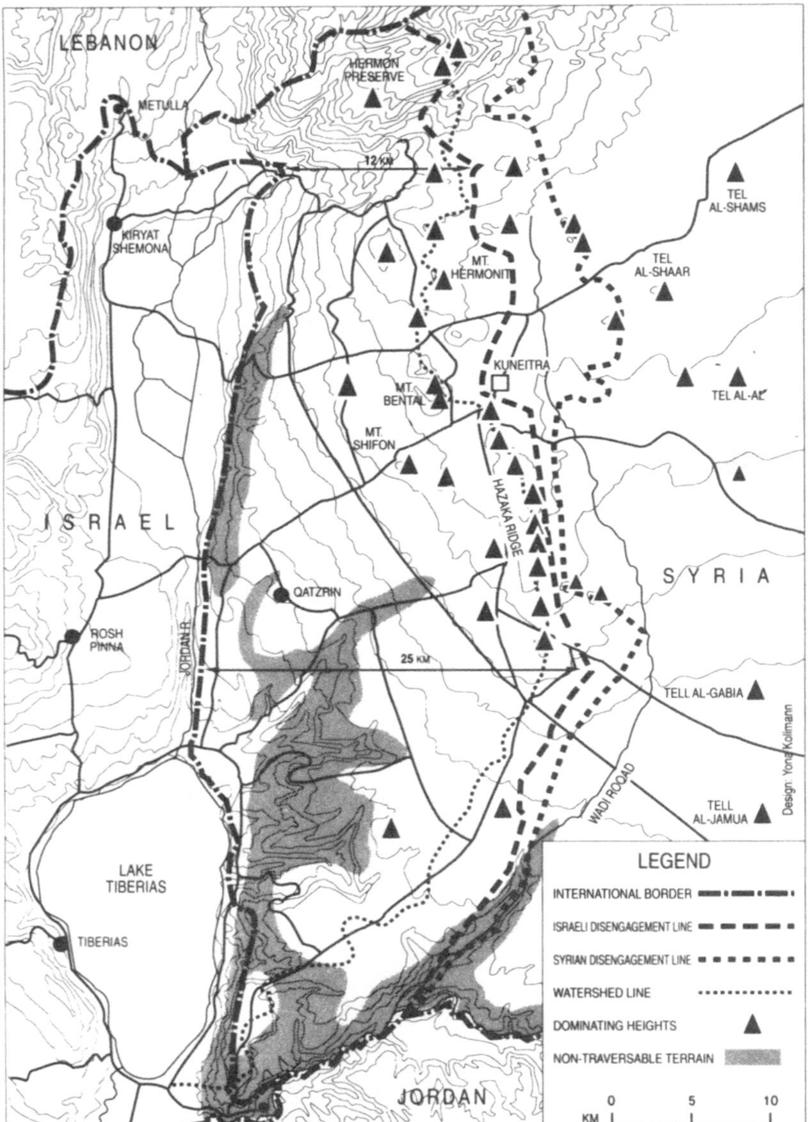

MAP NO. 8
OBSERVATION DISTANCES FROM MT. BENTAL (KMS.)

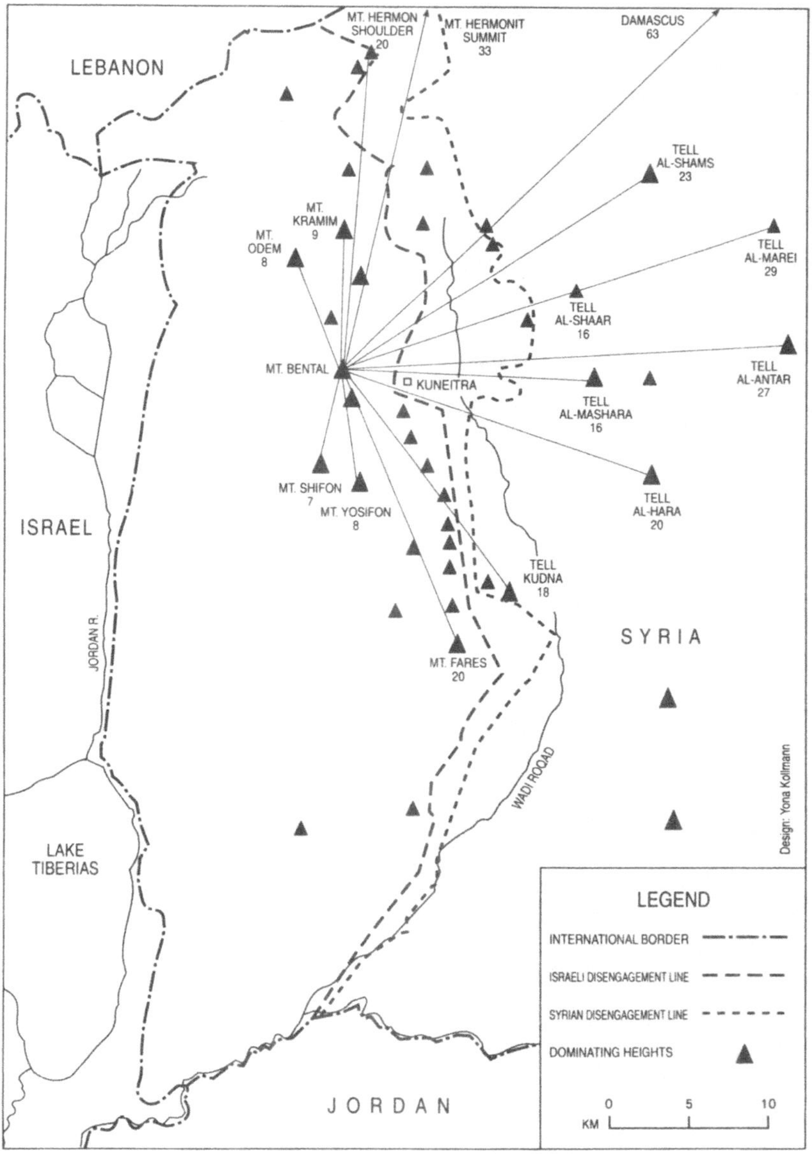

MAP NO. 9
OBSERVATION DISTANCES FROM MT. FARES (KMS.)

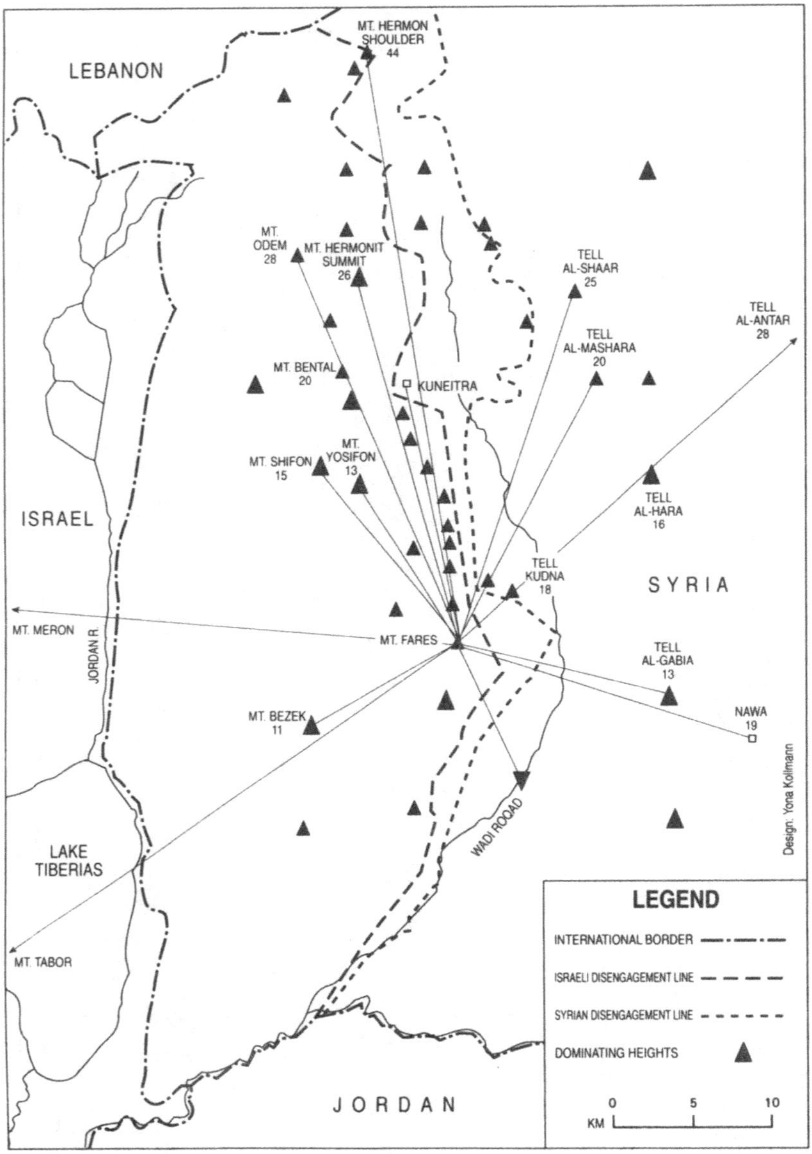

MAP NO. 10

THE ISRAELI-EGYPTIAN PEACE AGREEMENT 26 MARCH 1979

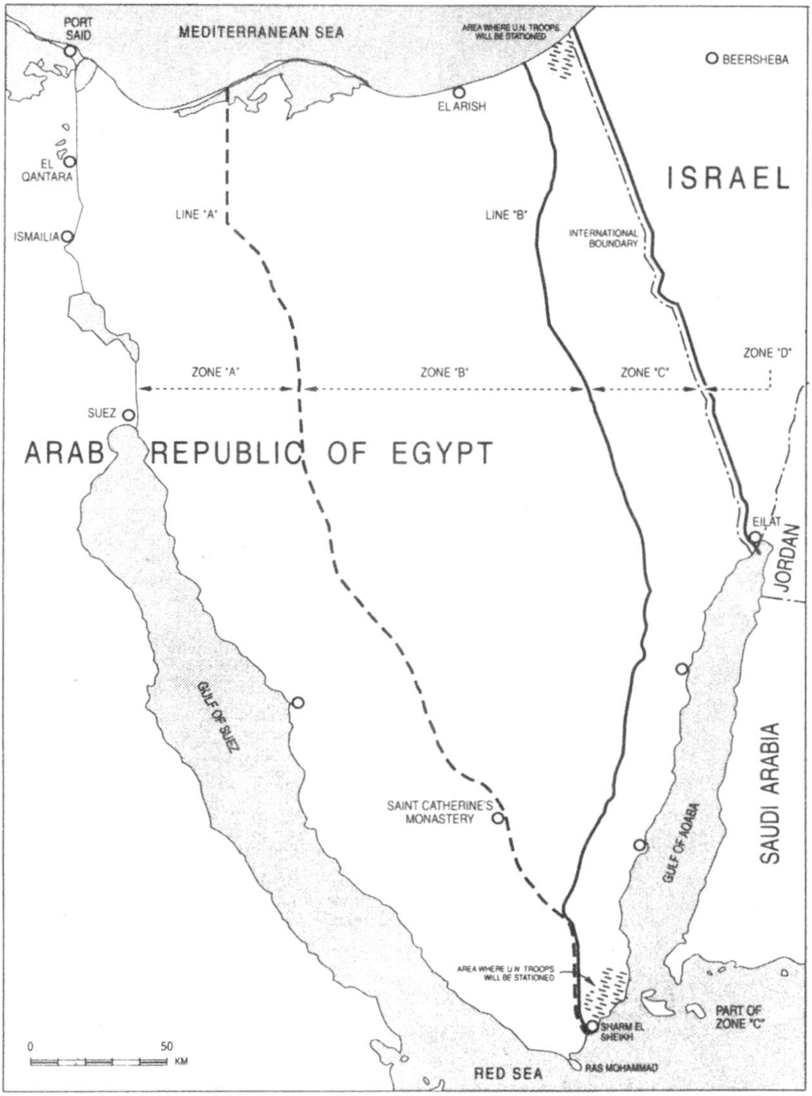

FIGURE NO. 1
TOPOGRAPHIC STRUCTURE OF THE GOLAN: SECTIONS

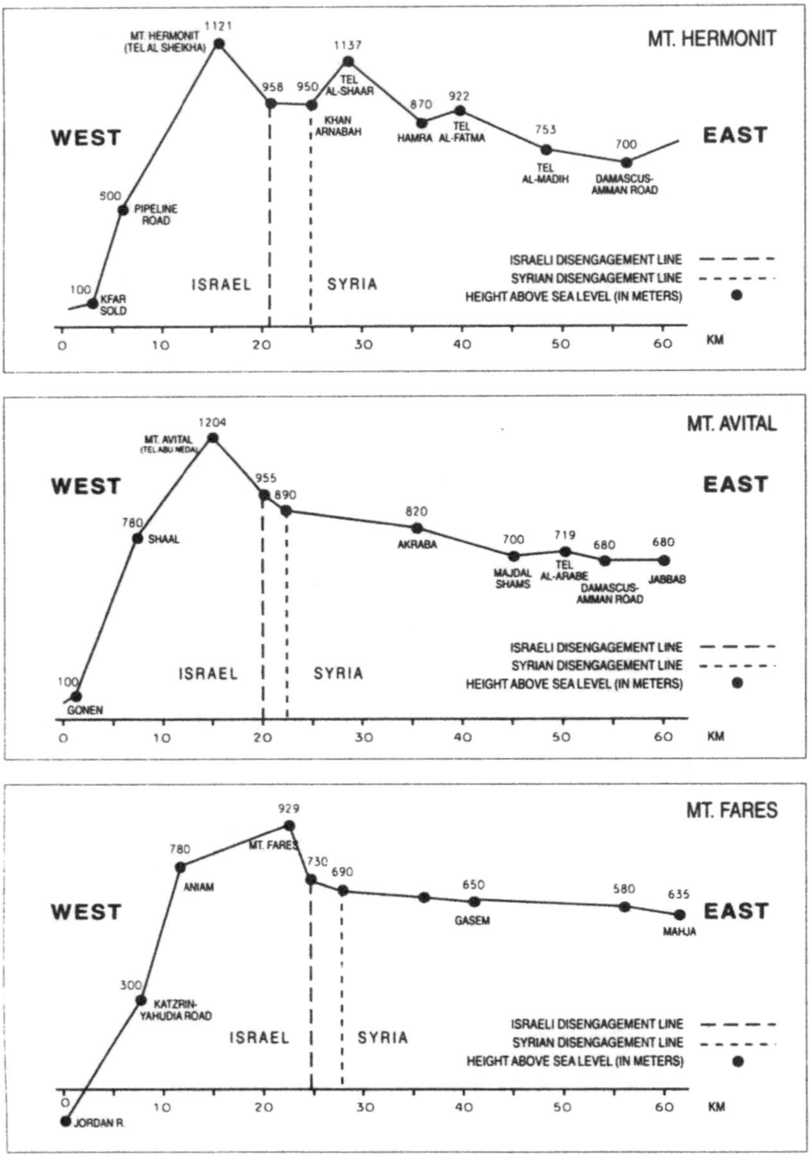

Part IV

Security Risks for Israel

If Israel and Syria sign a peace agreement and it is implemented smoothly (including the normalization clauses), hopefully two important processes will gradually develop: the risk of war between Israel and Syria--and the other Arab states--will decline; and the prospects for terminating the Arab-Israel conflict will be augmented.

By the same token, if the negotiations fail, and particularly if the cause is what the United States perceives as Israeli intransigence in the face of partial Arab flexibility, the Arab states could conclude that negotiations with Israel are futile. And they would continue to find it difficult to accept indefinitely Israel's occupation of their territories.

Failure of the peace negotiations with Syria (and with the other parties) could, therefore, entail negative consequences for Israel. One would be deterioration in relations with the United States and with Western Europe--and improved relations between them and the Arab states--leading to reduced support for Israel and quite possibly to diminished strategic backing (political and military), particularly if, as noted, Israel is seen to be the intransigent party. Another could be the long term loss of any opportunity to make peace with the Arab states on the basis of territories for peace. Finally, Syria and the other Arab states would become convinced that the only viable alternative vis-a-vis Israel was the military option. Within a few years of deadlocked talks, the risk of war could loom again.

It follows that if Syria and other Arab parties display flexibility toward the substance of peace, and Israel's stand is based on preserving the status quo, especially in the territorial sphere, rather than encouraging mutual concessions toward the attainment of a peace treaty--then Israel will court considerable risk.

Chapter 13. Probable Risks in the Aftermath of a Peace Treaty

An examination of potential security risks to Israel following the signing of a peace treaty with Syria is usefully preceded by an analysis of the argument which is occasionally voiced (albeit, by a distinct minority) that, despite previous hostile relations, the treaty will create a new situation in which the risk of war between Israel and any Arab state will be eliminated. Some might claim that the so-called "new world order" of the post-Gulf War era will eliminate all risk of war anywhere. Everyone hopes that this will be the case, but for the present it is a premature conclusion.

Historically, Israel and the Arab states have understood peace differently. For Israel peace is the goal, whereas for the Arab states (as illustrated in the case of Egypt) peace is a means toward at least two ends: Israeli withdrawal from the territories it captured in 1967, and improved relations with the United States, expressed in the form of long-term aid from Washington. Since the Arabs view peace not as a goal but as a price to be paid, it makes sense, from their point of view, to pay as little as possible--again, we note the precedent of Egypt and the "cold peace" since the 1979 peace treaty with Israel. It strains credulity that peace agreements would radically alter that approach overnight, with Arab states immediately accepting Israel's right to exist and rushing to establish normal relations which, in short order, would reduce and finally eliminate war risks. It is sobering, in this context, to consider Iraq's invasion of another Arab state, Kuwait (August 1990), even though no state of war existed between the two countries. Although that example raises questions about the value of a signed and sealed peace treaty as a means to prevent war in the Middle East, and certainly where Israel is concerned, it is clear that war risks are fewer in a situation of peace and the absence of conflict, than in a situation of no peace and a conflict generated by vital interests.

The author's point of departure is that a Syrian-Israeli peace agreement will not in itself terminate the Arab-Israel conflict. Israel will continue to face security risks for a lengthy period. In other words, until a Middle East peace develops that is comparable to the situation in Western Europe, the risk of an Arab attack on Israel will remain. The author basically agrees with the opinion of a leading Israeli dove, Aryeh Eliav: "Not even a binding contractual agreement will uproot from our hearts the dread of the next round."[1]

That risk will probably not be uniform and fixed for the entire transition period. It will become more moderate or more acute as the peace process advances or regresses. Certainly the risk will be gradually reduced if a number of developments take place. These include the signing and implementation of peace treaties with all the confrontation states (Syria, Jordan, Iraq, Lebanon), including the development of normalization; agreement on a permanent (not merely an interim) solution of the Palestinian problem, with the majority of Palestinian refugees being rehabilitated in the Arab states and the refugee camps razed; and the beginning of Arab state reconciliation with Israel's existence. The peace treaties must contain compromises that address vital interests of Israel and the Arab states, yet must not be perceived as harmful, and must help reduce the mutual threat. And finally, indeed ultimately, basic transformation must occur in the Arab world's concept regarding the legitimacy of the use of force to resolve disputes, either among themselves or with others. As a consequence, peaceful relations must develop **within** the Arab world.

This may entail an incipient shift in the direction of democratic regimes in the Arab states. One school of thought in Israel maintains that democracies can more easily resolve conflicts peacefully, whereas non-democracies (such as Syria) may have to resort to violence in conflict resolution. It follows, according to this approach, that Israel should wait for the emergence of democratic regimes in Syria and in other Arab states before making peace.[2] Yet the democratic experiment in Algeria, which was stifled in 1991 following the electoral victory of Islamic fundamentalists, did not prove itself conducive to moderation and suggests, perhaps, that a democratic regime in an Arab state may actually harm the prospects for peace.

Although in 1991 there were increasing calls in Syria for a transition to democracy, and President Assad dwelt on the subject at length in a speech he delivered in March 1992, no such transition is foreseeable any time soon. Assad advocates greater political and economic openness but balks at the idea of genuinely free elections. "Democracy," he stated in the aforementioned speech, "derives from local conditions, and there is no place to import it, since we do not import foreign and artificial political frameworks."[3]

Even if "local conditions" changed in this direction, much time would elapse before the emergence of a fundamentally new situation. In that period the leader of an Arab state bordering on Israel (perhaps even Syria) might launch an attack against it, if regional and world conditions are convenient and if he thinks the prospects for success are high and the risks low. In this regard, war risks will increase during the lengthy transition period if, for example, the two sides are unable to bridge fundamental disputes during the peace talks, as occurred in the 1949 armistice negotiations between Israel and its neighbors. The compromise reached at that time between Israel and Syria on the creation of a demilitarized zone west of the international boundary, but without agreement on the zone's political status, had the effect of exacerbating the dispute. The same pattern may repeat itself in the current negotiations. If, for example, a peace treaty did not involve the return to Syria of all or most of the Golan Heights (though Syria would probably not sign such a treaty in the first place), it could, instead of advancing mutual reconciliation, induce Syria to attempt a military action which would not necessarily stop at the Green Line.

By the same token, neither President Assad, Syria's ruling Ba'th Party, nor any other Damascus government which posits as its primary interest hegemony in the Levant, would agree to a separate peace with Israel. Peace, from the Syrians' point of view, would be conditional on the resolution of the Palestinian problem. Here an interim agreement would not suffice. Yet attainment of a full solution of the Palestinian problem--in a manner acceptable to the Palestinians, Israel and the Arab states--is exceedingly difficult, if not impossible. Only the more distant future, and presently unforeseeable conditions, may see a substantive change in Syria's approach, toward nonlinkage with the Palestinian question.

Even if Israel and the Palestinians could reach a compromise on a permanent solution, the concessions each side would have to make would be heavy and painful. Implementation of the agreement would encounter serious difficulties which might hamper its prospects for success and possibly cause its collapse. This, in turn, would adversely affect the ability of Israel and Syria to maintain and develop their peace. War risks could therefore be magnified.

Moreover, it is a safe assumption that Arab enmity toward Israel will not fade away as soon as peace treaties are signed. The desire to "get rid" of Israel, or to reduce its size by means of an aggressive action, could persist. If a coalition based on nationalist regimes in Syria, Iran and Iraq were to emerge, and if the three states perceived an identity of interests, pressure for such an action could grow even in an era of "peace."

In any event, war risks will increase if a peace treaty does not include security arrangements that prevent the emergence of conditions congenial to a Syrian offensive; or if the treaty does not increase the price to be paid for failure in such a move; or if a balance of forces favorable to Syria develops. Hence the importance of security arrangements as a deterrent to possible future hostilities.

Although this study is concerned with potential security risks to Israel and arrangements to offset them, we should remember that from Syria's perspective Israel was the aggressor in the majority of its wars. In other words, Syria has its own security sensitivities, and the subject will be raised for discussion in the peace negotiations. The major current risk in Syrian eyes lies in the fact that the IDF is poised on the Golan Heights only

60 km from the Syrian capital, a situation Damascus perceives as a strategic threat which must be eliminated.

In the light of the working assumption that a peace treaty will not do away with war risks (although they may well be considerably reduced and perhaps pave the way to more positive developments), we turn now to examine the possible risks to Israel of a specific scenario: a political agreement stipulating the return of the Golan Heights to Syrian sovereignty, and the complete demilitarization of the Golan, together with areas to its east and west.

Chapter 14. Absence of Early-Warning Intelligence

A major strategic risk that will be created if the IDF leaves the Golan Heights is the loss to Israel of early-warning information about an impending attack. Although the IDF has good intelligence, a surprise is always possible. There is no certainty that Israeli intelligence will foresee an attack on the Golan in time to enable the IDF to mobilize and contain the Syrian offensive. Thus Israel could face a surprise attack.

We shall first consider intelligence evaluation and early warning at the national level. Three modes should be distinguished: (1) current situation assessment; (2) assessment of new enemy capabilities in view of changes in the current picture; (3) evaluation of the enemy's intentions. Of these, the last two involve early warning. The assessment of capabilities derives from changes that have occurred in the current situation. In contrast, the evaluation of intentions stems not from any new option the enemy may have acquired, but from the outlook and considerations of its leadership. As explained below, although mistakes are possible in both types of assessment, the probability of error is greater in the area of intentions, which involve leadership decisions, whereas in assessing capabilities the risk of error can be reduced and even prevented.

Forming the current assessment estimate is the simplest of the three modes, as it deals only with facts and not with their implications. Here, too, however, error is possible, usually due to insufficient information. At least one precedent exists in which Israel was surprised by a military move because it lacked information about a change in deployment and preparations by the Egyptian army.[1] A mistake can be made even if reasonable information is available.[2] It is the author's conclusion that improved intelligence-gathering capabilities render this type of surprise in the current situation assessment improbable in the future.

The other two levels of evaluation constitute intelligence early warning. They seek to assess what is expected, or possible, based on information and its analysis, research experience, intuition and the like. The assessment can refer to the other side's capabilities or intentions.

Evaluation of an armed forces' capacity relies chiefly on the current situation assessment, including changes in order of battle, weapons systems, deployment, training, level of commanding officers, etc. Also taken into account are logistical and other preparations carried out in the army and country in question, and potential new abilities inherent in those changes. Even if all, or most, of a state's forces are deployed within the framework of a regular army (rather than reserves), certain modifications must be executed prior to launching an attack. If Israeli intelligence, for example, can collect information attesting to these preparations at their very outset, then shortly after evaluating their significance it would be able to warn that the enemy has acquired an attack option.

Before launching a surprise attack, the Syrian Army would have to make several last-minute preparations, e.g., moving up bridging equipment for fording the Roqad by armored divisions; advancing artillery batteries to cover a wider range of enemy territory, and particularly readying artillery ammunition stores; and deploying short-range surface-to-surface missiles (Frog 7, SS-21) at launch sites relatively close to the front, again to achieve a better range.

It is difficult to estimate the minimum time these preparations would require (not including basic preparations, which would undoubtedly take place long before, such as planning, maneuvers, inter-Arab coordination, etc.), but we are probably talking about 12 to 24 hours. Even if Israeli intelligence receives most of the relevant information, a few hours could elapse before an assessment is completed. Moreover, the enemy preparations could take even less time if some were accomplished in advance. Incoming reports may not be unequivocal, giving rise to differing interpretations about the purposes behind the enemy's redeployment and other moves. It may not be possible to say definitively that the purpose of the preparations in question is to attack Israel.

Syrian deception could also make it difficult for Israel to formulate a correct assessment. Repeated deceptions, to which Israel could become "habituated," could, over time, reduce alertness and, consequently, Israel's early-warning capability and its capacity to meet the threat (mobilization of reserves, preemptive air strike, etc.). Still, Syria would have to exercise caution, since its preparations could prompt an Israeli preemptive strike. Continuous intelligence "coverage" can enhance the ability to distinguish between deceptive moves and real war preparations.

Thus it might take some hours after Syria begins practical preparations before Israel assesses that these are meant to build an offensive option. To minimize that time, extensive intelligence is required about preparations by the Syrian Army. Information must be comprehensive--it is not enough to know what a single division is up to--and should cover the air arm as well as land forces. The information must arrive shortly after preparations have begun.

The assessment of intentions--i.e., forecasting the decisions that the leader of the other side will make--is a complicated and complex task and has often been bungled by Israeli intelligence.[3] This assessment is based largely on agents' reports and far less on electronically acquired information. The most glaring Israeli mistake occurred in October 1973, on the eve of what became known as the Yom Kippur War. The blunder involved the evaluation of intentions, i.e., the understanding of the decision taken by Sadat and Assad to launch a war. Whether such a mistake could recur regarding a Syrian attack, or an offensive on the eastern front in general, is not easy to say in the current state of affairs, since "there is no guarantee against errors and mistakes."[4] At the same time, it should be stressed that the mistake in October 1973 lay in the assessment of Egypt's decisionmaking, i.e., its intentions, not its war capability.[5] One can conclude from the events on the eve of the Yom Kippur War that in the future, too, Israeli military intelligence will be able to supply in good time an assessment regarding the development of an offensive option by an Arab state against Israel, based on reports of practical preparations.

There is a good possibility that by means of intensive in-depth information-gathering Israel would be able to learn about preparations by Syria to launch a war, and on that basis would be able within hours to evaluate whether the practical ability to attack exists. Nevertheless, enemy concealment and deception may deprive Israel of this information. Furthermore, correct information could be wrongly interpreted, with the attack plan being detected only after the enemy's forces are already on the move. What follows, then, deals mainly with the measures required to obtain a pre-attack warning.

How important is the Golan Heights for obtaining information from which an accurate current situation evaluation could warn in advance of a Syrian attack option? We have noted that the key is to spot practical preparations as early as possible. Intelligence views such preparations as "indications" of a possible attack. Before it is possible to assess that certain preparations can enable a war to be launched, it is essential to detect and understand them, and to "read" them for possible changes in the situation.

A major, perhaps crucial source for obtaining early warning lies in technological intelligence (SIGINT, or signals intelligence, referring to communications and electronic intelligence) and observation using optical and electro-optic instruments. Another element is ground-based observation radar, including long-range radar, which can locate and identify movement by armored vehicles, other vehicles and personnel. The combination of three conditions is required to produce such intelligence: First, a full "line of vision" for observation, and an almost full line of vision for SIGINT, between the instruments that are collecting the information and each of the sources they are targeting. Secondly, continuous collection-contact with the sources: this is the only way to know whether certain facts are new and the situation has changed, and if it has--how and to what degree. And third, in order to pinpoint the exact location where ground activity is underway (redeployment, clearing of axes through minefields, movement of forces, etc.), it is essential to monitor (by observation and especially with electronic equipment) the activity from at least two sites. This is particularly important regarding movement of enemy forces, which may be a primary element in early warning.

The advantage of the high mounds in the eastern Golan Heights is that the line of vision they offer across long distances toward the east enables the large-scale collection of accurate data. Elevations further to the west in Israel are not an adequate substitute. Because of their distance from the front and because their lines of vision are, at least in part, blocked (by the mounds in the eastern Golan), they allow the collection of only incomplete intelligence. Similarly, as we shall see, the use of balloons and monitoring aircraft (devices universally employed) is inadequate. It is therefore essential for Israel to maintain a number of electronic-intelligence bases on the Golan Heights to meet the early-warning and intelligence needs of the air force, as long as there is a risk that Syria may launch a war.

Visual observation posts based on the eastern Golan mounds are another essential element. They can detect, at a distance of up to several dozen km, the movement of forces and weapons, including surface-to-air missiles, the low-altitude approach of combat aircraft and helicopters, including helicopter gunships, and even aircraft on the ground. The removal of this intelligence-collection means (if Israel is denied access to observation sites on some of the eastern mounds) can only partially be compensated for by airborne surveillance.

Until the 1967 war, the IDF's collection installations were located on high terrain west of the international boundary. True, Israel "muddled through" with that situation. But since then considerable changes have taken place. For one, today's Syrian Army is larger by far than in 1967, and is almost entirely armored and mechanized; its combat equipment has been modernized and it possesses offensive capability, whereas prior to 1967 its orientation was primarily defensive. It follows that the danger today is greater, that the time required for pre-attack preparations--as well as the elapsed time between the start of movement for an attack and the attack itself--can be far shorter. Early warning therefore becomes critically important.

Secondly, until 1967 a large part of the Syrian Army was deployed on the Golan Heights, and priority in coverage to detect indications of Syrian preparations for an attack was directed toward that area. This was possible from elevated locations inside Israel, which offer a line of vision to the western Golan. Again, however, the situation has changed: the Syrian Army is now east of the Golan, and, as explained above, the mounds in the eastern Golan block the line of vision from Israel to those areas. (One may assume that a peace agreement that demilitarizes the Golan would perpetuate this situation.) Therefore, a system for collecting early-warning information that is based on elevated sites inside Israel cannot meet current assessment needs.

Finally, radio communications in the Middle East have undergone a change. Until 1967 the Syrian and Egyptian armies used primarily HF communications instruments at the tactical level. VHF was just being introduced. When the Yom Kippur War opened up the possibility of advanced and sophisticated tactical communications, western and Soviet alike, communications technology, and especially military communications, underwent considerable development. Thus, SIGINT sources ceased to operate on HF some time ago. Tactical communications are mainly VHF and their reception requires a line of vision, i.e., high altitude. Here again, Syrian VHF communications cannot be received from Sefat and the Galilee hills because they are blocked by the mounds in the eastern Golan. Such reception is possible only from the highest points in the eastern Golan.

One possibility, which needs further examination, is to raise the altitude of the receiving stations several km above the Golan Heights. A variety of conditions could place severe limitations on some of these alternatives, but they merit examination. Balloons, for example, enjoy an advantage over aircraft in their ability to provide continuity. Their disadvantage lies in their sensitivity to bad weather and their propensity for technical hitches. Even if several balloons were launched simultaneously, severe weather over northern Israel could defeat their purpose. A further complication is that balloons would interfere with both military and civilian flights.

Monitoring and surveillance aircraft, on the other hand, lack total continuity. Such aircraft can only supplement, not replace, ground-based collection facilities, since continuous coverage is essential to detect changes in real time. Aerial photographs, although important, are no substitute for visual observation posts--which allow a continuous stream of activity to be identified--because they provide a static picture of a given moment. A steady continuity of photographs would be very problematic because that requires frequent surveillance flights.

Turning to the option of satellites, even if Israel acquires all the advanced technologies needed to build and orbit one or more satellites, and has the financial means required, it is very doubtful whether this means, for all its importance, can replace ground-based early-warning stations. To illustrate the problems involved, we will examine the effectiveness of a static (geostationary) satellite, i.e., one which orbits the earth above a constant site, at high speed and a high altitude. Because the satellite has to maintain an altitude of 36,000 km, this limits its use for intelligence purposes. Thus it cannot be used for aerial photography, which requires a satellite orbiting at no more than a few hundred km altitude. And it is very improbable that the satellite would be able to pick up VHF transmissions from the ground, although HF transmissions may occasionally be received, because of the great distance, and because satellites can be outfitted with only small antennas (they can serve for communications if the ground transmission uses large antennas, enabling good reception by satellites).

If static satellites are not useful for early-warning purposes, what about a satellite orbiting at a relatively low altitude?[6] Such a satellite can cruise above the same point approximately once every seven hours (3.5 times per day). It orbits the earth in 90 minutes and requires five to six orbits before returning to the same point. Its cruising speed is 10 km per second. A photograph taken from an altitude of over 300 km covers an area of 20 sq km. Therefore, two or three satellites are needed in order to photograph an area of several dozen sq km. Individual objects, such as jeeps, can be identified from such a photograph, which can be transmitted to the ground. Night photography is possible using infrared equipment, though the quality is inferior to daylight photography.

A few satellites of this type can provide important information through aerial photography, but their effectiveness in obtaining advance warning through listening is very limited, since every seven hours they overfly Syria for only a few minutes. To provide continuity of both photography and radio monitoring over every part of Syria would require a few dozen satellites--an unlikely proposition. It costs $1 billion to develop a system of low-altitude satellites, a prodigious investment. Every satellite costs $20-30 million, and a launch costs some $30 million.

Another option could involve unmanned installations at some of the high mounds in the eastern Golan. Technologically, it is possible to install unmanned sensors at some of these sites and to receive information through them via a transmission back to Israel. However, a number of limitations cast doubt on the efficacy of this alternative. Thus, for example, the installations would neither be staffed nor protected by the IDF if they were located in an area outside its control. They would be vulnerable to sabotage and to electromagnetic disturbances. And proper maintenance (servicing defective parts, replacing equipment, etc.) would be very problematic. Moreover, because of anticipated developments in Syrian communications systems, it would be necessary--to ensure continuous early-warning capability--occasionally to renew the equipment at the relay sites, including installation of additional technologies and antennas. Syria would almost certainly object to this.

In theory, of course, it is possible to install sensors that will transmit back to Israel even what is observed from long-range unmanned observation points. But if their locations are known to the adversary, it becomes a comparatively simple matter to disrupt, if not prevent, their collecting capability. And even if the disruption itself could be regarded as a form of warning, Israel would find it virtually impossible to rely on this important source of SIGINT and long-range observation.

We have seen, then, just how essential the SIGINT stations on the mounds of the eastern Golan Heights are, and the importance of long-range observation posts there. Before concluding, we will examine two more alternatives: one is to receive early-warning information from American intelligence. This assumes that the peace treaty stipulates the presence of an American force on the Golan with SIGINT stations, and that the United States undertakes to transmit to Israel in real time all intelligence raw material pertaining to Syria. Yet even in the best case, if the United States were ready to make a commitment to Israel in this regard, Israel would not be able to rely on early-warning intelligence based solely on information from a foreign source pertaining to a potential existential danger from a regional enemy on its border.

The second possibility is to rely on the early detection of Syrian war preparations by the Israeli embassy in Damascus that would be established as part of the normalization process. Although this might be sufficient to cover the area around the capital, and perhaps some other important sources, the Syrians could be expected to engage in a counter-effort to reduce the potential damage they might sustain. Syria could restrict the embassy's activity--though, again, this in itself could be regarded as a warning signal. In any event, Israeli freedom of activity inside Syria is liable to be limited from the outset, and it would be difficult to rely on that presence as a substitute for electronic installations on the Golan Heights. An embassy or other official legation cannot serve as a basis for intelligence collection, since the adversary will do all in his power to foil such activity. By way of comparison, if the superpowers could rely on their embassies abroad to collect intelligence information for early-warning purposes, they could dispense with the vast array of expensive espionage devices that they employ.

Conclusion

Early warning will remain critical for Israel as long as the risk of a war with Syria exists. This is because of the time Israel requires to mobilize its reserves. In contrast, Syria needs to make only a few preparations before launching an attack, and can cross the relatively narrow Golan Heights (12 to 25 km) in a short time.

An analysis of the possibilities in this critical realm shows that the only effective option by which Israel can meet its early-warning needs is by using the high mounds on the eastern Golan, and particularly Mount Hermon. Satellites, balloons, surveillance aircraft, reports from foreign sources and other means can be supplementary elements--but by no means substitutes.

Thus the crucial areas for installing early-warning stations during the period when war risks continue to exist are Mount Hermon in the north and several places on the line of mounds. In order to obtain Syria's consent to this arrangement, Israel will have to consider whether it could allow Syria to meet its own early-warning needs by installing an identical number of SIGINT and observation stations on the Golan, and perhaps also in Eastern Galilee. Compared with the loss to Israel if it is forced to withdraw its early-warning stations from the Golan, the benefit to Syria from installing a station there would be marginal.

Chapter 15. Threat from the Air

Generally speaking, the emerging balance of air power in the Middle East is to Israel's disadvantage. Not only numbers of combat aircraft must be taken into account, but also quality, i.e., the introduction of advanced aircraft into the Arab states' order of battle, at a time when Israel finds it difficult to compete because of budgetary constraints.

With 620 combat aircraft, Syria has the largest air force of the countries bordering Israel. By comparison, Egypt has 540 and Israel 640. Syria has twice as many interceptors as Israel (340 vs. 170), but 40 percent fewer strike aircraft (280 vs. 470).[1] True, the Syrian Air Force has not proved its mettle in confrontations with the Israel Air Force (IAF), but it has taken an active part in the Arab-Israeli wars. Its size, training efforts and advanced aircraft mean that it cannot be dismissed as a potential threat.

Syria has nearly twice as many military airfields as Israel (21 vs. 11), and in terms of distance from targets inside Israel, all of them can accommodate strike aircraft. Thus, in order to neutralize (and, if possible, destroy) Israeli air power in a war, Syria would have to attack half the number of airfields that Israel would have to attack in Syria. Syria, then, could allocate more planes per target, while Israel would have to disperse its strike capability.

There is no doubt that the Syrian Air Force will take part in any future war between Syria and Israel, including attack missions. Because of its size, even if only one-third of its strike aircraft bomb their targets, heavy damage and large numbers of casualties will result. For this reason it is important to examine the contribution of the Golan Heights to the air war, and to inquire how important it may be for Israel to retain the Golan even after signing a peace treaty with Syria. Thus we turn now to examine Israel's operational needs from this point of view.

Early warning and intelligence were covered in Chapter 14.

Ground radar. Good radar can cover an area of more than 250 sq km. It is not necessary to install radar stations on the Golan Heights, since such stations based on the high ground in Israel can achieve control, command and early-warning. Israel should oppose any Syrian request to install radar on the Golan, since it would be able to scan all of Israel. Of course the Syrians could mount airborne radar, but its cost is prohibitive.

Aerial photography. The May 1974 Separation of Forces Agreement between Syria and Israel permits each country to fly up to the forward line of its ground forces (Israel to Line A, Syria to Line B; see Map 4). Using oblique aerial photography, each country can cover the other to a depth of 40 to 45 km. If the terms of a peace treaty allow Israel to fly only as far as a line west of the Golan Heights (not to the present Line A), aerial photography would be able to cover to a depth of only 20 to 25 km of the area east of the Heights, meaning a loss of information. This could be overcome in a number of ways.

One possibility is that the peace treaty would allow Israel to go on flying, at least for the purpose of aerial photography (and for observation and ELINT, i.e. electronic intelligence derived from electromagnetic radiation) as far as Line A. This would be Israel's preference, as its aerial photography capability is far greater than Syria's.

Alternatively, the US could pledge, within the framework of the peace agreement, to supply each side with aerial photographs weekly (taken from planes or satellites) of an area covering 40 km on each side of the Golan Heights. In situations of tension, the Americans would provide such photographs with greater frequency, even one per day, at Syrian or Israeli request.

This alternative is less advantageous for Israel, since the coverage in the hands of both sides would be identical. There are indications that the United States already supplies Syria and Israel, once every few weeks, with aerial photographs of the limited-forces zones, though naturally this does not replace each country's right to carry out its own aerial photography missions.

Finally, Israel could compensate itself for a reduction in its aerial photography capability, by employing its own reconnaissance satellites.

Surface-to-air missile batteries. The separation-of-forces agreement prohibits both sides from placing surface-to-air missiles closer than 25 km from the separation lines. Both sides respect this limitation. The major risk in the realm of air warfare if the Golan is demilitarized within the framework of a peace treaty, is that surface-to-air missile batteries could be moved forward. If the present limitation on their placement is maintained, this risk will be reduced.

It should be noted that the Patriot surface-to-air missiles now in Israel's possession, with a range of about 100 km for intercepting aircraft (vs. 40 km for the HAWK), could be situated in the Galilee.

Israel's air-strike capability. In a war, the IAF does not require an Israeli military presence on the Golan Heights in order to attack airfields and other targets in Syria. Even if Israel and Jordan reach a peace agreement, the IAF may wish, for operational reasons, to send part of its strike force from Israel into Syria through northern Jordan. It would therefore be useful for Israel to obtain Jordan's agreement that, if Syria attacks Israel, the IAF will be allowed to overfly northern Jordan en route to Syria. In any event, such an agreement would be of conditional military significance, since it is doubtful whether Israel could rely on it automatically, to fly over Jordan's missile-protected area.

Syrian observation from the Golan. New Syrian settlements, built on the Golan Heights following its evacuation by Israel under the terms of a peace treaty, could serve as a cover for installing observation points and perhaps even laser guidance devices to help direct air attacks.[2] An effective supervision mechanism would be essential to deal with possible violations in the demilitarized zone, and particularly to ensure that no laser guidance devices were installed.

Air-training areas.[3] As small as the Golan Heights is, its airspace, as well as that of Judea and Samaria, assumed new importance for IAF training flights following Israel's withdrawal from Sinai. The IAF is presumably obliged already to make considerable use of simulators for training purposes (because of space and budget constraints). Loss of the Golan would necessitate a further cutback in this area. One possible alternative, besides simulators, would be to conduct training flights over the Mediterranean Sea; this is feasible for air combat exercises but not for practicing air-to-surface attacks or low-altitude navigation.

Conclusion

The IDF's presence or nonpresence on the Golan Heights will have almost no effect on Syria's potential to attack targets in Israel in a war. The main ground factor in this regard would be the location of surface-to-air missiles. A peace treaty which leaves intact the current arrangement (contained in the 1974 separation-of-forces agreement), according to which Syria may not deploy missile batteries closer than 25 km east of Line B (with Israeli batteries no closer than 25 km west of Line A), would have no negative implications. It would also be necessary for Israel to install on the Golan Heights a number of long-range electronic and observation early-warning posts. These would considerably enhance its ability to obtain advance intelligence about an impending Syrian attack (including an air attack). Finally, Israeli flights as far as Line A for aerial photography, covering an area of 40 to 45 km east of Line B, should be allowed to continue.

Chapter 16. War

This chapter examines the possibilities of an attack on Israel in the more distant future, an attack in which Syria plays a central or exclusive role. In this scenario, even though Israel has signed a peace treaty with Syria and with other Arab states, war nevertheless erupts within a few years.

Impact of the Future Battlefield

We begin by considering the impact that precision weapons will have on the battlefield of the future. The question is examined first at the strategic level and then at the operational-tactical level.

At the strategic level, during the five weeks of the Gulf War (January 18-February 25, 1991) Iraq launched about 40 Al-Hussein (Improved Scud) surface-to-surface missiles at densely populated Israeli cities. The attacks caused tremendous dislocations. It was the first time since 1948 that the civilian sector in Israel "became the front," so to speak, and that an Arab state did not hesitate to use strategic weapons against Israeli cities.

Iraq's action dramatized the fact that Israel has no defense against such missiles and that it was unable to deter a distant Arab state from using them. Nor did Israel try to eliminate the Iraqi missile batteries, one reason being the operational difficulties involved. Should Iraq's use of surface-to-surface missiles to achieve strategic objectives be seen as a turning point in the Arab states' military modus operandi against Israel?

According to Maj. Gen. (Res.) Yisrael Tal, the Arab states "have reached the strategic parity they desire, in other words, strategic deterrent capability, and they have done so by means of surface-to-surface missiles." In the past, Israel's air power gave it a monopoly on strategic deterrence. Today, however, "we have lost our monopoly on strategic deterrence and the danger is that it will pass to the [Arab states remote from Israel.]"[1]

According to this view, the danger in the future is that the Arab states, with their vast financial resources, will obtain western technologies which enable them to acquire precision surface-to-surface missiles. They would then be able to hit point targets in Israel such as airfields, POMCUSes, command-and-control centers, supply bases and power stations, and to disrupt the mobilization of IDF reserves. On the day that they are capable of neutralizing the IAF with the use of precision weapons, they will be able "to set the rules of the game of war, in other words, to choose total war"[2] and advance the strategic phase of applied firepower to the stage of movement and preparations for attack.

The conclusion is that at the strategic level precision weapons (surface-to-surface missiles) will play a major role in a future Arab-Israeli war, and that Israel could lose its deterrent capability vis-a-vis remote states. In a possible future war with states on the eastern front, Syria and perhaps others would probably use surface-to-surface missiles against strategic targets, perhaps even from the very start of hostilities. It would be total war and the civilian sector would no longer be immune, as it was in the pre-Gulf War era. Syria would undoubtedly pay a very heavy price if it mounted a strategic attack using missiles. However, it could launch such an attack together with other Arab states. And the threat from the IAF would be reduced "if the Arabs have smart precision missiles that can hit airfields in Israel and impair its air power."[3]

There are two main schools of thought about how precision munitions would influence future warfare. According to one view, strategy determines activity at the operative level and operative considerations, in turn, determine tactics. Modern weapons systems, including precision anti-tank weapons, are not relevant here because they belong to the tactical level. The Arabs' firepower will be decisive even in the ground battle at the tactical-operative level if the IAF is neutralized by precision missiles. In this view, "the new battlefield will not give the Syrians additional options at the tactical and operative level, other than better defense against fighter aircraft thanks to more effective anti-aircraft weapons."[4]

A similar view holds that "territory will have tremendous significance for the future battlefield," and "the fighting will be to capture territory and prevent the enemy from doing the same."[5] Even though the future battlefield will give preference to firepower on the front, in the rear, and between the two, this will not affect the defense of the Golan Heights.

The second and perhaps conflicting view[6] is that the traditional battlefield will be basically the same in the coming years, with a few changes. The transition to a new doctrine capable of deciding a war based on the use of long-range precision weapons, will be extremely costly and entail decisions of principle by the government. This option could be actualized within nine or ten years if decisions are not put off. The shift to precision-guided munitions (PGMs), besides its cost, will also involve a considerable scaledown of the traditional army. The transition will not be possible while the risk of war remains. It may be possible in an era of peace and reduced risks, enabling resources to be reallocated from the traditional army to PGMs. In that instance, however, the government will not give the IDF priority in the allocation of state resources and may even slash the defense budget.

If indeed the future battlefield is characterized by long-range precision firepower, then operational gains (such as neutralizing the enemy's reserves at all levels) will be possible with the use of precision weapons at various depths. At the same time, tank crews will operate at a range of 3 to 4 km using tactical precision munitions. Dominant terrain will become far less significant. In the initial period after acquiring PGM capability the enemy may be tempted, in a situation of rising tension, to occupy the Golan Heights by force. If Syria's economic situation improves dramatically (which does not seem likely at present), it may be able to develop PGM capabilities while continuing to maintain a large traditional army. If so, this would pose a grave threat to Israel. Even if that scenario is not actualized, Israel's working assumption must be that Syria will acquire PGM capabilities and that in a war PGMs will constitute the major weapons systems of both sides. To defeat Syria under these conditions, Israel would require many thousands of precision weapons with ranges of 5 km and more. The cost would be prohibitive.

Taking into account the differences of opinion and the conflicting scenarios, the author's point of departure is that in the coming years, at least, the Middle Eastern battlefield will retain its traditional character. It follows that territory and the ability to threaten vital interests of the enemy will continue to be important.

Objectives of an Attack

Syria might launch an attack in two basic situations: on its own, or jointly and in a single front with Jordan, Iraq and perhaps other Arab states and/or Iran. In each case the war aims will be different. If Syria attacks alone and other Arab states do not join afterward, its approach will be more cautious; the ground offensive will not seek to occupy territory west of the Golan Heights (subject to change if the advancing Syrian forces encounter few difficulties). In contrast, if a coordinated attack is mounted by Arab forces in other sectors as well, Syria's objective might be to seize territory west of the international boundary, i.e., in the Galilee. Some experts believe that this was Syria's real goal in the 1973 Yom Kippur War. Syrian Defense Minister Mustafa Tlas stated in 1984: "In the October War eleven years ago we wanted to cross the Jordan [west of the international boundary]."[7] Similarly, Mahmoud Riad, who was Egypt's foreign minister in 1973, wrote: "The Plan agreed upon between the two countries had been that Egyptian forces should reach the passes and beyond if possible, to enable Syria to liberate the Golan and pose a threat to north Israel."[8] One may well ask what Riad means by "pose a threat to north Israel," but if this is combined with Tlas's remark, one can conclude that there was a genuine threat to the Galilee. In any event, the essential premise here is that Syria, having regained a demilitarized Golan in a peace agreement with Israel, decides to cancel the peace and create a new military threat to Israel, with the option of consolidating its gains and advancing into Israeli territory in the Galilee.

Mode of Attack

The opening of the ground war and of the entire offensive would depend, again, on whether Syria were acting alone or in concert with others. If the latter, Syrian ground forces would try to seize at least the Golan Heights, with the Jordanians attempting to capture Judea and Samaria. An Iraqi expeditionary force would operate in either or both of the sectors as a secondary strategic echelon.

Such an attack might be launched from one of two basic situations: First, Syrian and Jordanian ground forces might attack from their permanent deployment posture in order to maximize the element of surprise and achieve successes in the first two critical days (until the IDF can mobilize and deploy its reserves). Alternatively, the attack would be launched after a large part of the Syrian Army (including artillery, surface-to-air missiles and ammunition stores) assumed an emergency defensive deployment (from which it could also mount an offensive) between Damascus and the front, while Iraqi expeditionary forces entered Syria and Jordan. The aim would be to provoke the IDF into attacking the heavily entrenched Syrian emergency array, consisting of five to six divisions. Once the Israeli attack was broken, Syria would take the offensive in more congenial operational conditions, with the Iraqi units helping consolidate the gains.[9]

The second mode would pose high risks to Syria, and even more to Jordan, in the form of the possible prior mobilization of the IDF and even a preemptive Israeli strike against the advancing Syrian forces before they could complete their emergency deployment.

How, then, could Syria achieve strategic surprise in the first mode of operation, whether acting alone or as part of an Arab coalition? From the Syrians' point of view, an attack is most conveniently launched in the morning, when the sun is in the east and thus behind them and in the IDF's eyes. During the two nights preceding zero-hour the Syrians would move up and deploy artillery, missile batteries and other forces to provide covering fire for the attacking units. Syrian artillery comprises up to 1,700 guns (belonging to the six divisions stationed between Damascus and the Golan Heights and to the General Staff artillery brigade), towed surface-to-air missile batteries (the mobile batteries are assigned to the attacking divisions), and engineering units to breach obstacles.

Even if we assume that under the terms of a peace treaty the Golan Heights is demilitarized, Damascus would have to take into account the likelihood that Israel would discover its war preparations, some of which would begin several days before the attack. Syria, then, must make its preparations on the basis of a worst-case scenario from its standpoint, namely that some IDF units succeed in entering the Golan Heights and taking up positions before the attack begins.

A few hours before dawn the divisions assigned to invade the Golan Heights would set out. At dawn Syrian fighters would attack Israeli airfields and other strategic targets (joined by Iraqi and perhaps also Jordanian planes). At the same time, or slightly later, Syria and Iraq could begin firing surface-to-surface missiles deep into Israel, mainly targeting sites crucial to the mobilization of the reserves and perhaps larger strategic targets. Syria would have at its disposal three types of missiles: Scud B (range: 280 km), Scud C (500 km) and SS-21 (80 km).

Syrian helicopters could land a large number of paratroops and commando units in two areas: the western Golan, in order to isolate the entire Golan sector and delay advancing IDF units; and on the dominant terrain in the eastern Golan. Simultaneously an artillery barrage could target sites west of the international boundary, making use of two long-range guns: the 180-mm S-23 (range: 32 km) and the 130-mm M-46 (27.1 km).[10] Concurrently three divisions could attempt to break through into the Golan Heights, with three divisions behind them as the secondary attack echelon.

As the offensive began, four or five Iraqi divisions would move out of their home bases on the way to take part in the battle for the Golan Heights (and possibly also the West Bank). The first division could arrive within forty-eight hours.

Syrian ground forces are trained to attack either from a contact line or from a mobile base. In the former case the attacking forces advance to the contact line (forward line) of the army, organize and then launch the offensive. Arab armies, including the Syrian Army, are better trained in this type of attack, hence its advantage for the Syrians. The problem is the probable loss of the element of surprise: the Syrians must assume that Israel would immediately spot the forward movement of their forces and certainly their preparations once at the forward line. The second possibility, an attack launched from a mobile base, affords a greater likelihood of surprise, but is far more difficult to execute. Nevertheless, it is feasible, particularly if the Golan is demilitarized and the IDF is not deployed there in advance. In that situation the Syrians could hope to move unimpeded, at least in the initial stages of their thrust into the Golan. This study takes as its premise a Syrian mobile attack.

Momentarily ignoring IDF interference and countermeasures, if we allow a relatively slow technical time for operational movement, and taking into account the Golan's narrow width of between 12 and 25 km, it is the author's assessment that Syrian forces could capture the Golan Heights in less than 12 hours under conditions of demilitarization and complete surprise.

As for possible Israeli interference: in a Syrian surprise attack along the lines described above, including the blocking by commando units of the five steep axes of ascent from west to east (with an elevation difference of about 500 meters) along two or three km at the Golan's western extremity, Israeli regular forces would have to breach at least some of the barriers in order to advance into the Golan and do battle with the advancing main Syrian force. The IDF could also interfere by means of artillery fire and especially air strikes against Syrian strategic targets, against surface-to-air missile batteries on and near the Golan, and against advancing mechanized units. It is impossible to evaluate the results of these countermeasures.

Were Syrians to attack before the IDF had mobilized reserves, and to capture all or most of the Golan, a counterattack would be required to dislodge them. It is most unlikely that Israel, in order to avert bloodshed or perhaps to create the backdrop for another round of war, would turn to the political arena in order to force the Syrians to retreat. For the consolidation of Syrian control on the Golan would mean the loss of Israel's deterrent capability and the risk of additional military moves against it in the future.

In a counterattack the IDF's primary difficulty would be the terrain. The topography of the area affords a clear advantage to the defender (in this case the Syrians) against a force coming from the west. This advantage would in part be offset by the fact that at this stage the Syrians would not yet be dug in, somewhat limiting their defensive ability.

Conclusion

Although the probability of a Syrian attack may decrease after a peace treaty is signed, it cannot be ruled out completely. Israel's primary objective should be to ensure that the political and military conditions are such that Syria avoids opting for war.

One important way to induce the Syrians not to attack, particularly during a lengthy transitional period in which full peace does not yet prevail, is security arrangements. If they do decide to attack, the Syrians will make every effort to achieve surprise. It is therefore essential that the security arrangements allow for the early detection of preparations for an attack, thus preventing a surprise, and enable the IDF to deploy in advance on dominant terrain of the Golan, i.e., its eastern area.

Chapter 17. Extension of the Front to Lebanon

In the course of attacking the Golan, Syria might also launch an offensive through Lebanon. This risk has been on Israel's agenda since 1976. It was on the night of May 31-June 1, 1976 that Syria first moved army units--a reinforced armored division--into Lebanon. Although this was primarily a politically motivated invasion (exploitation of the civil war in Lebanon to extend hegemony there), Syria had long since set it sights on Lebanon as an important security element in the event of war with Israel. Lebanon, in this conception, would be transformed from an "auxiliary front" into a "confrontation front," and would be integrated into a single front extending from Rosh Hanikra on the Mediterranean coast to Jordan's port of Aqaba, covering Israel's northern and eastern borders.

Following Operation Peace for Galilee (1982), in which the IDF attacked Syrian forces in Lebanon, the Lebanese Bekaa took on greater importance. The Bekaa, which lies between Mount Lebanon in the west and Anti-Lebanon and Mount Hermon in the east, is 120 km long and ranges in width from 12 km in the south to 30 km in the north. Although maneuverability in the Bekaa is difficult because of irrigation ditches and concentrated agriculture, armored combat is possible. The Barda River divides the hills east of the Bekaa from the Anti-Lebanon hills to the north and Mount Hermon to the south. There are no longitudinal axes in these hills; the principal lateral axis is the Damascus-Shtoura-Beirut road which traverses the southern part of the Anti-Lebanon hills. According to Damascus, the Bekaa is a Syrian security zone because through it Israel could flank the well-fortified Golan front and threaten both Damascus and northern Syria, while Syria could strike at the Galilee Panhandle via the Bekaa. The Syrian leadership therefore views the Bekaa as a security area of military and strategic importance.

Israel is liable to face a number of risks from Syria through southern Lebanon, and particularly through the Bekaa, during an attack on the Golan Heights. One is an attack directed at the Galilee Panhandle parallel to a main effort aimed at capturing the Golan Heights and, if possible, territory west of the international boundary. An attack via the Bekaa axis would probably be mounted by the Syrian force in Lebanon, comprising two and a half to three divisions.

First, however, the Syrians would presumably weigh the pros and cons of launching a parallel offensive through the Bekaa in order to capture the Galilee Panhandle, or, alternatively, sufficing with a defensive alignment there. The arguments against an offensive would include the difficulty of justifying the capture of Israeli territory in the international arena; the danger posed to Syrian gains in Lebanon if the attack fails; and the likelihood that Syrian forces in Lebanon would become a legitimate long-term target for Israeli attacks if Syria made use of Lebanese territory in an unsuccessful war.

Moreover, while a Syrian force could move down the Lebanese coast south of the Awali River in order to threaten Israel and keep IDF units occupied, this would involve crossing "red lines" (such as the Awali) that could trigger a military clash with Israel in Lebanon. Syria's respect for the red lines is likely to persist, at least as long as Syria does not attack the Golan. The principal red lines about which understanding was reached in 1976 with the aid of the United States were: Syrian forces will not move south of the existing line toward the Lebanon-Israel border; Syria will not introduce surface-to-air missiles into Lebanon and Syrian aircraft will not overfly Lebanon; and the arrangements in the security zone of southern Lebanon will remain intact and the South Lebanon Army (SLA) will be free to assist residents in the Djezzine enclave.

Another alternative for Syria would be to activate terrorist forces from Lebanon in support of an offensive against the Golan and to pose a concrete threat to population centers in northern Israel. To this end, Syria could enlist the aid of Palestinian groups and Hizballah. Their operational options could including firing of rockets at Israel, with virtually no preparation needed, and with a small number of terrorist squads slipping into the Galilee to carry out attacks; and sending a large number of squads across the border to carry out attacks and "quality operations"--a move requiring several weeks of preparations.

Syria could also move surface-to-air missile batteries into the Bekaa or, less probably, into southern Lebanon, in order to protect the Damascus area and limit the IAF's freedom of the air. This might be done even if it slightly weakened Syria's anti-aircraft deployment between the Golan and Damascus. Because Syria is aware of the risk to which its missiles would be exposed if they were moved into the Bekaa, it would probably take such a step only under special circumstances.

Finally, if the entire Golan Heights were returned to Syria, Lebanon might cooperate with Damascus and at its behest divert the waters of the Hatzbani River (together with Syria's diversion of the Banias) to prevent them from reaching Israel.

Military Risks: Conclusion

The preceding four chapters demonstrate that the strategic importance of the Golan Heights lies in three spheres:

Defense: The Golan constitutes a defense buffer for the Jordan Valley and Eastern Galilee and for their civilian populations. Without the Golan it would be difficult, if not impossible, to defend these areas against the Syrian Army, which has become much stronger since the 1973 war, let alone defend them against an entire eastern front. In other words, as long as the risk of war exists, the Golan affords some depth (of an operational character) for defending northern Israel and thus preventing the capture of cities such as Tiberias and Sefat and, ultimately, Haifa.

Here the military balance enters the picture. The Syrian Army, the potential enemy for a war across the Golan, is nearly four times as large as the Jordanian Army (the potential enemy for a war in Judea and Samaria). In a war, Israel's entire north would be endangered. It is therefore essential that the security arrangements be such as to prevent the Syrian Army from seizing the Golan in a surprise attack.

Deterrence. The IDF's presence on the Golan Heights has major deterrence value because of the potential threat it poses to Damascus, 60 km away.

Bargaining asset. The Golan, or large parts of it, could be an asset to be used politically by Israel as a quid pro quo for peace.

Chapter 18. Israel's Water Resources

Water is a crucial issue for several Middle Eastern states, but for none, perhaps, more than Israel. The leadership of the pre-state Yishuv and afterward of Israel considered water a strategic, indeed an existential asset. It was the compromise reached in the 1920s by the two Mandatory Powers, Britain and France, over the Syria-Palestine boundary, that created the potential for conflict and for Syrian interference on the water question. Three main factors are involved. First, a large portion of the sources of the Jordan (Hatzbani and Banias) remained across the border, in Lebanon and Syria. Secondly, the third source of the Jordan (Dan) ran very close to the border with Syria. And third, the border in the east lay very close to the Jordan and the natural water reservoirs (Lake Hula, Lake Tiberias [Kinneret]), and the area's topography allowed for Syrian dominance in observation and fire. Although the boundary ran ten meters east of Lake Tiberias' northeastern section, in practice the Syrians controlled this strip.

A brief look at the three tributaries that combine to form the Jordan will be useful:

The **Dan**, the main and richest source of the Jordan, is the only one of the three that is completely within pre-1967 Israel, albeit adjacent to the international boundary. It is fed by the springs at Tell Dan, which are 198 meters above sea level. Deriving from a large subterranean basin, they are not immediately dependent on precipitation. As a result, the Dan's flow is stable and its yield is the same almost the whole year round. Its total annual yield is 272 m^3, including base flow--equivalent to the Hermon and Snir streams combined.

The **Hermon** (**Banias**) originates on the slopes of Mount Hermon at a height of 320 meters above sea level, adjacent to the Banias cave, one km east of the international boundary. It is fed by surface runoff and from a spring near the village of Banias. The stream's flow is heavily dependent on precipitation and its supply displays radical fluctuations: from 16 million m^3 per month in the spring to one-quarter of that amount in the fall. It contributes about 121 million m^3 of water annually to the Jordan.

The **Snir (Hatzbani)** originates in Lebanon at the Hasbeya springs, some 17 km from the Israel-Lebanon border. It is fed by spring water, rain and snow, and is more heavily dependent on precipitation than the Dan or Hermon. The flow differences in summer and winter are extreme. Flash floods in winter can generate 21.5 million m^3 of water a day. Snir contributes about 122 million m^3 of water a year to the Jordan.[1]

An additional source is waters that descend from the Golan to the Hula Valley, Lake Tiberias and the Jordan Valley. The Golan is rich in precipitation, with an annual average rainfall of 1,000 mm in the north and 600 mm in the south. There are about 100 springs of varying yields on the Golan. The streams and springs in the eastern basin of Lake Tiberias have a potential of approximately 105 million m^3 annually. Much of the water from the springs serves the Golan settlements; very little of it reaches Lake Tiberias.

Our analysis of the possible future risks to Israel's access to water will be preceded by a glance at past (pre-1967) experience, with the emphasis on the Syrian (and other Arab) efforts to divert the waters of the Jordan in order to deprive Israel of their use.

The Historical Record

The struggle over water sources was a major characteristic of the armistice regime. For Israel this was an issue of strategic importance which brooked no compromises. In contrast, Israel could accept, for example, albeit with great reluctance, Syrian influence and control in several Arab villages (such as al-Hamma and Nuqeib) in the Demilitarized Zone (DZ) proximate to the international boundary.

The climax of the struggle over water sources came later (beginning in late 1964), when the Syrians (and other Arab states) attempted to divert the Jordan headwaters in order to prevent Israel from implementing its project to divert water from the

Jordan to the Negev desert. This protracted conflict was a major cause of the deterioration in Israeli-Syrian security relations that culminated in the Six-Day War.

Water, then, has been and will continue to be a subject of the greatest importance for Israel. The experience of the past is of the essence here. Based on that experience, Israel must ensure that in a peace treaty with Syria its vital interests in this area are not harmed. We begin with a brief description of four issues which were paramount in the struggle over water sources.

First, the Anglo-French border agreement of 1923 placed the whole of Lake Tiberias and a ten-meter strip on its eastern shore (from the northern end of the southern DZ to the meeting point of the Jordan and Lake Tiberias) in Israel. Until the 1948 war Syrian villagers living near and east of Lake Tiberias used the lake for pleasure boating, fishing and drinking water, based on the arrangements between France and England.[2]

In the first years following the signing of the armistice agreement, Syria acknowledged that it did not have access either to Lake Tiberias or to the ten-meter strip and did not have the right to interfere with Israeli activity in those areas. Still, the ten-meter strip was a source of disagreement as early as 1950. Syria argued that the water line shifted as the lake's water level changed, whereas Israel said that the line was fixed at ten meters east of the highest level of the water.[3] In any event Damascus changed its position with regard to access to Lake Tiberias in late 1953, sparking a violent struggle for the northeastern area of Lake Tiberias.

Secondly, the clash over Israel's project to drain Lake Hula (March-May 1951) had its origins in a Turkish concession of 1914 which a Jewish society purchased from the Syrians in 1934. In early 1951 Israel began draining the Hula and the marshes to its north. The first stage of the project, planned for the area of the DZ south of Lake Hula, was meant to broaden, deepen and straighten the bed of the Jordan for 4.5 km in order to accelerate the water flow. Syria objected to the project and local incidents flared up; these erupted into a sharp military confrontation in two areas, al-Hamma and northwest of Lake

Tiberias. Only after a resolution by the UN Security Council (May 18, 1951) and an Israeli decision to carry out the work on the western side of the Jordan alone, and not on Arab land there, was Israel able to complete the project, against Syria's will but without its interference.[4]

A fourth key issue was the conflict over the diversion of water from the Jordan River inside Israel by means of a canal beginning south of Banat Yaqub Bridge, continuing to Lake Tiberias and from there to the south of the country. On September 2, 1953, following coordination with the UN-appointed chairman of the Mixed Armistice Commission, Israel began earthworks on non-Arab land in the DZ south of Banat Yaqub Bridge. Syria objected vehemently to the project (after previously agreeing to it in March 1952, in secret talks the two countries held on dividing the DZ). The COS of the UN Truce Observation Team, General Bennike, was also opposed to the project. The issue was referred to the Security Council and Israel temporarily suspended work on October 27, 1951, even though the Syrians had not tried to stop the project by force. On January 22, 1954 the Soviet Union cast its first Security Council veto on a Middle East issue to prevent passage of a draft resolution that would have allowed Israel to resume the project.[5] As a result, Israel was forced to revise the plan substantially.

Fourth and lastly, Israel, prevented from diverting the Jordan waters in the DZ, decided to forego that part of the project and launch the National Water Carrier by means of pumping from Lake Tiberias. Large pumps, dug deep into the earth, were installed in the northwest section of Lake Tiberias in order to draw water into a canal extending to the center and south of the country. The water system began to operate on May 26, 1964.

The first Arab summit meeting, held in Cairo in January 1964, decided to step up the general Arab military buildup, implement a coordinated program for diverting the sources of the Jordan--which would deprive Israel of half the river's water and render the National Water Carrier inoperative--and to create, for the first time, a Palestinian political and military authority.[6] These decisions derived from the Arab leaders' assessment that they were not yet ready for a full-scale war with Israel (though Syria demanded a decision on war).

The second summit meeting, held that September in Alexandria, formulated a two-stage program designed to prevent so much as a drop of water reaching Israel from Arab territory. In the first, short-term, stage, which was to last a year and a half to two years, the waters of the Jordan would be diverted but would not be collected for use by Arab states; in the second stage, which would take eight to ten years to implement, dams, reservoirs and hydroelectric stations would be built to exploit the water. The short-term stage comprised diversion of the Hatzbani River in Lebanon, with part of the water going for agricultural use in the Nabatiya area and part to Syria; and diversion of the Banias and of water from the Hatzbani in Syria, involving the digging of a canal 73 km long (and tunnels 4.5 km in length) as far as Wadi Roqad, which spills into the Yarmuk. The canal was to be cut into the western slopes of the Golan at heights ranging from 300 to 350 meters above sea level, at some points very near the border with Israel.

The timetable for completing the work on the Hatzbani was 18 months, while the Banias would require a longer period. Syrian bulldozers began preparing the ground north and south of the Banias in November 1964. Syria now claimed that both Tell Dan and the Dan stream were in its territory, but this was rejected by the UN.

In the ensuing confrontation, Israel took advantage of four border clashes to attack Syrian heavy machinery 2.5 to 12 km east of the border. On March 17, 1965, after the Syrians opened fire on an Israeli patrol near Tell Dan, Israeli tanks responded with direct fire at Syrian machinery working at the foot of the Hermon about 2.5 km from the border. The equipment was hit and the work was moved further south. On May 13, 1965, following a Syrian attack on a patrol east of Mishmar Hayarden, Israeli tanks again went into action, this time knocking out machinery working some 3.5 km from the border. Israel's successful exploitation of border incidents to disrupt the Syrians' work prompted President Nasser to declare (May 31, 1965) that the diversion project entailed the risk of a premature war. Nevertheless, the Syrians went on with their efforts.

On August 12, 1965, the Syrians opened fire at an Israeli tractor working north of the point where the Jordan spills into Lake Tiberias. Israel responded by using tanks and aircraft to attack Syrian machinery 11 km from the border. The fourth and final incident occurred on July 14, 1966. In reaction to a Syrian attack on Israeli tractors, Israeli aircraft destroyed heavy machinery that was working east of Lake Tiberias about 12 km from the border. The Syrians then stopped the water diversion works.

The Syrian diversion project was thus scuttled primarily by means of improved tank gunnery, enabling accuracy to be achieved at ranges which were exceptional in that period.

Possible Risks for Israel

Israel's chronic water shortage accounts for the strategic importance of the Jordan River, the main source of the country's flowing water. It is therefore essential to examine the possible risks to Israel if it has to leave the Golan Heights under the terms of a peace treaty.

The first risk is a renewed Syrian attempt to divert the Banias. This could be done in the same way that an attempt was made in 1964-1965 to deprive Israel of the water and turn it to other uses. By digging a canal 70 to 80 km long--as they began to do in 1964--the Syrians could divert the Banias and deprive Israel of 100 million^3 of water a year. Implementation would require two to three years. Alternatively, Syria could dig a canal along a more easterly route, rendering it difficult for Israel to hit the Syrians' equipment with flat-trajectory fire. Water could be drawn into the canal from the Banias with the use of large pumps. The drawback for the Syrians is that the pumps, unless given elaborate protection, would be close to the border and hence vulnerable to Israeli attack.

As an alternative to diverting the Banias, to deprive Israel of water, Syria could execute a large number of drillings at a depth of hundreds of meters, drawing water from the basin of the Banias, and perhaps also from that of the Dan and the Hatzbani, and then transporting the water through one or more canals. The Banias basin is located beneath the Syrian Hermon, while the Hatzbani receives all its water from an aquifer beneath the Lebanese Hermon. (It is not known whether the three streams are fed by a single underground runoff or a number of separate reservoirs.)

The Syrians could probably accomplish this using technology already available or by means that are easily obtainable. They would have to take into account the possibility that by drilling in order to rob Israel of water, they might reduce the water supply in the Awaj Stream and consequently diminish the flow from there to Damascus. In addition, because the aquifers are very large, considerable time (several years, perhaps) would elapse from the time drilling and pumping begin until the amount of water in the Banias and the other streams was actually reduced. According to expert estimates, the cost of each drilling project would be about one million dollars.

A third possibility is for Syria to block up to 80 million of the 200 million m^3 of water from the sources on the Golan Heights. Technically, it would probably not be feasible for the Syrians to divert springs from west of the cliff (Jalabina, Darbashiya, etc.), which have an output of between 40 and 50 million m^3 a year. Of the remainder, half cannot be blocked because it derives from sporadic floods. But some 80 million m^3 could be blocked by technical means (closure of wadis, for example), and 40 to 50 million m^3 of that amount could be blocked more simply, by using Israeli-built reservoirs.

Possible Countermeasures

Before looking at possible countermeasures to these risks, we will explain briefly the importance of the water reaching Israel from the Golan Heights (primarily from the Banias). True, the Banias represents less than nine percent of Israel's potential water supply (120 million m^3 out of a total of 1,770 million). However, in a situation of a prolonged shortage of water and limitations on its use for agriculture, together with a population increase because of immigration from the former Soviet Union and the expansion of industry that this necessitates, nine percent becomes economically significant.

Nor is this merely a question of economics. Legal-historical rights of use anchored in the Helsinki Convention are involved. It is virtually unheard of for a country to give away natural resources--particularly if a longtime state of war has existed with the recipient. There is no reason for Israel to behave differently.

Over the years, the water issue has come to symbolize an overriding national interest. We have already described the struggles with Syria, often involving violence, for control of water sources, of which the most important was Israel's scuttling of Syria's attempt to divert the waters of the Banias and the Hatzbani. Clearly, then, economic, national and legal reasons--as well as the need to deter Syria--dictate that a peace treaty include clauses to ensure the continued natural flow of water into the Jordan River and to Israel.

Israelis with a security orientation are divided as to how much of the Golan Heights Israel must retain within a peace treaty framework in order to secure the water sources. There are a number of schools of thought on this subject, and they cross party-political lines.

According to a view expressed long ago by Deputy Prime Minister Yigal Allon, Israeli control of the Golan is vital "in order to guarantee us a considerable portion of the water sources."[7] A second opinion, which has several variations, holds that it is sufficient to maintain physical protection close to the water sources and that this does not require holding the entire Golan Heights.

One variation on this theme, expressed by Maj. Gen. (Res.) Yitzhak Hofi, is that the water sources cannot be safeguarded only from one side, as was the case in 1967; a physical presence must be retained on the Golan Heights for this purpose.[8] Another variation is that for Israel to ensure the water sources in the northern Golan close physical proximity is essential, entailing a presence on the shoulder of the Hermon, at least.[9] Maj. Gen. (Res.) Herzl Shafir adds that, as Lake Tiberias is Israel's major water supply, the Syrians must not be allowed a presence on or close to the water line, even in a peace agreement. The water is too important to allow such an inveterate enemy to gain a foothold there. Israel must therefore retain, even in a peace treaty, the plateau above Lake Tiberias which links Syria with Jordan and allows Lake Tiberias to be protected.[10]

According to a third view, although the Golan is vital to Israel for security reasons and for its water sources, the water problem can be resolved by political means within the framework of a peace treaty, and the territory ceded. Thus, Prof. Yuval Ne'eman agrees that the water issue is a crucial one, but believes it may find its solution in a peace settlement.[11] Former chief of staff Mordechai Gur concurs that an agreement on the water problem can be reached with the Syrians in a treaty, and that this issue does not require Israel's presence on the Golan.[12] Maj. Gen. (Res.) Yossi Peled believes that a solution can be found to the water problem and that it is not a crucial issue for Israel.[13]

Conclusion

Water is of existential importance for Israel. It is essential that the flow of water from the sources of the Jordan to Israel continue uninterrupted. The risk that the Syrians will divert the Banias waters will be relevant only if Syria is willing to hazard a war with Israel. There are two reasons for this, both of which are undoubtedly known to Damascus. For one, it will take several years, at least, of drilling and other work before results can be achieved. This rules out the possibility of a Syrian surprise designed to produce a fait accompli. Secondly, precisely because any such move would constitute a clear casus belli for Israel, Syria would initiate it only as part of a plan for war.

If regional water cooperation arrangements can be worked out in the years ahead among the countries of the Middle East, including Israel, it stands to reason that the countries involved will want to maintain them, and will set up supervisory mechanisms accordingly. This would reduce the need for Israel to protect the sources of water reaching it from Syria and Lebanon. In the meantime, to ensure that the water sources remain intact, Israel needs to deploy three forces: in the areas dominating the Banias, in order to prevent its diversion or attempts to pump water from it; in the dominating areas of the Hermon, in order to prevent drilling and pumping of the groundwater that feeds the Banias; and on the escarpment east of the Jordan River and Lake Tiberias, in order to prevent Syria from realizing an ancient ambition: to become Israel's partner in the use of those water sources.

Part V

Security Arrangements in the Transition Period

Chapter 19. Solutions Proposed to Date

An Israeli-Syrian settlement will require a lengthy transition period, though it is still too early to estimate its exact duration. The process would begin following the signing of peace treaties and would, it is hoped, ultimately evolve into genuinely peaceful relations--like those prevailing within the European Union--between Israel and the Arab states and within the Arab world. Some argue that this is an unattainable goal because it depends on the will of the Syrian people and not just its leadership; consequently, they say, Israel should reduce its aspirations in the realm of peace and strive for long-term security arrangements. The author does not share this view. He believes that peace is essential between peoples and not only between leaderships. Visitors to Syria have come away with the impression that the Syrian people themselves want peace with Israel. Yet it would require a lengthy period to cement peace between the two peoples. Obviously, the Syrian government's position will be of crucial influence in the peace process. Damascus' desire for Israel's withdrawal from most of the Golan Heights could spur it to work toward normalization.

If and when true peace (of the Western European variety) prevails in the Middle East, security risks will disappear and borders will assume administrative significance. Until then much time will pass--a transition period--during which war risks will continue to exist in the region, and could erupt into full-scale hostilities. To reduce the probability of a Syrian attack, and to allow Israel to defend itself effectively and with minimal casualties in a possible future war, three elements are required.

The first is a basic change in Syria's political stand toward Israel, entailing acceptance of its existence and readiness to resolve the Arab-Israel conflict. This would inherently lead to the gradual building of peace, i.e., normal and even close ties between Syria and Israel in a broad range of areas: political, economic, cultural, commercial, tourism, etc.

Secondly, progress must be made toward a resolution of the Palestinian problem, involving the rehabilitation and integration of the 1948 refugees in Arab states and the elimination of the refugee camps.

Third, the nature of security arrangements on the Golan and to its east and west, should make Syria consider seriously before attacking. Indeed, they should induce it to avoid that course, while at the same time enabling Israel to withstand such an attack if it does occur (whether a purely Syrian endeavor, or one involving a Jordanian sweep into Judea-Samaria and support from an Iraqi expeditionary force).

This and the ensuing chapters will describe security arrangements that the author believes Israel must insist upon in peace talks with Syria. They are based on the following principles:

* Security arrangements must meet Israel's minimum needs and must be irrevocable.
* They must be the greatest possible deterrent to a Syrian or Arab attack; contribute to preventing a surprise attack; enable Israel to mobilize and deploy its reserves in advance of an attack; and allow Israel to withstand even a surprise attack.
* They will not necessarily be fixed for the entire duration of the transition period, but will be gradually abridged as the risks decline thanks to the (hoped-for) evolution toward true peace.

The possible solutions considered here for the security risks that Israel will face during a lengthy transition period are: superpower guarantees and the stationing of an American force on the Golan; military restrictions to be assumed by Syria; and an Israeli deterrent and defensive alignment on the Golan. Finally, the author's own proposal for security arrangements is based on two major components. One is preventive-defensive arrangements which, if implemented by Israel (or by a third party) would probably prevent or thwart a Syrian offensive. These involve

Israeli early-warning installations on the Golan Heights and deployment by the IDF (or a foreign force) on the Golan. The other involves limitations that Syria would take upon itself to reduce its offensive options and in particular the possibility of launching a surprise attack. These measures, to be applied to the east of the Golan Heights, would include the downscaling of the Syrian regular army, the deployment of a large part of that army along Syria's other borders, and the creation of a large demilitarized zone.

Views in Israel and Syria

Public comments in Israel and in Syria--particularly the latter--on the question of security arrangements remain scarce. Nevertheless, the Syrian authorities know this is a topic the two countries will have to discuss and resolve; and they are well aware that the US clearly supports the need to consider Israeli sensitivity on this issue. Among the few Syrian ideas about security arrangements which have so far been made public is the demilitarization of part, and perhaps all, of the Golan Heights, provided an equal area is demilitarized in Upper Galilee,[1] or, in another variation, with the addition of an area of 10 km on both sides of the Golan.[2] Syrian sources have also suggested that if Israel agreed to Syrian sovereignty on the Golan, Damascus would be able to agree to: an Israeli military presence on the Golan of a size too small to pose an offensive threat, for a predetermined period of five years, until a peace treaty is signed; international and Israeli early-warning installations and observers for a period of between ten and 15 years;[3] and a tripwire force to be placed on both sides of the international boundary by the five permanent members of the Security Council, which would reinforce the UN forces already in the field and prevent the eruption of hostilities.[4]

Ideas expressed in Israel about security arrangements have been more numerous and more diversified, as the following examples indicate. One proposal involves the stationing of forces of the Great Powers on the Golan and in Syria to guarantee that the Syrian Army does not attack Israel, together with a certain thinning out of IDF units on the Golan (since the Syrians would not agree to an IDF presence there).[5] Another insists that the Syrians deploy a large proportion of their forces far from the Golan (for example, two divisions near Tadmor and another near Alexandretta), leaving a relatively small force (two or three divisions) in the area between the front and Damascus.[6] Demilitarization of the Golan Heights is of course also broached, on condition that Syria demilitarize the area between the Golan and Damascus.[7] If so, Israel could make do with long-range observation posts on the Golan and would be able to consider (if Syria's agreement to the Israeli lookouts is contingent on this) agreeing to Syrian and UN observation posts on the Golan.[8]

Other Israeli security thinkers have insisted on entrusting security on the Golan Heights only to the IDF, as no other force could provide adequate security, and US forces must not be involved in Israel's defense.[9]

In addition, certain adjustments on the international boundary have been called for, such as: assuring Israel's control of the ten-meter strip east of Lake Tiberias (Kinneret); ensuring that the border runs two to three km east of the Jordan River and that the flow of the Banias water sources remains uninterrupted; holding the east bank of the Jordan River and maintaining observation posts on the Golan Heights, of which the most important are the Hermon shoulder and one or more of the high mounds.[10]

Finally, it is frequently mentioned in Israel that, because the building of peace will be a lengthy process in which war risks continue to exist, it is essential for the IDF to be deployed for ten to 15 years on the eastern line of the Golan's high mounds. Following this transition period compromises could be considered, depending on the situation.[11]

Chapter 20. Egypt and Israel: Security and Normalization

Security Arrangements

The Israeli-Egyptian peace treaty, signed at the White House on March 26, 1979, contains a military annex relating, among other subjects, to security arrangements (see Appendix 5). We shall first consider how relevant these arrangements are to a future Israeli-Syrian peace. The military annex stipulated Israeli withdrawal in two stages from the entire Sinai Peninsula. Even after that withdrawal, the majority of the Egyptian Army remained west of the Suez Canal with no restrictions on its positioning. The peninsula itself, which is some 250 km wide, was divided into three zones (see Map 10), with a fourth inside Israel:

Zone A--extending 50 to 60 km from the Suez Canal. In this zone Egypt may maintain one mechanized division (consisting of three mechanized infantry brigades and one armored brigade), up to 126 artillery pieces, up to 126 anti-aircraft guns, several surface-to-air missiles, up to 230 tanks and other materiel.

Zone B--extending east of Zone A for 100 to 130 km. Here Egypt may maintain border units of four battalions equipped with light weapons.

Zone C--extending from the eastern end of Zone B to the international boundary line between Israel and Egypt and ranging from 16 to 30 km in width. This zone is limited to UN forces and Egyptian civil police, the latter equipped with light weapons.

Zone D--a narrow strip of a few km running parallel to and east of the international boundary line on the Israeli side. Israeli forces in this zone are limited to four infantry battalions and may not include tanks, artillery and anti-aircraft missiles (man-portable surface-to-air missiles are permitted).

As for overflights, the annex stipulates that no Egyptian combat or reconnaissance flights will take place east of Zone A, nor Israeli flights west of Zone D. Practically speaking, this means that neither country can take aerial photographs of any area in which the other side maintains military forces. Similarly, "Egypt and Israel may establish and operate early warning systems only in Zones A and D, respectively." Such facilities, in other words, are located at a considerable distance, 150 km, from the forward forces of the other side.

The annex stipulates that UN forces and observers [in reality a non-UN force, the MFO, was established for this purpose; A.S.] will supervise the implementation of the military annex, operating "check points, reconnaissance patrols, and observation posts along the international boundary" and in Zone C (not in Zones A and B). Periodic inspections are held in Zones A and B and in Zone D (in the latter only by UN Observers), with the findings reported to both sides.

The majority of the security arrangements in the Israeli-Egyptian peace treaty are inappropriate for the Golan Heights for the following reasons:

First, because the Golan is about one-tenth the width of Sinai, the time Israel would have at its disposal in the event of an Egyptian attack is far greater than would be the case in a Syrian attack. Israel might even have sufficient time to organize a parallel, if not a preemptive, attack before Egyptian troops could cross the international boundary. In contrast, if Israel does not maintain troops on the Golan the time required for a preemptive strike, or even to mobilize the reserves, might be too short.

Secondly, forces on the Golan Heights could pose an immediate danger to nearby Israeli towns, whereas the eastern extremity of Sinai is 40 km away from the nearest Israeli city, Beersheba (Eilat is adjacent to Sinai but access to the city via Sinai is limited).

Third, Sinai's desert terrain enables the IAF to disrupt advancing enemy forces far more readily than on the Golan.

Israeli-Egyptian Normalization

A second aspect of the Israeli-Egyptian peace that bears examination is the state of normalization between the two countries. In the Israeli perception, normalization helps instill security and therefore increases the prospects for peace. As Moshe Arens explained in 1992 (when he was minister of defense), "The purpose of [establishing] relations with Egypt is to create a pattern that will lead to a one-way peace, without any possible U-turns."[1] During the peace negotiations Egypt accepted the idea of normal relations with Israel. In the peace treaty, Par. 3 of Article III states that the two sides "agree that the normal relationship established between them will include full recognition, diplomatic, economic and cultural relations," and other elements. Annex III, titled "Protocol Concerning Relations of the Parties," elaborates on this subject and contains general agreements in eight areas: diplomatic and consular relations, economic and trade relations, cultural relations, freedom of movement, cooperation for development and good-neighborly relations, transportation and telecommunications, respect for human rights, and territorial waters.

After the signing of the peace treaty, a joint meeting held on January 31, 1980, between an Israeli delegation (headed by Maj. Gen. Avraham Tamir) and its Egyptian counterpart (led by Ambassador Taha al-Magdoub) decided to establish a high-level committee to discuss "normalization of relations between Egypt and Israel." The joint committee met alternately in Cairo and in Tel Aviv from February 6 to May 8, 1980, and concluded eight agreements, on: flights of civil aircraft (Annex III), postal and telecommunications ties (Annex IV), tourism relations (Annex V), agriculture (Annex VI), border checkpoints (Annex VII), culture (Annex VIII), trade (Annex IX) and air transport (Annex X). The stated purpose of the agreements is "to normalize and promote relations between their two countries in accordance with the Treaty of Peace at Washington, D.C. done on March 26, 1979." The agreements were to be implemented upon completion of Israel's interim withdrawal to the El Arish-Ras Mohammad line. In the two years that followed, several additional agreements were signed: on exchange visits by youth and youth counselors, a protocol for cooperation on levying tariffs, a memorandum of understanding on meteorology, and others.

In the ensuing years, however, Egypt did not fulfill "in language and in spirit its part in implementing the normalization arrangements which should have prevailed between [the two countries]."[2] The result has been the emergence of a "cold peace" in which many of the important agreements which were intended to bring about full normalization have not been implemented. According to Avraham Tamir, who coordinated the negotiations with Egypt on normalization, the implementation of "several of these agreements, and in particular those dealing with trade and culture, did not conform with their spirit, and some crucial elements, such as banking, were actually frozen."[3] The failures of normalization, Tamir added, lay in the fact that the Egyptians evaded "the agreements and the assurances that President Sadat gave at the time to Prime Minister Begin."[4]

In Tamir's view, the Egyptians were lavish in their assurances concerning normalization, but the Egyptian Foreign Ministry "fulfilled the assurances with regard to Egypt's problems in the Arab world and not in accordance with its commitment deriving from the peace treaty."[5] Egypt created a clear connection between execution of the normalization agreements which had been signed with Israel, the development of its relations with the Arab world and progress in the autonomy talks.

Moshe Arens noted in 1992 that "trade, academic, cultural and tourism relations need to be developed.... The Egyptian government does not encourage a pattern of relations of that kind. My impression is that the pattern is very meager."[6] A sharper reaction came from Defense Ministry director-general David Ivri: "The peace with Egypt is not peace in the full sense of the word. It is in effect a ceasefire which has lasted for 14 years."[7]

Another evaluation maintains that, with the exception of Egyptian oil sales to Israel, trade is limited, totaling about $15 million annually. This is because the Egyptian government forbids the public sector, which comprises 80 percent of the economy, to maintain relations with Israel; Egyptian banks, including the state bank, refuse to do business with Israeli banks; and the Egyptian government has prohibited the establishment of an Egyptian-Israeli chamber of commerce.[8]

Also noteworthy is the fact that while tens of thousands of Israelis visit Egypt every year, Egyptian tourism to Israel is nonexistent. Egypt has also tried to prevent the renewal of diplomatic relations between Israel and African states.

Conclusion

The security provisions of the Israel-Egypt peace treaty are largely inapplicable to an Israeli-Syrian peace, due to radical geographic differences. However, the principle of demilitarization embodied in the Israeli-Egyptian treaty is relevant.

Because it will be even more difficult for Syria than for Egypt to enter into a process of normalization with Israel, the lessons derived from the experience with Egypt must be applied in double measure in a peace treaty with Syria.

First, it is imperative that the clauses on normalization be as detailed as possible, and be worded in a manner both binding and amenable to implementation. Although lucid formulation cannot guarantee smooth implementation, whatever is worded in general, non-binding terms will almost certainly not be carried out.

Secondly, there must be a close and conditional connection between the normalization process and the process of Israel's withdrawal from those parts of the Golan Heights that are agreed on by the two countries. Syria's interest in receiving areas of the Golan may induce it to pay with the coin of normalization to ensure that the phases of the withdrawal are executed. It can be argued that even if the Syrians are forced to enter into normal relations in various spheres, they can terminate the process after Israel has withdrawn from areas on the Golan. One possible way around this problem is for the withdrawal and normalization processes to be carried out simultaneously over a lengthy period, in the course of which norms of relationships, not easily broken, will gradually evolve. For the same reason, the peace treaty should include not only a clear and unequivocal commitment to carry out normalization as one of the two pillars of the agreement (the other being security), but it should also state that if that basic element is not honored even after it is put to arbitration, Israel will have the right not to fulfill the agreement's second basic element.

Chapter 21. Superpower Guarantees, a US Force, Limitations on Syria

Israel must look for answers to the security risks in four spheres: superpower guarantees, the stationing of an American force in the area, security limitations to be assumed by Syria, and an Israeli early-warning and defense system. The latter is discussed in Chapter 22; as for the first three components, because a direct connection exists between security arrangements and the terms of the peace treaty, it is imperative to build a "package" of security arrangements that integrates elements from all four spheres. For example, if Syria were to accept broader limitations on its armed forces the immediate risk to Israel would be reduced and it could display greater flexibility regarding the scope of the defensive system and perhaps even agree to its being manned in part by an American force. By the same token, if Syria agrees to fewer limitations, this will necessitate a more potent Israeli defensive alignment.

Superpower Guarantees

This provision envisages a situation in which, to replace the IDF's deployment on the Golan Heights (neither Israel nor Syria will maintain forces there), the major powers, especially the United States, provide guarantees to ensure the upholding of the peace treaty's military clauses and the security of the states in the region. We shall now examine several of the major elements of the question of superpower guarantees.[1]

Great Power guarantees for the security of weak states were widespread in the nineteenth century. Alan Dowty[2] has counted 115 commitments since 1815 which can be defined as political guarantees. These are of two types: a joint guarantee by Great Powers; and a guarantee by one or more Powers against other Powers. Only seven of the 115 guarantees were of the first type and five of those predate World War I. Guarantees of the first type were given only twice after World War II. The first was the tripartite guarantee of 1950, given by Britain, France and the United States, at that time the only Powers with influence in the Middle East, to prevent the supply of arms related to the Arab-Israel conflict. That guarantee expired at the time of the Suez Campaign (1956) when the disunity among the three Powers, which was already apparent, was aggravated by Soviet encroachment in the region, and a new situation emerged in which one of the elements was Soviet influence. The second instance involved the Western Powers' guarantee, over Soviet objections, for direct UN action in the Congo from 1960 to 1964. This was successful because of a unique evolution of circumstances. It is a situation unlikely to recur and therefore this type of guarantee cannot serve as a model.[3]

Dowty notes that the majority of the guarantees given in the past were based on Great Power rivalries, i.e., a guarantee given by one or more Powers to a state (or states) against attempted expansion by a rival Power. In 17 cases the guarantee was directed against a local adversary of the recipient state. In most cases, Dowty finds, the guarantees of Great Powers in local or regional conflicts are not upheld.[4] Among the difficulties and possible developments liable to impede the implementation of guarantees, Dowty points to international flash points, interpower cooperation, and shifts in the military balance. He concludes that international guarantees should not be viewed in isolation from the dynamics of interpower relations and realpolitik.[5]

Another expert, N.A. Pelcovits, believes that the purpose of a guarantee is to reduce but not eliminate the potential risks to a small state that knowingly foregoes security advantages. Pelcovits links such a guarantee to the guarantor state's maintenance of a military presence on the borders of the recipient state; this, in order to avert a war or prevent a surprise attack, and to give the defender ample time to organize defenses (mobilization of reserves). To that end a multinational force is required that is ready to confront an aggressor. Summing up, Pelcovits explains that "guarantees can provide supplementary insurance that is useful, though not worth a high premium."[6]

Although historically Great Power guarantees have generally proved disappointing, they can still have a deterrent effect and therefore should not be rejected out of hand.[7] The author's view is that, in any event, if the Arab states decide to attack Israel in a war or by terrorist raids and thus violate the peace treaty and the demilitarization of the Golan Heights, Israel will not be able to count on the guarantees acting as a deterrent. The lesson of the past is that any state that has wanted to violate its commitment to the territorial integrity of another state has always found a way to do so.[8]

Of the three possible guarantors--the UN, Western Europe (with or without the United States) or the United States alone--the latter is definitely to be preferred. A multinational guarantee such as may be provided by the UN or by Western European states, which are not superpowers and are heavily dependent on the Arab states (oil and assets), is not credible. Only the sole remaining superpower, the United States, can give a credible guarantee of security. As to whether the United States would intervene on behalf of Israel if this were stipulated by the guarantee, that question is best addressed with reference to public opinion polls conducted in the US, on the assumption that they reflect the will of the American people.

Such surveys consistently reflect opposition to any form of commitment that is liable to involve the use of American forces in the Middle East. In polls conducted after the 1973 war, only 12 percent favored sending in US troops if Israel were in danger of destruction. The majority even opposed sending US forces to Europe, if it were attacked.

Washington's decision to intervene militarily to save Kuwait following the Iraqi invasion is not a model from which one can draw conclusions about the prospects of intervention in Israel's favor. In the Kuwaiti case the decision was influenced by conditions not applicable to the Israeli case, particularly the oil issue and President Bush's successful mobilization of an international coalition. Most recently, the reordering of American priorities (in favor of domestic needs) under the Clinton administration, coupled with the move to "downsize" the US military in general, only add weight to this assessment.

In his article "Superpower Guarantees in the 1980's," Shai Feldman noted that in public opinion polls conducted in the United States (1978) 22 percent of those questioned supported American intervention if the Arab states were to invade Israel, while 25 percent were in favor of US intervention if Cuban troops were to invade Rhodesia.[9] In December 1979, following the Soviet invasion of Afghanistan, 40 percent of those polled said they would support intervention on behalf of Israel,[10] but this fell to 29 percent in October 1980.[11] Public opinion polls conducted in the United States during the 1980s show a decline in the percentage of those who would support American military intervention to assist Israel in the event of an Arab invasion. A *Los Angeles Times* poll in September 1986[12] showed 48 percent against and only 29 percent in favor. A majority of Americans said they would oppose such intervention in a poll taken by the Chicago Council for Foreign Relations in March 1987.[13] If such polls are a true indication of the American nation's readiness to assist Israel militarily if it is attacked, in a no-war situation that readiness does not exceed 30 percent, and it is doubtful whether Israel can rely on such support.

Past Israeli experience with guarantees is not positive. In 1957 the United States assured Israel freedom of navigation in the Straits of Tiran. According to Undersecretary of State Lucius Battle, "We promised Israel that we would continue to view [the Straits] as an international waterway."[14] Israeli Foreign Minister Abba Eban stated: "The US commitments were given to us explicitly in 1957 by [Secretary of State] John Foster Dulles."[15] In 1967, however, Washington knew nothing about any such commitment, lacking even the minutes of the 1957 talks, which were finally retrieved from former President Eisenhower's private archives. In practice, the United States did not use force in 1967 in order to ensure freedom of passage in the Straits of Tiran and did not uphold its commitment to Israel.[16]

The underlying concept of a guarantee--to deter a potential aggressor state and avert war--appears to be logical. But for two reasons it is inadequate. For one, the guarantor state might disavow the guarantee in the future, either because new political conditions have arisen or because of domestic considerations. Secondly, and here the doubts are even greater, there is a credibility problem regarding implementation. The track record of superpower guarantees has been disappointing. Moreover, there is not necessarily an identity of interests in this regard between the United States and Israel: the enemies of the latter are not necessarily also the enemies of the former. Thus, the United States could be faced with a severe dilemma if confronted with a demand to make good on its guarantee to Israel.

An additional consideration is that the likelihood of deterring Syria from attacking by means of US guarantees to Israel is far lower than it would be, for example, in the case of similar guarantees against an attack by Jordan. The Syrian Army is three times as large as Jordan's, and the risk undertaken by Damascus in attacking Israel would be proportionally smaller. Besides, Syria's dependence on the United States is still quite limited. In view of the risks involved, Israel cannot base its security and existence exclusively on external guarantees. Israel must be able to face all future risks from the Arab states by itself, and not trade security measures for guarantees. Nevertheless, such guarantees would be acceptable as part of a "package" of security arrangements, in the knowledge that guarantees may have a certain deterrent effect, even if the prospects of their realization in a crisis are negligible.

A US Force on the Golan Heights

UN forces have been part of the peacekeeping arrangements in the Middle East since 1957 (the UN force in Sinai). For the most part they are composed of units from small states. History shows that they have been useful as long as the parties wished to maintain quiet (for example, on the Golan Heights since the 1974 separation-of-forces agreement). But they are unable to warn against or prevent belligerent action or war. This is because a UN force lacks deterrence if its units are not from a superpower, and has no authority to fight in order to stop an attack by any side. Under its mandate it may open fire only in self-defense. This did not change even in 1992, when the scope of UN military activity was vastly expanded.

For example, in 1967 the UN force in Sinai did not prevent Egypt from closing the Straits of Tiran to Israeli navigation or from sending troops into Sinai. Nor could it prevent the Six-Day War (indeed, the UN withdrew its forces from Sinai upon Egypt's demand). Fifteen years later the presence of a UN force in southern Lebanon did not deter Israel from launching its large-scale Operation Peace for Galilee, during which the IDF even captured the Lebanese capital, Beirut. The UN force did not interfere in any way with the IDF's advance.

Thus the only option that appears to be worthy of examination here is the stationing of a military force, consisting of two brigades, by the United States, the only remaining superpower,[17] in the eastern Golan, presumably in conjunction with NATO troops or as part of a multinational force. Its purpose would be to separate the Israeli and Syrian forces and, by its very presence, prevent violations of the agreement and deter hostilities. This option is also based on the assessment that Syria would prefer an American force on the Golan rather than an Israeli military presence. Moreover some observers argue that if the new world order does not evolve according to expectations, the United States would be willing to send troops outside a UN framework.

Yet, as with guarantees, there is no certainty that world political conditions or domestic developments in the United States would allow Washington to commit a military force on the Golan Heights for a prolonged period. It is not clear, in other words, whether the United States, in addition to or as part of a guarantee to Israel, would be ready to station forces on the Golan and assume responsibility to separate Israeli and Syrian unim and to deter both sides from violating a demilitarization arrangement. Nor is there any way to know in advance whether, in case this tripwire fails, Washington would be willing to use force against Syrian troops entering the Golan Heights. And even if the United States stations forces on the Golan, future conditions could conceivably dictate a decision on their removal, creating a vacuum.

We turn now to consider the advantages and disadvantages to Israel of US troops being stationed in the eastern Golan Heights.

Possible advantages. An American force stationed in the eastern Golan in a defensive alignment would probably deter Syria from attacking across the Golan Heights. If the deterrence failed, the United States would become a side in the war and its force on the Golan would be sufficiently large to enable it to fight and delay the advancing forces.

Possible disadvantages. In return for stationing its troops on the Golan Heights in order to defend vital areas of Israel (the country's north and its water sources), Washington would undoubtedly exact a heavy political price. Israel's freedom of maneuver, already now reduced (among other reasons because of its political, economic and security dependence on the United States), would shrink even further. In this situation Israelis might lose faith in the state's ability to exist independently; Israel would be weakened internally. Moreover, Washington might conclude that the presence of American forces on the Golan considerably reduced the strategic threat to Israel and therefore that a major cut in its military aid to Israel was in order. The effect of this would probably be to aggravate the military balance between Israel and the Arab states and thus to increase the risk of war--peace treaties notwithstanding.

Further, while the presence of a large US force on the eastern Golan Heights would greatly reduce the risk of a Syrian attack, it could, by the same token, increase the possibility of limited Syrian military operations such as terrorist raids. Since signing the separation-of-forces agreement in 1974, Syria has preserved quiet along the Golan boundary and has not permitted terrorist groups to enter the area to attack Israeli targets there or to cross it into Israel. Damascus has adopted this line because, based on past experience, it fears a possible premature slide into war. The presence of a foreign (US) force between the two armies would, from Syria's point of view, greatly reduce the risk that terrorist acts launched across its border against Israel might lead to war. In other words, a US military presence could not physically prevent terrorist raids against Israel, and could constrain Israel's anti-terrorist deterrent in two ways. First, it would limit Israel's option to execute punitive cross-border operations to put a stop to hostile actions originating from inside Syria. And secondly, it would reduce the likelihood of war breaking out as a consequence of terrorist provocations.

At the same time, political considerations could also make Syria more cautious, and anxious to avoid a possible confrontation with the United States that could be sparked by terrorist raids perpetrated under American "cover." The risk of such raids would be greatest in the first years after the signing of a peace treaty, when difficulties are liable to crop up in its implementation and internal pressures could lead either side to look for ways, however limited, to pressure the other. For example, even after a treaty is signed Syria might decide to support terrorist operations against an Israeli population still remaining on the Golan at that stage in order to hasten their departure.

In any event, a US military presence on the Golan Heights cannot supply one of the crucial elements in Israel's security needs: early-warning intelligence. Although cooperation undoubtedly exists between the Israeli and US intelligence services, Israel cannot rely on foreign intelligence for an advance warning about an impending Syrian attack. Israel can and should draw on reports and evaluations of other intelligence services, particularly the United States, but it must retain its own independent ability to produce early-warning intelligence. To the argument that protection by a US force reduces the importance of early warning, the author responds that precisely because it is impossible to rely on a permanent American presence, Israel must maintain an independent early-warning capability, even when American troops are present on the Golan Heights.

The author's conclusion is that at least during the period when the risks are still great--in other words, during the initial period after the treaty is signed, before the peace stabilizes--Israel will not be able to rely for its security on the presence of an American force on the Golan Heights in place of the IDF.

Military Limitations on Syria

A number of limitations to which Syria might agree would reduce the risk of attack on Israel--particularly a surprise attack--via the Golan Heights. Such limitations would be written into the peace treaty and their violation, in whole or in part, would constitute a casus belli, and justify Israel acting in self-defense. Thus, from Israel's point of view, it would be desirable to **reduce the size of the Syrian regular army by half** in order to reduce its offensive ability and the risk it poses to Israel, especially the risk of a surprise attack. This is the optimal way to reduce the possibility of a Syrian attack.

Syria would resist this idea, not only because it would wish to remain in a position of strength toward Israel and be able to deal with possible perceived threats from it, even after a peace treaty, but also because of its disputes with neighboring states (Turkey, Iraq, and occasionally Jordan) and its ambition to achieve hegemony in the Levant. Another, perhaps less critical factor would be the Syrian leadership's desire to continue providing a livelihood to the officer corps that supports the regime.

If Syria did agree to reduce its regular army, Israel would not be able to reciprocate; already today it is at a considerable disadvantage vis-a-vis the size of the Arab regular armies. Nevertheless, Israel should be adamant in insisting on unilateral reduction of the Syrian Army.

A partial alternative limitation might be the **permanent deployment of a large portion of the Syrian forces far from the Golan Heights**. For Israel this option is less desirable, as Syria would be able to continue building its offensive capability and even possibly to use it. Still, this limitation would hamper Syria's capacity to launch a surprise attack and would perhaps give Israel time to mobilize its reserves. In an optimal scenario Syria would maintain two-thirds of its ground forces near its borders with Iraq and Turkey--500 km and 400 km, respectively, from Damascus--leaving a total of no more than four divisions in the Damascus area, Lebanon and opposite Jordan. The distant units would require at least two or three days to reach the front.

It is doubtful whether Syria would agree permanently to maintain the bulk of its land forces far from the region it considers vital: Israel, Lebanon and Jordan. If Damascus were to agree, Israel could accept fewer security arrangements on the ground.

Demilitarization of a large area inside Syria east of the Golan Heights (in addition to the demilitarization of the Golan) is another possible limitation. The area demilitarized must be sufficiently large to rule out a Syrian surprise attack and to enable Israel to spot Syrian troop movements immediately (the assumption being that Israel would maintain an early-warning system on the Golan Heights to provide information about the initiation of Syrian troop movements and the final preparations preceding them). Israel would need about 24 hours to deploy its regular forces defensively on the Golan to meet a Syrian attack--based on the necessary assumption that the peace treaty permits Israel to return its forces to the Golan if Syrian forces enter the demilitarized zone. This means that the size of the demilitarized zone in Syria east of the Golan Heights must be sufficient that it would take advancing Syrian forces at least 24 hours to traverse the entire demilitarized zone, including the Golan. This posits the addition of some 100 km of demilitarized Syrian territory east of the Golan. Syria would probably be unwilling or unable to agree to such a wide zone, which would include Damascus. As a quid pro quo, Syria would probably demand that Israel demilitarize an area of equal or nearly equal size west of the Golan Heights. This would be opposed by Israel, because if the Golan Heights is demilitarized Israel must have the ability to deploy there quickly should Syria attempt to seize the area.

An alternative limitation would involve the **downscaling of the arms race between Syria and Israel** in order to reduce the risks of war, as long as both the Arab-Israel conflict and violent inter-Arab disputes persist. It is unlikely that Israel and Syria (and other Arab states) would be able, concurrently with the signing of peace treaties, to reach agreement on a military balance that gives all parties security and at the same time renders another war less likely. Syria and the Arab states would almost certainly demand that Israel eliminate its weapons of mass destruction--they believe that Israel has a clear advantage in this sphere--but would be unwilling to forego their quantitative advantage in conventional munitions.

Under additional limitations, Syria could be asked to **pledge not to allow Iraqi or other external forces to enter its territory**, and/or to **undertake not to assume any commitment that would conflict with the terms of the peace treaty**. In other words, Syria would not be a member of alliances, and would not enter into military or political treaties with Arab or Muslim states, that are directed against Israel. Finally, under the terms of the peace treaty **Israeli diplomats would be posted in Syria and the government there would not restrict their movements**. The diplomats would thus be able to report on any preparations for war that they discern.

These seven limitations could help preserve calm in the region. The more limitations Syria assumed, the smaller the security risk to Israel in a withdrawal from most of the Golan Heights. It is very doubtful, however, whether Syria would agree to most of these limitations (with the exception of the last three), especially if called upon to do so concurrent with the signing of a peace treaty.

Chapter 22. Early-Warning Facilities and the IDF's Deployment

Early-warning and Observation Facilities

This chapter examines the possibility of setting up IDF early-warning and observation facilities in the eastern Golan Heights, on Mount Hermon and on some of the high mounds. Our underlying assumption is that there will be no Syrian military forces on the Golan. The purpose of the installations would be to provide the IDF with early-warning intelligence in time to allow it to take countermeasures, i.e., mobilize reserves and deploy them defensively on the Golan. Clearly Israel should try to acquire maximum early-warning intelligence about an impending Syrian attack, particularly if the peace treaty prohibits IDF deployment on the Golan Heights, or even in a situation of limited deployment (such as exists today). As already explained, Israel needs this capability because of the Arab regular armies' overwhelming advantage in size of ground forces. The presence of early-warning facilities on the Golan Heights, with Syria's knowledge, would act as a deterrent because Damascus would know that it has little prospect of launching a surprise attack.

Because the high areas are at the Golan's eastern extremity, it is there that the IDF must be able to set up and man a number of long-range electronic early-warning and observation stations. Unmanned facilities are not recommended because they will not be accessible for maintenance, repairs, replacement and installation of new instruments, etc. Deterrence would be achieved because the Golan offers an observation range of several dozen kilometers into Syria, while from the Hermon the range of vision extends as far as Damascus. At least three such stations, combining observation and electronic surveillance, would be needed: on Mount Hermon, which because of its altitude is the most important site, although the southern part of the front cannot be covered from there; at Tell abu Neda, located in the center of the sector; and at Mount Fares, in the south. This alignment would also provide a degree of overlap between the stations.

Syria is likely to follow the example of Egypt, which objected to Israel's establishment of long-term early-warning stations in Sinai. It will not be easy to overcome this opposition. Ezer Weizman, the defense minister at the time, has recounted a discussion held on this point with his Egyptian counterpart, Gen. Gamasi. Israel's chief of Military Intelligence, Maj. Gen. Shlomo Gazit, suggested that "Israel should maintain in Sinai three early-warning stations until it becomes absolutely clear that this is truly a stable peace." The Egyptians objected, arguing that Israel had agreed to withdraw completely from Sinai and, in Gamasi's words, "There is no country on earth that places early-warning stations in another country."[1] Gamasi did not reject another proposal by Gazit--that Egypt, in return, would be able to establish at least one early-warning station in Israel--but the idea was not pursued.[2]

As for air early-warning activity, for Israel to be able to survey a large part of the Syrian alignment west of Damascus and detect possible modifications, the IAF would have to continue flying as far as the current Line A.

Although early-warning intelligence of an impending attack is certainly a high priority, on the Golan Heights front (because of its narrow width, and in view of the large Syrian force deployment to the east) this would not suffice without an IDF presence there. Nor would the proposed early-warning facilities necessarily provide a warning of 48 hours preceding an attack. Even reports about preparations for movement in the Syrian Army may prove difficult to link with a Syrian intention to attack. In other words, the existence of a warning system is not a foolproof guarantee against a successful Syrian--or combined Arab--surprise attack. It follows that the mere emplacement of early-warning and observation stations on the Golan Heights (without Israeli forces) cannot ensure that a warning would be received in time for the IDF to seize the dominant high mounds in the eastern Golan before the attacking Syrian forces could reach them.

Nevertheless, reliance on IDF early-warning and observation facilities by themselves might be acceptable to Israel if Syria were to agree to a number of conditions. First, to concur with the majority of the security limitations suggested above, particularly: to halve its regular army and turn it into a defensive force, or to deploy much of its standing army permanently along its borders with Iraq and Turkey; and to demilitarize the area between Damascus and the Golan Heights. Secondly, Syria would have to undertake officially not to permit Iraqi (or other) forces to enter its territory. And third, Syria should agree to allow the IDF to deploy permanently in a strip 3 to 4 km wide east of the international boundary (i.e., in the westernmost strip of the Golan) where there is a steep ascent from the Israeli side. Thus, if an intelligence warning is received, IDF forces would be able to make the ascent from the Jordan Valley and the Hula Valley without resistance. Ideally, this strip should in fact become part of Israel, but here again Syrian concurrence is doubtful.

IDF Deployment in the Eastern Golan Heights

Without an IDF presence, electronic intelligence facilities and observation posts on high mounds in the eastern Golan may be insufficient to meet Israel's security needs. To contain a Syrian attack, even a surprise attack, until the reserves can be mobilized, the IDF must be deployed on the high mounds at the Golan's eastern extremity. A topographical analysis shows that only from that line is it possible to achieve operational and intelligence observation dominance toward the east. The area to the west is a continuous decline and contains few alternative sites for defense against an attack from the east.

It is essential that for a few years following the signing of a peace treaty, when the risk of a Syrian and Arab attack will be greatest, the IDF maintain a force the size of two armored brigades on the eastern Golan. Where the terrain permits, they should deploy in two lines, i.e., on the eastern line of high mounds and on the second line of mounds. Early-warning intelligence facilities would naturally be included in this deployment and on the Hermon, and the security of Israel's water sources would thereby also be assured.

This form of deployment has two principal advantages. First, it offers a reasonable defense against a Syrian attack. And secondly, it would deter Damascus from launching an attack with a high risk of failure: such an attack could be broken by the Israeli defensive alignment and generate a counterattack against Damascus. But the idea has its drawbacks as well. Syria would certainly not agree to a long-term deployment of this kind, as it would enshrine the status quo on the Golan Heights (including the continued presence of the Jewish settlements). Indeed, even though it is a deterrent deployment, it could actually generate military action, because Syria would find it less tolerable in a situation of peace than in the present situation of no war and no peace.

In the author's view, then, this arrangement would only be viable for a relatively limited period.

Table III illustrates the security implications for the IDF of the various solutions for a lengthy transition period and the probability of their acceptance by Syria.

Table III. Possible Transition Security Arrangements and their Ramifications

Possible Solution	***Probability of Syrian Acceptance***	***Effect of Solution on:***		
		Anti-Terrorism Defense	***Early-Warning Possibility***	***Defensive Capability***
Superpower Guarantees	High	Extremely low	Low	Low
Military limitations on Syria	Low to improbable	Low	Low	Intermediate
IDF early-warning and observation	Less than intermediate	Very low	High	Low
US Forces on the Golan	Reasonable	Very low	Low	High
IDF deployment in eastern Golan plus early-warning elements	Low	Intermediate to high	High	High

Chapter 23. Author's Proposal and Conclusion

Basic Assumptions

The security arrangements proposed below reflect the author's views. They are based solely on security considerations. Underlying them are several basic assumptions.

The first assumption is of prior agreement between Syria and Israel on the overall solution of the Golan Heights question and on the content of the peaceful relations between them, from which the phased arrangements would be derived. At each phase the operational aspect would include three main elements: Israeli withdrawal, security arrangements and, simultaneously, a process in which Israel's existence is accepted by Syria and the two countries advance toward peace. Both states would undoubtedly find it difficult to achieve an agreement along these lines. Israel would have to agree that at the end of a lengthy process it would withdraw from most of the Golan Heights, while Syria would have to agree to build a structure of peace with Israel and implement it concurrent with the latter's withdrawal. Whether the two countries would agree to the modalities proposed here cannot be known, but it may be the only practical compromise.

Admittedly, there is no chance that Syria would agree to a full and deep peace with Israel, at least until the latter agrees to remove all its forces and settlements from the Golan Heights. Indeed, it is doubtful whether Syria would agree to a peace of this kind even if Israel were willing to withdraw completely.

Secondly, as long as there is no full and stable peace, the risks of war will remain and security arrangements will be needed to meet those risks and perhaps to avert war. To work, such arrangements must meet the needs of both states and be agreed on by both. Basically, both Israel and Syria would be permitted to maintain a certain level of forces on the Golan Heights even after signing a peace treaty. On this point the two states are polarized: Syria's goal is to restore its full sovereignty on the Golan and bring about a complete Israeli withdrawal within a specified period. Israel, in contrast, wants to eliminate the possibility that the Golan Heights will be a staging ground for a Syrian attack or for the harassment of its north. Israel would thus insist on long-term security arrangements with which it could deter Syria from going to war, allow it to detect Syrian preparations for an attack, and enable it to contain a Syrian advance until it could mobilize the reserves.

Third, there is no reason to expect Syria to agree to a long-term Israeli military presence on the Golan Heights without Israel's prior concession on the territorial issue. It may be possible to talk about security arrangements, but no agreement on their content is possible before agreement is reached on an IDF withdrawal and on the content of the peace. Syria would have to agree that the process will culminate in a full peace, i.e., peace between peoples and not only between leaders. The peace would develop gradually, serve common interests, and give Israel security. Israel would have to agree that at the end of the peace process it would transfer sovereignty over most of the Golan to Syria. Without an agreed foundation along these lines, bridging the conflicting basic interests of the two states, no agreement could be reached on security arrangements even with American help.

Furthermore, from the viewpoint of both Syria and Israel, a self-contained interim accord on the Golan does not seem probable without a prior agreement stipulating the content of the peace and resolving in full the territorial question. Were Israel, say, to agree to a partial withdrawal, not within the framework of a comprehensive agreement, in a small area that poses neither a political nor a security risk, it would want a Syrian quid pro quo in the realm of peace provisions. But it is unlikely that Syria would be ready to offer a political equivalent before Israel agrees to withdraw from the entire Golan.

Israel, too, would find it difficult to pay the price, in terms of withdrawal, of full Syrian compliance with its wishes. In this sense it is not possible to say whether in peace negotiations Israel would agree to withdraw from all or most of the Golan Heights in return for full peace, and whether Syria would agree to a full and deep peace if Israel agreed to withdraw from the entire Golan. Thus the outcome remains cloudy. Nonetheless it is clear that the sphere in which Syria is interested and Israel has something to offer is that of territory; while the sphere in which Israel is interested and in which Syria has something to offer is the content of the peace. This is the only possible basis for a deal between Syria and Israel.

A fourth assumption holds that if there is a gradual evolution toward full peace, it is likely that the risks will still be high at the start of the process, perhaps diminishing over time. It follows that the security arrangements should be more stringent in the first years, and be gradually mitigated as the peace becomes rooted. For the same reason, arrangements concerning both security and peace should be implemented simultaneously, not consecutively. Thus Syria's desire for Israel to leave the Golan would obligate it (in complete contrast to its longtime stand) to agree to the implementation of various elements of peace and the start of normalization parallel to the start of an Israeli withdrawal. Syria will have little chance to get back large areas of the Golan Heights if it does not agree to a parallel process of peacemaking with Israel. If Syria is adamant that peace be established only at the conclusion of a lengthy transition period, it is doubtful whether the two countries will be able to arrive at a peace treaty.

Finally, as the peace process develops it will be possible gradually to reduce the security arrangements, which by their nature impose restrictions on the Syrian Armed Forces and grant the IDF certain advantages on the Golan Heights. The problem is that neither Syria nor, for that matter, the United States (assuming it is intimately involved in the negotiations and/or transition security arrangements) would agree to have security arrangements that were intended for the initial, high-risk period, continue throughout the lengthy transition. At the same time, it is impossible to determine in advance a timetable for the gradual lifting of the security arrangements, for the simple reason that it is impossible to know how long the political thaw between the two countries would take. It is, however, possible to determine in advance a correlation between the security arrangements and the changes that must occur in the political relations between the two states. For example, the security arrangements could be modified in accordance with the development of the peace process between Syria and Israel and between Israel and other Arab states and the Palestinians.

Content of the Security Arrangements

Changes in the international boundary. Our working assumption is that the peace treaty would take as its point of departure the international boundary between Syria and Palestine-Eretz Yisrael as the permanent border. It follows that Israel would agree to Syrian sovereignty over the majority of the Golan Heights. The major modification would be the relocation of the international boundary three to four km to the east along its entire length. This strip would become part of Israel for two reasons: first, so that in an emergency Israel could safely move troops to the Golan Heights on the few steep roads of ascent from west to east; and secondly, to ensure that Syria does not interfere with the flow of the Banias and to protect that water source physically.

Syria would certainly resist the idea of conceding a few kilometers of the Golan and would insist on receiving the entire area. Here Israel could hold out the "carrot" of southern Lebanon--i.e., agree to withdraw from that region, albeit under conditions that would allow for the security of northern Galilee--as an inducement for Syria to forego, as a quid pro quo, a narrow strip on the ascent to the Golan Heights.

Prohibiting Syrian forces on the Golan. No Syrian troops would be permitted into the areas evacuated by Israel under the agreement. An additional area in Syria to the east of the Golan Heights would also be demilitarized, as would a small area in Israel west of the international boundary. The larger the demilitarized area inside Syria, the smaller the force that the IDF would maintain on the Golan. If the agreement permitted Syrian civilians to return to the Golan, a local police force equipped with light weapons only could be stationed there.

Phases in IDF withdrawal and in the establishment of peace. Because of the military and political conditions, the lengthy transition period would be divided into interim periods. As peace progresses, changes in the security arrangements pertaining to each period would be affected. Syria's consent to the two following limitations in the area east of the Golan would create a new situation: halving the size of its standing army, or stationing a large portion of its units on other borders so that the force between the Golan and Damascus is too small to threaten Israel (one to two divisions); and demilitarizing the area between the Golan and Damascus. In this situation Israel could agree to move up one phase of the withdrawal from the Golan, i.e., to forego the first phase and begin the implementation directly from Phase II (see below). However, in what follows it is assumed that Syria would not accept the limitations just described. Therefore, implementation of both processes (peace and withdrawal) would take place in a number of phases.

The mutual transition from phase to phase would depend on the execution of each phase and not on a predetermined timetable. Syria and Israel would have to reach prior agreement on the phases, which may have the following structure.

Phase I

This would begin with the signing of the peace treaty. Israel would undertake to withdraw from most of the Golan Heights at the conclusion of a lengthy process, upon the establishment of a broad-based, comprehensive peace between the two states. This phase would comprise the following bilateral elements:

- Agreement on the termination of the state of war and its replacement by a state of peace.
- Termination of economic or other boycott of Israel by Syria.
- Termination of anti-Israel propaganda by Syria.

* It would be very desirable if diplomatic relations were established, but this would probably not be attainable in the first phase. The Israeli-Egyptian peace treaty stipulated that diplomatic relations would be established upon completion of the interim withdrawal by Israel (i.e., to the El-Arish--Ras Mohammad line). Israeli-Syrian diplomatic relations could therefore be established in the second phase (see below).
* Cooperation between the two states to prevent violent incidents. Within this framework Syria and Israel would coordinate with regard to military maneuvers involving a force of brigade size or greater, and unusual flight or navigation patterns.

IDF withdrawal and deployment. Phase I would involve limited withdrawal by the IDF of up to several hundred meters from two or three points near the separation-of-forces line in the southern Golan--not in the area of the eastern high mounds. To deter Syria from launching an attack or from perpetrating or abetting terrorist raids, and to contain a surprise attack until the mobilization of reserves, the IDF would continue to deploy in areas of suitable terrain on the Golan (i.e., on the high mounds in the east). Deployment in this phase could be based on existing fortifications and obstacles. Two armored or mechanized brigades would be required to fulfill this mission.

Palestinian sphere. Phase I calls for the rehabilitation of half the Palestinian refugees living in Syria (150,000 out of 300,000). Rehabilitation of the refugees is the most important index of a true reduction of hostility in Syria and the Arab world toward Israel.

Phase II

Phase II would begin with a political thaw with Syria that includes, at a minimum, the following bilateral elements:

* Establishment of diplomatic relations, including embassies.
* Revision by Syria of its propaganda approach to Israel, and issuance of a declaration regarding Israel's right to exist.
* Rewriting of Syrian textbooks to reflect the acceptance of Israel.
* Open borders between the two states in both directions and unimpeded passage of people and goods across them.

IDF withdrawal and deployment. In this situation, following considerable progress in the peace process and in normalization, and a certain decline in the risk of a Syrian attack, Israel could agree to withdraw its force on the high mounds in the eastern Golan to the second line of mounds. It would be replaced on the high mounds by a division-size American force, or a multinational force with a dominant American component.

Palestinian sphere. Phase II would involve completion of rehabilitation of the Palestinian refugees in Syria and simultaneous implementation of an advanced stage of their rehabilitation in the other Arab states, i.e., rehabilitation of up to a quarter of the total number of refugees there.

Phase III

The peace process would continue to evolve bilaterally, and would comprise:

* Trade relations.
* Creation of a joint regime on exploiting the region's water.
* Syrian-Israeli economic and political cooperation.
* Cooperation in tourism, agriculture, medicine, etc.
* Halving the size of the Syrian Army or relocating a large portion of its units to distant borders, and agreement on mutual arms limitations.

IDF withdrawal and deployment. If all the above conditions were met, the IDF would be replaced on the second line of high mounds by a US or multinational force (which would continue to hold the first line as well). In the southern sector the IDF would withdraw from the Purple Line and deploy in the Nahal Golan-El Al pass located east of Maaleh Gamla, in the pass between Afik and Givat Yoav, and in the pass south of the settlement of Metzar.

Palestinian sphere. Phase III calls for the rehabilitation of three-quarters of the Palestinian refugees in the Arab states.

Phase IV

In the bilateral and regional spheres, this phase would include:

* Development of the peace process to the stage that exists among the Western European states.
* Final rehabilitation of all Palestinian refugees in Arab states.
* Strategic cooperation between Israel and Syria and between Israel and other Arab states within a regional strategic framework.
* Regional cooperation between Israel and the Arab states.
* Emergence of democratic, or at least more liberal regimes in the Arab states (despite the risk of victory in elections by fundamentalist Muslim forces).
* Thaw in relations among the Arab states.

Israeli withdrawal. If all the above were implemented, Israel would withdraw to the new border (three to four km east of the Syria-Palestine international boundary). This would include withdrawal of the IDF and removal of the Jewish settlements from the Golan Heights.

Early-warning intelligence facilities. Early-warning intelligence would be vital to Israel as long as war risks exist, i.e., throughout the lengthy transition period. Topographical conditions require three Israeli intelligence facilities containing electronic devices and long-range observation. The suitable locations are: Mount Hermon in the north, Tell abu Neda in the center and Mount Fares in the south.

These facilities would be necessary even if gradual progress were made in peaceful relations and normalization. The peace treaty would include a definition and prior agreement on the state of political relations between Syria and Israel, beginning from Phase III, and between the Arab states and Israel, in which Israel would cut back the number of intelligence facilities from three to two as the peace process develops and war risks are reduced. In any event, Israel would continue to retain the relevant area of Mount Hermon for early-warning intelligence and to preserve its interests in the area's water sources. If Syria accepts and implements in its own territory the limitations already described--reduction of its regular army or stationing much of it on alternative borders, and cutting the size of the force to the west of Damascus--Israel might be able to agree to reduce the number of early-warning stations to two beginning in Phase II.

If Syria demands a quid pro quo for agreeing to allow Israel to operate early-warning stations on the Golan, Israel could agree that beginning in Phase II Syria could operate early-warning facilities of its own on the Golan and perhaps even in Israeli territory, west of the international boundary.

Flights. Until the end of Phase III the IAF would be able to continue flying as far as Line A for aerial photography and intelligence production by other means (COMINT, ELINT, etc.). The Syrian Air Force would be able to fly as far as Line B.

Jewish settlements. Israel would have to agree in a peace treaty that at the conclusion of the process all (or most) of its settlements would be removed from the Golan Heights. This would be a major concession for Israel, and exceedingly difficult to implement. However, as long as the peace process has not entered its advanced stage (Phase IV) Jewish settlements would continue to exist, even after US troops had replaced the IDF on the eastern line of high mounds. Because of the negative Israeli domestic implications of the evacuation, it would not be executed in stages over a lengthy period, but in one swift move.

Lebanon. The security arrangements regarding southern Lebanon, to be agreed on with Syria and/or with Lebanon, must include, at the least, the following elements:

* Withdrawal of Syrian units from the Bekaa and their replacement by a multinational force (not a US force, because it is unlikely that Washington would want to send troops to Lebanon in addition to those on the Golan Heights). This, in order to prevent an Israeli attack on Damascus from the flank and to prevent a Syrian attack on the Galilee Panhandle.
* A gradual IDF pullout from Southern Lebanon, but only after the Lebanese government brings the Palestinian and other guerrilla forces (Hizballah) there under its authority, and assumes direct responsibility for quiet on the border with Israel. This would probably be easier to accomplish with the Palestinians, if their negotiations with Israel had made good progress and after the Palestinian refugees now residing in southern Lebanon were rehabilitated. The major difficulty would arise in preventing terrorist activity by Hizballah. This would probably require direct Syrian involvement if Israel left southern Lebanon. Israel, however, would find it difficult to accept a situation in which the price for a quiet border was a Syrian takeover of southern Lebanon.

Conclusion

The security arrangements examined in this study are those which the author believes Israel must insist upon in order to preserve its security even after the signing of a peace treaty with

Syria. Basically, these are preventive-defensive arrangements on the Golan Heights, predicated on the assumption that Syria would not easily agree to security arrangements that imposed limitations on its forces east of the Golan. If Syria agreed to those limitations, particularly to a major reduction of its standing armed forces, Israel would be able to accept a certain mitigation in the defensive security arrangements.

In any event, the foundation of the security arrangements between the two countries would necessarily be a peace treaty, of which the central elements would be the gradual restoration of most of the Golan Heights to Syria in return for a full and deep peace, to be established concurrent with Israel's withdrawal. The peace treaty would stipulate the phases of execution of the two elements and specify each side's role in parallel with the other side. Implementation of each stage would thus be mutually concurrent, rather than automatic or subject to a fixed timetable.

This method has the advantage of being a catalyst for implementing the agreement. Each side has a greater interest to move to the next stage in order to secure, in return for its concession, its primary goal (for the Syrians, Israeli withdrawal; for Israel, a stable peace). The danger of this method is that the process could break down in the middle. This could result, for example, from a disagreement between the two states over whether a particular phase had been completed by one or both of them, hence whether they were obligated to start the next phase. A dispute of this kind could arise at any stage and might require arbitration. There appear to be two possible ways to break such an impasse. The first (and preferable) one is by means of an Israeli-Syrian control commission, perhaps chaired by an American; the second is to call in an international arbitrator, whose character and authority would be stipulated in advance in the peace treaty (e.g., an American arbitrator).

Despite this difficulty, it is not recommended to set a fixed timetable for implementing each phase, for it is impossible to assess how much time each phase would actually require. For example, there is no way to know how long it would take for the Arab states to agree to rehabilitate one-quarter of the Palestinian refugees, thereby facilitating implementation of Phase II. The only practical way to proceed is therefore to define the content of each phase and each side's obligations regarding its implementation, without reference to a fixed timetable.

According to the security arrangements proposed here, Syria would have to agree to an Israeli military presence on the Golan Heights during a lengthy transition period, while the risk of war is still high. Syria would undoubtedly object to this and would demand a considerable reduction of the Israeli presence following the signing of the treaty.

Whether, or to what degree, the sides would agree to the proposals put forward in this study is difficult to determine. Syria, even under American pressure, might not accept the central concept of a parallel process involving three elements: the peace process, Israeli withdrawal and security arrangements. In this event it is doubtful whether the two countries would be able to sign a peace treaty. Faced with hard options, though, Syria might conceivably display greater flexibility in this area.

To facilitate the Syrian acceptance of the proposal, Israel would have to make major concessions. It would have to agree to withdraw from most of the Golan Heights (including removal of the Jewish settlements) at the conclusion of the transition period, and to transfer sovereignty to Syria. And it would have to agree that a US or multinational force (of scaled-down division size) replace, in the transition stage, the IDF in the area of the eastern high mounds; and to withdraw from most of the remaining area not at the end of the process but gradually, parallel to the development of the peace process.

Clearly, these would be painful concessions for Israel. They would involve loss of the Golan Heights, evacuation of the Jewish settlements and a revision of the security arrangements currently made possible by Israel's control of the Golan. The mode of phases and the checks and balances proposed in this study could mitigate the difficulties and open the way to obtain both peace and security. It is based on a gradual withdrawal over a very lengthy period, with each phase conditional upon the development of the peace between Syria and Israel, with the assurance of security arrangements suited to current risks.

As this lengthy road unfolds, security arrangements are a crucial element for Israel's security, and for the prevention of another war with Syria both during and after the transition period.

Notes

Chapter 1

1. On the basic considerations for and against by Syria and Israel, and on the effect of the Gulf War on them, see Aryeh Shalev, "The Outlook for Substantive Syrian-Israeli Negotiations," in Joseph Alpher, ed., *War in the Gulf: Implications for Israel* (Jerusalem: Jerusalem Post and Boulder: Westview Press, 1992).
2. Interview by Syrian Defense Minister Mustafa Tlas to *Der Spiegel*, quoted in *Ha'aretz*, September 28, 1986.
3. Interview by President Assad to the Kuwaiti *Al-Qabas* on January 24, 1987, Hebrew translation in Hatsav 848/009, February 3, 1987.
4. The interview with Prof. Eli Kedourie is quoted in *Ha'aretz Weekly Magazine*, May 17, 1991.
5. President Assad's interview of May 16, 1986 to the *Washington Post* is translated into Hebrew in Hatsav 843/020, May 25, 1986.
6. Syrian Vice President Abd al-Halim Khaddam to *Kuwait Radio* on June 30, 1989, according to FBIS-NES-89-133, July 13, 1989, p. 42.
7. Assad, *Washington Post*, May 16, 1986.
8. President Assad's interview to *Damascus Television* on April 25, 1984 appears in SWB, ME/7629/A/2, April 28, 1984.
9. Tlas to *Der Spiegel*, quoted by *Ha'aretz*, September 21 and 23, 1984.
10. *Yediot Aharonot*, December 21, 1983, quotes Prof. Moshe Maoz: "Assad has decided to create a large military force which will enable him to deal with Israel defensively and afterward offensively as well."
11. Tlas, *Der Spiegel* (*Ha'aretz*), September 21 and 23, 1984.
12. Interview by Syrian Information Minister Ahmad Iskander Ahmad to *Al-Kafah al-Arabi*, Lebanon, October 13, 1980, Hebrew translation in Hatsav 843/057, October 30, 1980.
13. Hatsav 834/008, June 12, 1985, Hebrew translation of Assad's concept of strategic parity as explained by Ghassan al-Amam in *Al-Wattan al-Arabi*, Lebanon, May 10, 1985.
14. Tlas, *Der Spiegel* (*Ha'aretz*), September 21 and 23, 1984.

15. Background conversation with Patrick Seale, September 7, 1990.

16. Itamar Rabinovich, "Israel, Syria and Lebanon," *International Journal*, Vol. XLV, Summer 1990, p. 549.

17. Patrick Seale, *Asad of Syria: The Struggle for the Middle East* (Berkeley: 1988).

18. Moshe Maoz, *Assad--The Sphinx of Damascus* (Tel Aviv: 1988; Hebrew), p. 186.

Chapter 2

1. This section is based on the following sources: Pichon, *Le Partage de Proche Orient* (Paris: 1938); Raanan Frischwasser, *Frontiers of a Nation* (London: 1955); Shmuel Tolkovsky, *Political-Zionist Diary*: London 1915-1919 (Jerusalem: 1981; Hebrew); Moshe Brawer, *Palestine's Northern Boundary and its Demarcation During the Mandate Period* (Haifa: 1970; Hebrew) Gideon Biger, in *Ma'ariv*, December 18, 1981, and in *Ha'aretz*, December 29, 1981; Ya'akov Meron, "The Golan Heights 1918-1967," in Meir Shamgar, ed., *Military Government in the Territories Administered by Israel 1967-1980: The Legal Aspects*, Vol. I (Jerusalem: 1982; Hebrew); Moshe Brawer, *Israel's Borders* (Tel Aviv: 1988); *The Boundary with Lebanon and Syria* (1923; Hebrew); Gideon Biger, "The Political Demarcation of the Golan Heights During the Mandate Period," in Biger, *The Golan and the Hermon* (Avshalom Institute, Tel Aviv University; unpublished, Hebrew); conversations with Prof. Moshe Brawer, March-April 1992.

2. Letter from the chief political representative to the Minister of State for Foreign Affairs, Foreign Office, London, November 17, 1919; *Palestine Boundaries 1833-1947*, Vol. 2, ed. Archive (London: 1982), pp. 441-443.

3. Frischwasser, *Frontiers*, p. 89.

4. Tolkovsky, *Diary*, p. 10.

5. Eliezer Livneh, Yosef Nedava and Yoram Efrati, eds., *Nili: History of Political Audacity* (Tel Aviv: 1980; Hebrew), pp. 407-408.
6. *Palestine Boundaries*, pp. 213-222.
7. *Ibid.*, pp. 608-609, 631.
8. "Bon Voisinage Agreement concluded between the British and French governments on behalf of the territories of Palestine on the one hand, and on behalf of Syria and Great Lebanon on the other hand, signed at Jerusalem, 2 February 1926," see: League of Nations, Treaty Series, Vol. LVI, Nos. 1, 2, 3 and 4, pp. 80-87, 1926.
9. Aryeh Shalev, *Cooperation Under the Shadow of Conflict* (Tel Aviv: 1989; Hebrew), pp. 49-74.
10. *Ibid.*, p. 47.
11. Yemima Rosenthal, ed., "Minutes of the Third Meeting of the Delegations to the Negotiations which Preceded the Signing of the Armistice Agreement," *Documents of the Foreign Policy of Israel*, Israel State Archives, 3, p. 532.
12. Coded cable No. 26 from Henri Vigier, chairman on behalf of Dr. Bunche in the negotiations between Syria and Israel which preceded the signing of the armistice agreement, April 24, 1949, in Shalev, *Cooperation*, p. 47.
13. *Ibid.*, pp. 215-235.

Chapter 3

1. Shalev, *Cooperation*, p. 46.
2. *Ibid.*, p. 49.
3. *Ibid.*, pp. 99-150.
4. *Ibid.*, pp. 193, 203-204.
5. *Ibid.*, pp. 205-208.
6. *Ibid.*, pp. 215-253.
7. Henry Kissinger, *Years of Upheaval* (1982), pp. 935-1044.
8. Matti Golan, *The Secret Conversations of Henry Kissinger*, trans. Ruth Geyra Stern and Sol Stern (New York: 1976), p. 189.

9. Kissinger, *Years of Upheaval*, p. 104.

10. Background conversations held on February 27, 1987 and on July 23, 1990 with Maj. Gen. (Res.) Herzl Shafir, the senior IDF officer in the Israeli delegation to the Geneva talks, and on February 12, 1987 with Lt. Gen. (Res.) Mordechai Gur, the Israeli chief of staff during the negotiations.

11. Agreement on Disengagement Between Israel and Syrian Forces, May 31, 1974, and Annex 2 of the agreement.

12. Alan James, "The United Nations on Golan: Peacekeeping Paradox?" *International Relations*, Vol. IX, Book I (May 1987), pp. 73-82.

Chapter 4

1. Based on Shalev, *Cooperation*, pp. 297-298, 301-304, 329-331.

2. *Ibid.*, pp. 17-18.

3. *Ibid.*, pp. 297-298.

4. *Ibid.*, pp. 162-184.

5. Moshe Dayan, "Termination of the Crisis upon the Implementation of the Armistice Agreement with the Syrians," October 18, 1949, Israel State Archives.

6. Shalev, *Cooperation*, pp. 30-31.

Chapter 5

1. See *Davar*, June 2, 1987, for basic research by Meir Avidan, drawing on the diaries of Dr. Yaacov Herzog who in the period under discussion was the director-general of the Prime Minister's Office.

2. Background conversation with Meir Avidan, May 12, 1991.

3. Background conversation held on July 18, 1990 with

Mordechai Gazit, who in 1967 was the head of Middle East Division in the Foreign Ministry.

4. Gideon Raphael, *In the Secret of Nations* (Jerusalem: 1981; Hebrew), p. 156.

5. Avidan, *Davar*, June 2, 1987.

6. *Ibid.*

7. Reuven Pedatzur, *Ha'aretz*, May 3, 1991.

8. Abba Eban, *An Autobiography* (New York: 1977), p. 436.

9. Avidan, *Davar*, June 2, 1987.

10. *Ibid.*

11. The section on the 1970 plan is based on an article by Reuven Pedatzur, *Ha'aretz*, March 29, 1991.

Chapter 6

1. See, for example, Hatsav 843/024, April 16, 1981, for the Hebrew translation of a speech given by President Assad in Damascus and broadcast by *Damascus Radio* on April 11, 1981: "We actually want Palestine and only afterward the Golan."

2. According to SWB, ME/1171 A/8, September 7, 1991, Assad stated on September 5 to *Radio Damascus*, "Syria will not relinquish any land and will not allow anyone to relinquish any land or rights."

3. Syrian Foreign Minister Farouq al-Shara's remarks at the Madrid Peace Conference, quoted in *Ma'ariv*, November 1, 1991.

4. Interview with President Assad on British television, September 5, 1975, Hebrew translation in Hatsav 843/007, September 11, 1975.

5. Interview with Prime Minister Yitzhak Shamir, *Le Figaro*, March 1, 1991, English translation in FBIS-NES-91-043, March 5, 1991, p. 35.

6. The prime minister's message to residents of the Jordan Rift Valley appeared in *Davar*, November 15, 1991.

7. *Yediot Aharonot*, March 26, 1991.

8. Background conversation with Maj. Gen. (Res.) Yitzhak Hofi, February 10, 1987.

9. Knesset Members Shlomo Hillel and Edna Solodor quoted in *Ha'aretz*, November 5, 1991.

10. Labor Party leader Shimon Peres quoted in *Ha'aretz*, March 22, 1991.

11. Yitzhak Rabin quoted in *Yediot Aharonot*, December 27, 1991.

12. FBIS-NES-91-228, November 26, 1991, p. 32.

13. Interview with Maj. Gen. (Ret.) Yehoshua Saguy, *Yediot Aharonot*, March 22, 1991.

14. MK Reuven Rivlin, a close associate of Foreign Minister Levy, quoted in *Ha'ir*, September 1990.

15. Syrian Information Minister Muhammad Salman, quoted in FBIS-NES-91-236, December 9, 1991, p. 61.

16. Letter dated September 1, 1975, from U.S. President Gerald Ford to Prime Minister Yitzhak Rabin. See Michael Widlansky, ed., *Can Israel Survive a Palestinian State?* (Jerusalem: 1990), pp. 120-121.

17. Assad, British TV interview, September 5, 1975: "There is no international procedure or law and no resolutions by the U.N. which force a state to recognize another state."

18. Asked in 1991 whether he recognized the existence of Israel in the Middle East, President Assad replied: "This has to be put forward in the conference....This and other subjects will be tabled for discussion during the peace process." *Newsweek*, August 5, 1991, p. 18.

19. FBIS-MEA-72-142, July 25, 1977, p. H-1.

20. *Ibid.*

21. Interview with President Sadat, *New York Times*, December 28, 1970.

Chapter 7

1. Background conversations with the head of Katzrin local council, held on January 8 and November 30, 1992.

2. *Ha'aretz*, September 9, 1988.

3. Background conversations, Katzrin, January 8 and November 30, 1992.

4. "On Settlement and Security Before and After the Six-Day War--A Talk with Defense Minister Yitzhak Rabin," *Mibifnim: The United Kibbutz Movement* 49 (Summer 1987; Hebrew), p. 80.

5. Yehezkel Dror, "Security and Settlement," *ibid.*, p. 83.

6. Background conversation with Maj. Gen. (Ret.) Yisrael Tal, September 4, 1988.

7. "Seven Days" magazine, *Yediot Aharonot*, January 2, 1987.

8. Background conversation with MK Yossi Sarid, March 13, 1987.

9. Background conversation with Shimon Sheves, former adviser to the defense minister on settlement in the territories, December 6, 1987.

10. Conversation with Mordechai Gur, February 12, 1987.

11. *Ibid.*

12. Background conversation with Maj. Gen. (Res.) Yossi Peled, December 16, 1987.

13. Background conversation with a senior member of the Golan Settlements Regional Council, January 7, 1992.

14. Background conversation with Maj. Gen. (Res.) Ori Or, February 2, 1987. "Hedgehog" is defined as: "Concentration of an entrenched, fortified force, well equipped with anti-aircraft and anti-tank weapons and deployed for perimeter defense." See Yair Bourla, ed., *Dictionary of Military Terms* (Tel Aviv: 1988; Hebrew), p. 421.

15. Conversation with Golan Council member, January 7, 1992.

16. Conversation with Yitzhak Hofi, February 10, 1987.

17. *Ibid.*

18. Background conversation with Maj. Gen. (Res.) Moshe Bar-Kochba, November 15, 1987.

19. Conversation with Golan Council member, January 7, 1992.

20. Conversation with Katzrin Council head, January 8 and November 30, 1992.
21. Conversation with Mordechai Gur, February 12, 1987.
22. *Davar*, September 8, 1991.
23. *The Jerusalem Post*, May 3, 1991.
24. Background conversation with the chairman of the Golan Settlements Committee, January 21, 1991.

Chapter 8

1. *Official Gazette*, 1034, Jerusalem, December 15, 1981. SWB ME/6907/A/11, December 16, 1981.
2. SWB ME/6907/A/11, December 16, 1981, p. 12.
3. *Ibid.*
4. *Ibid.*
5. *Ibid.*, P. 13.
6. *Knesset Protocol*, Second Session, 32nd meeting of the Tenth Knesset, p. 767.
7. *Ibid.*, p. 771.
8. Background conversation with the adviser to the defense minister on settlement in the Territories, December 18, 1988.
9. *Knesset Protocol*, Tenth Knesset, p. 765.
10. *Ibid.*, p. 784.
11. Report by the UN Secretary-General, Security Council document No. S/14821, December 31, 1991, p. 3.
12. Yoram Dinstein, "Zion in International Law Shall Be Redeemed," *Hapraklit* 27, 3 (1971; Hebrew), p. 315.
13. *Ibid.*, p. 18.
14. Dr. Yehuda Zvi Blum, "Zion in International Law Has Been Redeemed," *ibid.*, p. 315.
15. FBIS, V, No. 242, December 17, 1981, p. H-3.
16. Letter from Syrian ambassador to the UN to the president of the Security Council, December 14, 1981, Security Council document No. S/14791, December 14, 1981.
17. Security Council document, December 31, 1991, p. 1.

18. Amended draft resolution by Jordan according to Security Council document No. S/14832/REV.1, January 19, 1982.
19. "Political and Security Questions," *Year Book of the United Nations 1982*, Vol. 36, p. 516.
20. Speech by President Assad at the opening of the Syrian Popular Council, February 27, 1986, Hebrew translation in Hatsav 843/004, March 3, 1986.
21. Background conversation with Prof. Amos Shapira, December 31, 1986.

Chapter 9

1. Maoz, *Sphinx*, p. 129.
2. Speech by President Assad on the anniversary of the Ba'th revolution, March 8, 1987, Hebrew translation in Hatsav 843/021, March 10, 1987.
3. Resolutions of the Syrian Ba'th Party conference, read by President Assad and quoted by *Damascus Radio*, January 6, 1980.
4. Remarks by President Assad, April 11, 1981, Hebrew translation in Hatsav 843/024, April 16, 1981.
5. Remarks by the Syrian foreign minister on *Amman Radio*, May 13, 1979, Hebrew translation in Hatsav 836/1341, May 13, 1979.
6. Interview with President Assad in *Der Spiegel*, quoted by *Damascus Radio*, August 27, 1979, Hebrew translation in Hatsav 836/2088, August 27, 1979.
7. Resolutions of the Palestinian Popular Conference held in April 1972 in Beirut, *Palestinian Arab Documents* 1972, p. 222.
8. Background conversation with Prof. Itamar Rabinovich, July 25, 1990.

Chapter 10

1. Aharon Daviza, background conversation, 1994.

2. Background conversation with Col. (Res.) Benny Ze'evi, March 19, 1987.
3. Aharon Daviza, *The Druse on the Golan Heights: Conflict of Misunderstanding 1978-1982* (Tel Aviv University: 1988; Hebrew), p. 29.
4. *Ibid.*, p. 6.
5. *Ibid.*
6. *Ibid.*, p. 26.
7. *Ibid.*, p. 33.
8. Conversation with Benny Ze'evi, March 19, 1987.

Chapter 11

1. The following sources were consulted in writing this chapter: G. Schumacher, C.E., *The Jaulan* (London: 1889), pp. 7-18, 61-65, 246-257; Geographical Section of the Naval Intelligence Division, *A Handbook of Syria* (London: 1920); Rene Dussaud, *Topographie Historique de la Syrie Antique et Medievale* (Paris: 1927), pp. 381-395; Zvi Ayalon, *Land of the Golan--A Guide* (Tel Aviv: 1969; Hebrew); *The Golan* (collection of articles), Kibbutz Movement Geography Section (Hebrew); "The Golan: A Profile," *Yediot Aharonot*, December 15, 1981; *The Golan Heights: Geographical and Historical Background* (Jerusalem: Information Center, 1982), pp. 5-7; Zvi Maoz, "Settlement and Security on the Golan Heights in Ancient Times," *Dapei Elazar* 7 (Tel Aviv: 1985; Hebrew), pp. 23-27; author's visits and tours of the Golan Heights and conversations with reserve officers who are well acquainted with the topography of the region.
2. A "rear defense stop line" is defined as: "Continuous rear defense systems at which the final effort to stop the enemy is made. The breaching of the line could lead to the fall of the region."
3. Conversation with Yisrael Tal, September 4, 1988.
4. Background conversation with Maj. Gen. (Res.) Yisrael Tal, March 1, 1992.

Chapter 12

1. Data furnished by the IDF's History Department via the IDF Spokesman, September 24, 1991.
2. David Ben-Gurion, *War Diary* 4 (Tel Aviv: 1983; Hebrew), p. 457.
3. Yehoshua Raviv, *The Israeli-Arab Military Balance after the Peace Treaty with Egypt* (Jaffee Center for Strategic Studies [hereafter: JCSS]: 1979; Hebrew), p. 21.
4. Joseph Alpher, ed., *The Middle East Military Balance 1989-1990* (Jerusalem: Jerusalem Post and Boulder: Westview Press, 1990), p. 366.
5. Interview with Director of Military Intelligence Yehoshua Saguy, *Ma'ariv*, April 17, 1992.
6. Remarks by head of Northern Command, Maj. Gen. Yitzhak Mordechai, *Hadashot*, May 6, 1992.
7. *Ibid.*
8. Alpher, *Military Balance*, p. 366.
9. Shlomo Gazit, ed., *The Middle East Military Balance 1990-1991* (Jerusalem: Jerusalem Post and Boulder: Westview Press, 1992), p. 388.
10. Aryeh Shalev, *Line of Defense in Judea and Samaria* (Tel Aviv: 1982; Hebrew), pp. 53-54.
11. *Ibid.*, p. 47.
12. Raviv, *Military Balance*, p. 21.
13. Alpher, *Military Balance*, pp. 366-367.

Chapter 13

1. Aryeh (Lova) Eliav, *Land of the Hart* (Tel Aviv: 1972; Hebrew), p. 161.
2. Background conversation with Yosef Ben-Aharon, director-general of the Prime Minister's Office, July 18, 1990.
3. Speech by President Assad, March 12, 1992, quoted by *Ha'aretz*, March 13, 1992.

Chapter 14

1. In early 1960, following a reprisal raid by the IDF on the Syrian border, Egypt moved an armored division and three infantry brigades into Sinai. Israeli Military Intelligence had no knowledge about the move or the preparations for it. Israel did not learn about the event until four days after the Egyptian force began to move. By then the advance force of the Egyptian armored division had already reached Jebel Libni.

2. On September 16, 1970, fighting broke out between the Jordanian Army and Palestinian terrorist organizations in Jordan, mainly in the center and north of the country. On September 25, after the withdrawal of Syrian units that had invaded Jordan, and at a time when the Jordanian Army had the upper hand in the fighting, the assessment of Israeli intelligence was that the Jordanians would not succeed in overcoming the Palestinian groups.

3. Prior to the Six-Day War there was no assessment in Israel that Nasser was prepared to take steps leading to war. Nor did Israeli intelligence have information that Egyptian forces were about to enter Sinai or that Nasser would close the Straits of Tiran to Israeli shipping. On the eve of the 1967 war, the Israeli assessment held that Syria would immediately join Egypt while Jordan would hesitate; the reality was the opposite. Israeli intelligence also failed to foresee that Egypt would launch a war of attrition (1968); that in-depth bombing of Egypt by the IAF would lead the Soviet Union to send military units to Egypt and render it assistance enabling it to pursue the War of Attrition (1970); that President Sadat would go to war, even though the IDF knew that Egypt and Syria had moved up forces and created an attack option (the 1973 war); or that Sadat would decide on a peace initiative (1977).

4. Interview with former Director of Military Intelligence Shlomo Gazit, in which he comments on the element of surprise, *Ma'ariv*, September 10, 1980.

5. On October 3, 1973, three days before the start of the Yom Kippur War, Israeli Military Intelligence reported that preparations already made by the Egyptian and Syrian armies gave

them a war option. The assessment was based on a large number of reports concerning modifications and changes in the deployment of the two armies and preparations of various kinds. In his autobiography, Moshe Dayan, the defense minister during the 1973 war, referring to a meeting of ministers with the prime minister on October 3, wrote: "The Intelligence representative emphasized that the Syrian and Egyptian armies were so deployed along the fronts that they were able at any moment to launch an attack, but he did not think they were about to do so." Moshe Dayan, *The Story of My Life* (London: 1978), p. 475.

6. Written on the basis of a background conversation with Prof. Yuval Ne'eman, July 8, 1992.

Chapter 15

1. Alpher, *Military Balance*, pp. 370-371.
2. Shalev, *Line of Defense*, p. 59.
3. *Ibid.*, p. 94.

Chapter 16

1. Conversation with Yisrael Tal, March 1, 1992.
2. *Ibid.*
3. Conversation with Yisrael Tal, March 29, 1992.
4. *Ibid.*, March 1, 1992.
5. Background conversation with a senior IDF officer, March 29, 1992.
6. Background conversation with a senior IDF officer, April 21, 1992.
7. Interview by Syrian Defense Minister Mustafa Tlas to *Der Spiegel*, quoted by *Ha'aretz*, September 21, 1984.
8. Mahmoud Riad, *The Struggle for Peace in the Middle East* (London: 1981), p. 289.
9. Shalev, *Line of Defense*, pp. 79-81.

10. Alpher, *Military Balance*, pp. 399.

Chapter 18

1. *The Water Problem in the Context of the Arrangements Between Israel and the Arab States* (JCSS, 1991; Hebrew, unpublished draft), p. 143.
2. Brawer, *Northern Boundary*, p. 10.
3. Shalev, *Line of Defense*, p. 283.
4. *Ibid.*, pp. 149-184.
5. *Ibid.*, pp. 263-279.
6. Yitzhak Rabin, "From the Battles over Water Sources to the Six-Day War," in *The IDF and its Corps: Encyclopedia of Army and Security*, I (Tel Aviv: 1982; Hebrew), pp. 183-184.
7. Yigal Allon's reply to a motion for the agenda by MK Menachem Begin, on reports about a plan for withdrawal to west of the Purple Line, appears in *Documents Annual 1974* (Hebrew), History Department of the Ministry of Foreign Affairs, p. 187.
8. Yitzhak Hofi, "Land of the Golan," *Dapei Elazar* 7 (Tel Aviv: 1985), p. 43.
9. Col. Eli, *Ma'arachot*, May 20, 1981, pp. 279-280.
10. Conversation with Herzl Shafir, February 27, 1987.
11. Background conversation with Prof. Yuval Ne'eman, May 21, 1987.
12. Background conversation with Lt. Gen. (Res.) Mordechai Gur, June 21, 1990.
13. Background conversation with Maj. Gen. (Res.) Yossi Peled, July 20, 1990.

Chapter 19

1. Assad interview, September 5, 1975.
2. The remarks of a Syrian senior official were quoted in *Yediot Aharonot*, June 11, 1992.

3. Report citing the views of a Syrian researcher, a former diplomat now living in Europe, taken from Initiative for Peace and Cooperation in the Middle East, discussions of a working group on security issues, held at Airlin House, England, February 26-27, 1992.

4. Zuhair Diab, "A Proposed Security Regime for the Arab-Israeli Conflict," November 1991, pp. 9-16. Diab is a Syrian living in London who claims to be a member of the Ba'th Party. The paper was presented at a conference held in Italy.

5. Conversation with Mordechai Gur, June 21, 1990; Brig. Gen. (Res.) Avigdor Kahalani quoted in *Ha'aretz*, October 29, 1991.

6. Conversation with Mordechai Gur, June 21, 1990.

7. Remarks by Chief of Staff Dan Shomron, *Yediot Aharonot*, August 3, 1990.

8. Conversation with Ori Or, February 2, 1987.

9. Background conversation with Lt. Gen. (Res.) Yitzhak Rabin, August 31, 1990; and with Yosef Ben-Aharon, July 18, 1990.

10. Background conversation with Maj. Gen. (Res.) Yisrael Tal, September 4, 1987; and with Ori Or, February 2, 1987.

11. Remarks by Maj. Gen. (Res.) Yossi Peled at a seminar on the Syrian-Israeli peace process, held by JCSS at Tel Aviv University, October 1991.

Chapter 20

1. Defense Minister Moshe Arens' reply to a parliamentary question was reported by *Yediot Aharonot*, April 15, 1992.

2. Avraham Tamir, *Soldier in Search of Peace* (Tel Aviv: 1988; Hebrew), p. 86.

3. *Ibid.*, p. 87.

4. *Ibid.*, p. 102.

5. *Ibid.*, p. 87.

6. Arens, *Yediot Aharonot*, April 15, 1992.

7. Maj. Gen. (Res.) David Ivri quoted in *Ha'aretz*, April 14, 1992.
8. Shaul Ramati quoted in *Jerusalem Post*, October 1, 1991.

Chapter 21

1. For the author's earlier analysis of this element of a political-security settlement in the West Bank, see his *The West Bank: Line of Defense*, pp. 115-116.
2. Alan Dowty, *The Role of Great Power Guarantees in International Peace Agreements* (Jerusalem: 1974), pp. 8-9.
3. *Ibid.*, pp. 10-11. The intervention was effective because of an identity of American motives and interests; the sketchy internal situation in the Congo; the general opposition to Belgian involvement; the fact that the UN secretary-general was an activist by nature; and the general objections to the detaching of Katanga from the Congo.
4. *Ibid.*, p. 18.
5. *Ibid.*, p. 27.
6. N.A. Pelcovits, *Security Guarantees in a Middle East Settlement*, Foreign Policy Paper No. 5 (London: 1976), pp. 48-55.
7. Shai Feldman, "Superpower Security Guarantees in the 1980's," in *Third World Conflict and International Security*, II, Adelphi Paper No. 167, London 1981.
8. Pelcovits, *Security Guarantees*, p. 27.
9. Feldman, "Superpower Security."
10. *Newsweek*, December 17, 1979.
11. *Ibid.*, October 27, 1980.
12. *Ha'aretz*, September 15, 1986.
13. *Ibid.*, March 9, 1987.
14. *Hatsofe*, May 15, 1975.
15. Michael Bar Zohar, *The Longest Month* (Tel Aviv, 1967), pp. 123-128.
16. Pelcovits, *Security Guarantees*, p. 21.

17. Prior to the evacuation of Sinai by the IDF in 1982, the UN was not prepared to deploy military units of its own to supervise execution of the Israel-Egypt peace treaty, and the task was carried out by an American civilian agency. But the US did create a precedent in the Middle East when it agreed to deploy an American Army battalion in Sinai, as part of the Multinational Force and Observers that commenced activity after the IDF had completed its withdrawal in 1982. This American precedent renders somewhat more likely the possibility that the US will agree to undertake a similar task in the future on the Golan.

Chapter 22

1. Ezer Weizman, *The Battle for Peace* (Jerusalem: 1981), p. 201.
2. Background conversation with Maj. Gen. (Res.) Shlomo Gazit, June 14, 1992. In contrast with Gazit, Weizman (*ibid.*) writes that the idea of reciprocal early warning stations also did not appeal to Gamasi.

About the Author

Brigadier General (res.) Aryeh Shalev served for 33 years in the IDF before joining JCSS in 1978. His final post was Military Governor of the West Bank. At JCSS he has published a number of works on the Arab-Israel peace process, including *The West Bank: Line of Defense* (Praeger/Greenwood, 1985), and *The Israel-Syria Armistice Regime, 1949-1955* (Jerusalem: The Jerusalem Post and Boulder: Westview Press, 1993). Early in his military career General Shalev served on, then commanded, the Israeli delegation to the Israel-Syria Mixed Armistice Commission.

Appendices

Appendix 1

Israel-Syria Disengagement Agreement

of 31 May 1974

A. Israel and Syria will scrupulously observe the ceasefire on land, sea and air and will refrain from all military actions against each other, from the time of the signing of this document, in implementation of United Nations Security Council Resolution 338 dated October 22, 1973.

B. The military forces of Israel and Syria will be separated in accordance with the following principles:

1. All Israeli military forces will be west of the line designated as Line A on the map attached hereto, except in the Quneitra area, where they will be west of Line A-1.

2. All territory east of Line A will be under Syrian administration, and Syrian civilians will return to this territory.

3. The area between Line A and the line designated as Line B on the attached map will be an area of separation. In this area will be stationed the United Nations Disengagement Observer Force established in accordance with the accompanying protocol.

4. All Syrian military forces will be east of the line designated as Line B on the attached map.

5. There will be two equal areas of limitation in armament and forces, one west of Line A and one east of Line B as agreed upon.

6. Air forces of the two sides will be permitted to operate up to their respective lines without interference from the other side.

C. In the area between Line A and Line A-1 on the attached map there shall be no military forces.

D. This agreement and the attached map will be signed by the military representatives of Israel and Syria in Geneva not later than May 31, 1974, in the Egyptian-Israeli Military Working Group of the Geneva Peace Conference under the aegis of the United Nations, after that group has been joined by a Syrian military representative, and with the participation of representatives of the United States and the Soviet Union. The precise delineation of a detailed map and a plan for the implementation of the disengagement of forces will be worked out by military representatives of Israel and Syria in the Egyptian-Israeli Military Working Group who will agree on the stages of this process. The Military Working Group described above will start their work for this purpose in Geneva under the aegis of the United Nations within 24 hours after the signing of this agreement. They will complete this task within five days. Disengagement will begin within 24 hours after the completion of the task of the Military Working Group. The process of disengagement will be completed not later than twenty days after it begins.

E. The provisions of paragraphs A, B and C shall be inspected by personnel of the United Nations comprising the United Nations Disengagement Observer Force under this agreement.

F. Within 24 hours after the signing of this agreement in Geneva all wounded prisoners of war which each side holds of the other as certified by the ICRC will be repatriated. The morning after the completion of the task of the Military Working Group, all remaining prisoners of war will be repatriated.

G. The bodies of all dead soldiers held by either side will be returned for burial in their respective countries within ten days after the signing of this agreement.

H. This agreement is not a peace agreement. It is a step toward a just and durable peace on the basis of Security Council Resolution 338 dated October 22, 1973.

For Israel:

For Syria:

Witness for the United Nations:

Ensio Siilasvuo Geneva 31 May 1974

Appendix 2

Statement by the Chairman of the Geneva Conference Regarding Agreement by the Parties Concerning the Details of the Disengagement Agreement and the UN Force, of 5 June 1974

1. A UNDOF forward H.Q. will be established in the area of separation dividing the forces at each phase. Israel and Syria will attach liason officers of the rank of Colonel to this H.Q. in order to facilitate its task in solving or settling any problem related to the implementation of the plan of disengagement.

2. Israel and Syria agree not to detain military or civilian personnel of the other side and undertake not to take prisoners of war during the period of implementation of the disengagement agreement. They agree to repatriate at end of same day through the good offices of UNDOF any member of the armed forces or any civilians who may fall in their hands.

3. UNDOF wil effect an inspection of redeployment of forces after completion of each phase on dates fixed in the Time-Table attached to the Plan of Separation of Forces and will report their findings forthwith to the parties, in order to determine that both Parties have redeployed their forces in the limited forces areas.

4. Israel and Syria will make available all information and maps of mine fields as far as their respective areas are concerned and the areas handed over by them.

5. Israel and Syria will co-operate with the ICRC in carrying out its mandate, including the exchange of dead bodies, which is to be completed on June 6th 1974.

6. Israel and Syria undertake to repatriate all prisoners of war still detained by them not later than June 6th 1974.

7. The UNDOF shall deny access to any military forces into the separation of forces area. It will deploy its forces in close co-operation with the Parties to the Agreement.

8. UNDOF will determine axes of access and exit for its forces from the Syrian and the Israeli held areas in close co-operation with the parties.

9. UNDOF will assume control, will establish and man observation posts in evacuated Israeli positions. It shall mark on the ground the respective lines shown on the map attached to the disengagement agreement.

10. The UNDOF will assist in the arrangements concerning the return of civilians to agreed locations in the separation of forces area.

11. The UNDOF will be permitted to construct a fenced off patrol road, with the assistance of the Parties, along the separation of forces area, and the use of former positions of both armies which are located in the separation area, between lines A and B.

12. In the Syrian administered inhabited localities of the area of separation, a local police force will operate. It will be responsible for normal police duties only. Police vehicles shall be light, soft and unarmed.

13. UNDOF will effect an inspection of redeployment of forces after completion of each of the phases in order to determine that both parties have redeployed their forces in the restricted forces areas, so that the remaining forces will be as follows:

(a) That the area of limitation in armament and forces west of Line A and east of Line B will be 10 kilometres in width. In each area, respectively the following are permitted:

(1) two brigades of armed forces, including 75 tanks and 36 pieces of short-range 122-mm or equivalent calibre artillery.

(2) the entire force of each party shall not exceed 6,000 men.

(b) That in the area between 10 and 20 kilometres west of Line A and east of Line B.

(1) there will be no artillery pieces whose range exceeds 20 kilometres.

(2) the total number of artillery pieces permitted is 162 with a range of not exceeding 20 kilometres and 450 tanks of all types

(3) surface-to-air missiles will be stationed no closer than 25 kilometres west of Line A and east of Line B.

14. UNDOF will carry out the following inspections during the separation period:

(a) Phase 2 - 16th June in No. 1 areas on both sides and in No. 4a area.

(b) Phase 3 - 20th June in No. 2 areas on both sides and in No. 1a and 4c areas.

(c) Phase 4 - 25th June in No. 3 areas and in 2a area and in the area between A and A-1 lines west of Kuneitra and in 4b area.

15. UNDOF will verify during these inspections that the level of forces does not exceed the following:

(a) At the end of phase 1, one-third of the final strength would remain in areas 1 and 4a, i.e. in the 10 km areas 2 infantry battalions, 25 tanks, 12 guns of short range on each side of the separation lines.

(b) At the end of the phase 2 on Israeli side two-thirds of the final strength would remain in areas 1 and 4a and 4c and No. 2 areas i.e. 4 infantry battalions, 50 tanks, 24 guns of short range. On Syrian side the final strength would remain in No. 1 and No. 2 areas within 10 km area and in 1a area;

(c) At the end of the phase 4 - in all the restricted forces areas on both sides of the separation lines (A and B) the final strength - i.e. 2 infantry brigades 75 tanks, 36 guns of short range and a total of 6,000 men only will remain within the 10 km line.

16. UNDOF will verify on the 26th June 1974 that the above mentioned limitations of forces are observed by the parties and will effect regular bi-weekly inspections of the 10 km restricted forces areas.

17. UNDOF will verify on the 27th June 1974 that no surface-to-air missile launchers and no missiles are deployed within the 25 kilometres west of Line A and east of Line B. UNDOF will also verify that in the 20 kilometres area there are no more than 162 artillery guns of a range not exceeding 20 kms and 150 tanks of all types only, and will effect regular bi-weekly inspections.

18. The Israel Army has stated that strict orders have been given not to cause any damage to civilian property in the area during the disengagement period.

This statement has been read in the presence of General Shafir and General Tayara and both Parties have accepted it.

Signed for the United Nations
in Geneva on 05 June 1974 by:

Lt. General Ensio Siilasvuo

Appendix 3

Golan Heights Jewish Population, 1991-1994

Name of Settlement	*Type*	*Population*				
		July 1991				*March 1994*
		Families	*Children*	*Single Adults*	*Total*	*Total*
Afik	Kibbutz	86	87	9	305	302
Alonei Habashan	Co-op Moshav	22	47	2	93	144
Aniam	Moshav	34	68	12	166	193
Avnei Eitan	Moshav	35	141	1	193	226
Bnei Yehuda	Regional Center	116	242	10	484	683
Bruhim Golan	Residential	19	0	0	64	62
Eliad	Moshav	45	107	7	204	246
Elrom	Kibbutz	56	114	40	326	352

Name of Settlement	*Type*	*Population*				
		July 1991				*March 1994*
		Families	*Children*	*Single Adults*	*Total*	*Total*
Ein Zivan	Kibbutz	40	118	6	212	265
Geshur	Kibbutz	30	68	22	150	172
Givat Yoav	Moshav	71	197	5	344	390
Hadnes	Residential	25	71	0	121	183
Hispin	Regional Center	75	150	0	335	594
Kanaf	Agricultural Co-op	19	21	3	62	102
Katzrin	City	1,000	0	0	4,000	4,400
Keshet	Co-op Moshav	47	238	6	358	445
Kfar Haruv	Kibbutz	45	104	37	231	341
Kidmat Zvi	Moshava	40	151	0	231	206
Ma'ale Gamla	Moshav	49	155	0	253	289

Merom Golan	Kibbutz	75	205	53	410	489
Metzar	Kibbutz	0	0	37	37	62
Mevo Hama	Kibbutz	80	160	55	375	422
Natur	Kibbutz	7	12	6	32	93
Neot Golan	Kibbutz	37	86	18	178	243
Neve Ativ	Moshav	31	60	1	123	162
Nov	Moshav	68	241	17	390	441
Odem	Village/Co-op Moshav	22	55	0	99	113
Ortal	Kibbutz	34	57	44	172	227
Ramot	Moshav	70	185	3	329	433
Ramat Magshimim	Co-op Moshav	74	244	45	437	496
Sha'al	Moshav	32	85	0	149	191
Yonatan	Co-op Moshav	32	85	0	154	193
TOTAL						13,160

Appendix 4

Golan Heights Mounds

I. In the Golan Heights, between the area north of the Khan Arnabah-Gonen Road and the foot of Mount Hermon, there are six mounds east of the watershed line and three west of it.

A. The eastern mounds are:

1. Mount Ram--1,188 meters above sea level.
2. Tel al-Manfuche--1,210m above sea level.
3. Mount Kramim (Tell Sader al-Arus)--1,198m above sea level. This is a large volcanic mound that rises 120-190m above its surroundings. Its crater opens toward the southwest.
4. Mount Varda (Tell al-Wardah)--1,226m above sea level. Rising 130-140m above its surroundings, it is the highest mound in the Golan Heights.
5. Tell Shueifri--1,141m above sea level.
6. Mount Hermonit (Tell al-Sheikha)--1,211m above see level. This volcanic mound rises 100-160m above its surroundings. Its crater opens toward the west.

B. The western mounds are:

1. Mount Odem (Tell al-Ahmar)--1,187m above sea level, it rises 80-110m above its surroundings. Its crater opens toward the west.
2. Mount Baron (Tell al-Baram)--1,055m above sea level. It rises to 70m above its surroundings and its crater opens toward the south. Although it is east of the watershed line, it is considered among the

western mounds due to its distance from the border.

3. Tell al-Hajal--1,060m above sea level. This is a small volcanic mound north of Mount Baron.

II. Between the Khan Arnabah-Gonen Road and the Kuneitra-Banat Yaqub Bridge Road there are four mounds to the east and four mounds to the west.

A. The eastern mounds are:

1. Tell al-Mahfi--1,056m above sea level. This is a small volcanic mountain with vineyards.
2. Mount Bental (Tell al-Uram)--1,165m above sea level. This is a large volcanic mount that rises 180-200m above its surroundings. Its crater opens toward the northwest.
3. Mount Avital (Tell abu Neda), the largest of the Golan mounds--1,204m above sea level. It rises 200-210m above its surroundings, and its crater is oblong.
4. Tell al-Rihaniya--1,018m above sea level. This small volcanic mound rises to 50m above its surroundings.

B. The western mounds are:

1. Tell al-Sheban--876m above sea level.
2. Two Dalwa mounds, located west of Kafr Dalwa, that are respectively 946 and 910m above sea level.
3. Mount Shifon (Tell abu Hanzir)--977m above sea level. This is a large, equilateral volcanic mound that rises 130-160m above its surroundings.

III. Between the Kuneitra-Banat Yaqub Bridge Road and the southern end of the Golan Heights there are 13 mounds along the eastern line, and four along the western line.

A. The eastern mounds are:

1. Tell al-Rasnniya--1,070m above sea level. This volcanic mound rises 80-110m above its surroundings.
2. Tell al-Hariya--1,110m above sea level. This is a large, prominent volcanic mound that rises 100-130m above its surroundings.
3. Mount Hozek (Tell Hazeika)--1,158m above sea level. This is a large volcanic mountain.
4. Tell al-Shu'af al-Kabir--1,135m above sea level.
5. Mount-Aqsha--1,029m above sea level. This is a large volcanic mound that rises to 130m above its surroundings.
6. Tell-Abbas--987m above sea level. This is a small volcanic mound.
7. Tell al-Shu'af Sindin--993m above sea level. This volcanic mound rises to 80m above its surroundings. Its crater opens toward the northwest.
8. Halil al-Shu'af--865m above sea level, these are two rocky hills.
9. Mount Fares (Tell al-Faras)--930m above sea level. This is a large isolated volcanic mound that is the most regular of the Golan Heights mounds. It rises 130-160m above its surroundings, and its crest affords good observation for great distances.
10. Tell al-Klaiat--727m above sea level; an oblong volcanic peaked crest that rises 30-40m above its surroundings.

11. Orha Hill (Tel Jokhadar)--68m above sea level; it rises to 40m above its surroundings.
12. Tell al Siqi--494m above sea level. This is a flat volcanic mound.
13. Tell abu al-Ritar--456m above sea level.

B. The western mounds are:

1. Mount Yosifon (Tell al-Yusef)--981m above sea level. This is a large, equilateral volcanic mound that rises 100-170m above its surroundings. Its crater opens toward the northwest.
2. Pazra Hill (Tell Pazra)--873m above sea level. This volcanic mound rises to 40m above its surroundings. Its crater opens toward the southwest.
3. Talya Hill--758m above sea level (located near the Keshet settlement).
4. Givat Natur--458m above sea level.

IV. The mounds east of the Israeli disengagement line (between the two disengagement lines):

1. Tell al-Ahmar--1,200m above sea level.
2. Tell al-Daoud--1,100m above sea level.
3. Tell al-Hawah--1,079m above sea level.
4. Tell al-Ahmar al-Gharbi--961m above sea level.
5. Tell al-Keva--1,029m above sea level.
6. Tell al-Karoum--1,011m above sea level.

The mounds east of (contiguous to) the Syrian disengagement line:

1. Tell al-Kudna--661m above sea level.
2. Tell al-Ahmar al-Sharki--885m above sea level.

Appendix 5

The Egyptian-Israeli Peace Treaty

The White House, Monday, March 26, 1979

The Government of the Arab Republic of Egypt and the Government of the State of Israel;

PREAMBLE

Convinced of the urgent necessity of the establishment of a just, comprehensive and lasting peace in the Middle East in accordance with Security Council Resolutions 242 and 338;

Reaffirming their adherence to the "Framework for Peace in the Middle East Agreed at Camp David," dated September 17, 1978:

Noting that the aforementioned Framework as appropriate is intended to constitute a basis for peace not only between Egypt and Israel but also between Israel and each of its other Arab neighbors which is prepared to negotiate peace with it on this basis:

Desiring to bring to an end the state of war between them and to establish a peace in which every state in the area can live in security;

Convinced that the conclusion of a Treaty of Peace between Egypt and Israel is an important step in the search for comprehensive peace in the area and for the attainment of the settlement of the Arab-Israeli conflict in all its aspects;

Inviting the other Arab parties to this dispute to join the peace process with Israel guided by and based on the principles of the aforementioned Framework;

Desiring as well to develop friendly relations and cooperation between themselves in accordance with the United Nations Charter and the principles of international law governing international relations in times of peace;

Agree to the following provisions in the free exercise of their sovereignty, in order to implement the "Framework for the Conclusion of a Peace Treaty Between Egypt and Israel";

Article I

1. The state of war between the Parties will be terminated and peace will be established between them upon the exchange of instruments of ratification of this Treaty.

2. Israel will withdraw all its armed forces and civilians from the Sinai behind the international boundary between Egypt and mandated Palestine, as provided in the annexed protocol (Annex I), and Egypt will resume the exercise of its full sovereignty over the Sinai.

3. Upon completion of the interim withdrawal provided for in Annex I, the Parties will establish normal and friendly relations, in accordance with Article III (3).

Article II

The permanent boundary between Egypt and Israel is the recognized international boundary between Egypt and the former mandated territory of Palestine, as shown on the map at Annex II, without prejudice to the issue of the status of the Gaza Strip. The Parties recognize this boundary as inviolable. Each will respect the territorial integrity of the other, including their territorial waters and airspace.

Article III

1. The Parties will apply between them the provisions of the Charter of the United Nations and the principles of international law governing relations among states in times of peace. In particular:

 a. They recognize and will respect each other's sovereignty, territorial integrity and political independence;

 b. They recognize and will respect each other's right to live in peace within their secure and recognized boundaries.

 c. They will refrain from the threat or use of force, directly or indirectly, against each other and will settle all disputes between them by peaceful means.

2. Each Party undertakes to ensure that acts or threats of belligerency, hostility, or violence do not originate from and are not committed from within its territory, or by any forces subject to its control or by any other forces stationed on its territory, against the population, citizens or property of the other Party. Each Party also undertakes to refrain from organizing, instigating, inciting, assisting or participating in acts or threats of belligerency, hostility, subversion or violence against the other Party, anywhere, and undertakes to ensure that perpetrators of such acts are brought to justice.

3. The Parties agree that the normal relationship established between them will include full recognition, diplomatic, economic and cultural relations, termination of economic boycotts and discriminatory barriers to the free movement of people and goods, and will guarantee the mutual enjoyment by citizens of the due process of law. The process by which they undertake to achieve such a relationship parallel to the implementation of other provisions of this Treaty is set out in the annexed protocol (Annex III).

Article IV

1. In order to provide maximum security for both Parties on the basis of reciprocity, agreed security arrangements will be established including limited force zones in Egyptian and Israeli territory, and United Nations forces and observers, described in detail as to nature and timing in Annex I, and other security arrangements the Parties may agree upon.

2. The Parties agree to the stationing of United Nations personnel in areas described in Annex I. The Parties agree not to request withdrawal of the United Nations personnel and that these personnel will not be removed unless such removal is approved by the Security Council of the United Nations, with the affirmative vote of the five Permanent Members, unless the Parties otherwise agree.

3. A Joint Commission will be established to facilitate the implementation of the Treaty, as provided for in Annex I.

4. The security arrangements provided for in paragraphs 1 and 2 of this Article may at the request of either party be reviewed and amended by mutual agreement of the Parties.

Article V

1. Ships of Israel, and cargoes destined for or coming from Israel, shall enjoy the right of free passage through the Suez Canal and its approaches through the Gulf of Suez and the Mediterranean Sea on the basis of the Constantinople Convention of 1888, applying to all nations. Israeli nationals, vessels and cargoes, as well as persons, vessels and cargoes destined for or coming from Israel, shall be accorded non-discriminatory treatment in all matters connected with usage of the canal.

2. The Parties consider the Strait of Tiran and the Gulf of Aqaba to be international waterways open to all nations for unimpeded and non suspendable freedom of navigation and overflight. The Parties will respect each other's right to navigation and overflight for access to either country through the Strait of Tiran and the Gulf of Aqaba.

Article VI

1. This Treaty does not affect and shall not be interpreted as affecting in any way the rights and obligations of the Parties under the Charter of the United Nations.

2. The Parties undertake to fulfill in good faith their obligations under this Treaty, without regard to action or inaction of any other party and independently of any instrument external to this Treaty.

3. They further undertake to take all the necessary measures for the application in their relations of the provisions of the multilateral conventions to which they are parties, including the submission of appropriate notification to the Secretary General of the United Nations and other depositaries of such conventions.

4. The Parties undertake not to enter into any obligation in conflict with this Treaty.

5. Subject to Article 103 of the United Nations Charter, in the event of a conflict between the obligations of the Parties under the present Treaty and any of their other obligations, the obligations under this Treaty will be binding and implemented.

Article VII

1. Disputes arising out of the application or interpretation of this Treaty shall be resolved by negotiations.

2. Any such disputes which cannot be settled by negotiations shall be resolved by conciliation or submitted to arbitration.

Article VIII

The Parties agree to establish a claims commission for the mutual settlement of all financial claims.

Article IX

1. This Treaty shall enter into force upon exchange of instruments of ratification.

2. This Treaty supersedes the Agreement between Egypt and Israel of September, 1975.

3. All protocols, annexes, and maps attached to this Treaty shall be regarded as an integral part hereof.

4. The Treaty shall be communicated to the Secretary General of the United Nations for registration in accordance with the provisions of Article 102 of the Charter of the United Nations.

Annex I — Protocol Concerning Israeli Withdrawal and Security Agreements

Article I

Concept of Withdrawal

1. Israel will complete withdrawal of all its armed forces and civilians from the Sinai not later than three years from the date of exchange of instruments of ratification of this Treaty.

2. To ensure the mutual security of the Parties, the implementation of phased withdrawal will be accompanied by the military measures and establishment of zones set out in this Annex and in Map 1, hereinafter referred to as "the Zones."

3. The withdrawal from the Sinai will be accomplished in two phases:

a. The interim withdrawal behind the line from east of El Arish to Ras Mohammed as delineated on Map 2 within nine months from the date of exchange of instruments of ratification of this Treaty.

b. The final withdrawal from the Sinai behind the international boundary not later than three years from the date of exchange of instruments of ratification of this Treaty.

4. A Joint Commission will be formed immediately after the exchange of instruments of ratification of this Treaty in order to supervise and coordinate movements and schedules during the withdrawal, and to adjust plans and timetables as necessary within the limits established by paragraph 3, above. Details relating to the Joint Commission are set out in Article IV of the attached Appendix. The Joint Commission will be dissolved upon completion of final Israeli withdrawal from the Sinai.

Article II

Determination of Final Lines and Zones

1. In order to provide maximum security for both Parties after the final withdrawal, the lines and the Zones delineated on Map 1 are to be established and organized as follows:

a. Zone A

(1) Zone A is bounded on the east by line A (red line) and on the west by the Suez Canal and the east coast of the Gulf of Suez, as shown on Map 1.

(2) An Egyptian armed force of one mechanized infantry division and its military installations, and field fortifications, will be in this Zone.

(3) The main elements of that Division will consist of:

(a) Three mechanized infantry brigades.

(b) One armed brigade.

(c) Seven field artillery battalions including up to 126 artillery pieces.

(d) Seven anti-aircraft artillery battalions including individual surface-to-air missiles and up to 126 anti-aircraft guns of 37 mm and above.

(e) Up to 230 tanks.

(f) Up to 480 armored personnel vehicles of all types.

(g) Up to a total of twenty-two thousand personnel.

b. Zone B

(1) Zone B is bounded by line B (green line) on the east and by line A (red line) on the west, as shown on Map 1.

(2) Egyptian border units of four batallions equipped with light weapons and wheeled vehicles will provide security and supplement the civil police in maintaining order in Zone B. The main elements in the four Border Batallions will consist of up to a

total of four thousand personnel.

(3) Land based, short range, low power, coastal warning points of the border patrol units may be established on the coast of this Zone.

(4) There will be in Zone B field fortifications and military installations for the four border batallions.

c. Zone C

(1) Zone C is bounded by line B (green line) on the west and the International Boundary and the Gulf of Aqaba on the east, as shown on Map 1.

(2) Only UnitedNationsforces and Egyptian civil police will be stationed in Zone C.

(3) The Egyptian civil police armed with light weapons will perform normal police functions within this Zone.

(4) The United Nations Force will be deployed within Zone C and perform its functions as defined in Article VI of this annex.

(5) The United Nations Force will be stationed mainly in camps located within the following stationing areas shown on Map 1, and will establish its precise locations after consultations with Egypt:

(a) In that part of the area in the Sinai lying within about 20 Km. of the Mediterranean Sea and adjacent to the International Boundary.

(b) In the Sharm el Sheikh area.

d. Zone D

(1) Zone D is bounded by line D (blue line) on the east and the international boundary on the west, as shown on Map 1.

(2) In this Zone there will be an Israeli limited force of four infantry battalions, their military installations, and field fortifications, and United Nations observers.

(3) The Israeli forces in Zone D will not include tanks, artillery and anti-aircraft missiles except individual surface-to-air missiles.

(4) The main elements of the four Israeli infantry battalions will consist of up to 180 armored personnel vehicles of all types and up to a total of four thousand personnel.

2. Access across the international boundary shall only be permitted through entry check points designated by each Party and under its control. Such access shall be in accordance with laws and regulations of each country.

3. Only those field fortifications, military installations, forces, and weapons specifically permitted by this Annex shall be in the Zones.

Article III

Aerial Military Regime

1. Flights of combat aircraft and reconnaissance flights of Egypt and Israel shall take place only over Zones A and D, respectively.

2. Only unarmed, non-combat aircraft of Egypt and Israel will be stationed in Zones A and D, respectively.

3. Only Egyptian unarmed transport aircraft will take off and land in Zone B and up to eight such aircraft may be maintained in Zone B. The Egyptian border units may be equipped with unarmed helicopters to perform their functions in Zone B.

4. The Egyptian civil police may be equipped with unarmed police helicopters to perform normal police functions in Zone C.

5. Only civilian airfields may be built in the Zones.

6. Without prejudice to the provisions of this Treaty, only those military aerial activities specifically permitted by this Annex shall be allowed in the Zones and the airspace above their territorial waters.

Article IV
Naval Regime

1. Egypt and Israel may base and operate naval vessels along the coasts of Zones A and D, respectively.

2. Egyptian coast guard boats, lightly armed, may be stationed and operate in the territorial waters of Zone B to assist the border units in performing their functions in this Zone.

3. Egyptian civil police equipped with light boats, lightly armed, shall perform normal police functions within the territorial waters of Zone C.

4. Nothing in this Annex shall be considered as derogating from the right of innocent passage of the naval vessels of either party.

5. Only civilian maritime ports and installations may be built in the Zones.

6. Without prejudice to the provisions of this Treaty, only those naval activities specifically permitted by this Annex shall be allowed in the Zones and in their territorial waters.

Article V
Early Warning Systems

Egypt and Israel may establish and operate early warning systems only in Zones A and D respectively.

Article VI
United Nations Operations

1. The Parties will request the United Nations to provide forces and observers to supervise the implementation of this Annex and employ their best efforts to prevent any violation of its terms.

2. With respect to these United Nations forces and observers, as appropriate, the Parties agree to rquest the following arrangements:

   a. Operation of check points, reconnaissance patrols, and observation posts along the international boundary and line B, and within Zone C.

   b. Periodic verification of the implementation of the provisions of this Annex will be carried out not less than twice a month unless otherwise agreed by the Parties.

   c. Additional verifications within 48 hours after the receipt of a request from either Party.

   d. Ensuring the freedom of navigation through the Strait of Tiran in accordance with Article V of the Treaty of Peace.

3. The arrangements described in this article for each zone will be implemented in Zones A, B, and C by the United Nations Force and in Zone D by the United Nations Observers.

4. United Nations verification teams shall be accompanied by liaison officers of the respective Party.

5. The United Nations Force and observers will report their findings to both Parties.

6. The United Nations Force and Observers operating in the Zones will enjoy

freedom of movement and other facilities necessary for the performance of their tasks.

7. The United Nations Force and Observers are not empowered to authorize the crossing of the international boundary.

8. The Parties shall agree on the nations from which the United Nations Force and Observers will be drawn. They will be drawn from nations other than those which are permanent members of the United Nations Security Council.

9. The Parties agree that the United Nations should make those command arrangements that will best assure the effective implementation of its responsibilities.

Article VII
Liaison System

1. Upon dissolution of the Joint Commission, a liaison system between the Parties will be established. This liaison system is intended to provide an effective method to assess progress in the implementation of obligations under the present Annex and to resolve any problem that may arise in the course of implementation, and refer other unresolved matters to the higher military authorities of the two countries respectively for consideration. It is also intended to prevent situations resulting from errors or misinterpretation on the part of either Party.

2. An Egyptian liaison office will be established in the city of El-Arish and an Israeli liaison office will be established in the city of Beer-Sheba. Each office will be headed by an officer of the respective country, and assisted by a number of officers.

3. A direct telephone link between the two offices will be set up and also direct telephone lines with the United Nations command will be maintained by both offices.

Article VIII
Respect for War Memorials

Each Party undertakes to preserve in good condition the War Memorials erected in the memory of soldiers of the other Party, namely those erected by Egypt in Israel, and shall permit access to such monuments.

Article IX
Interim Arrangements

The withdrawal of Israeli armed forces and civilians behind the interim withdrawal line, and the conduct of the forces of the Parties and the United Nations prior to the final withdrawal, will be governed by the attached Appendix and Map 2.

Annex III—Protocol Concerning Relations of the Parties

Article 1
Diplomatic and Consular Relations

The Parties agree to establish diplomatic and consular relations and to exchange ambassadors upon completion of the interim withdrawal.

Article 2
Economic and Trade Relations

1. The Parties agree to remove all discriminatory barriers to normal economic relations and to terminate economic boycotts of each other upon completion of the interim withdrawal.

2. As soon as possible, and not later than six months after the completion of the interim withdrawal, the Parties will enter negotiations with a view to concluding an agreement on trade and commerce for the purpose of promoting beneficial economic relations.

Article 3
Cultural Relations

1. The Parties agree to establish normal cultural relations following completion of the interim withdrawal.

2. They agree on the desirability of cultural exchanges in all fields, and shall, as soon as possible and not later than six months after completion of the interim withdrawal, enter into negotiations with a view to concluding a cultural agreement for this purpose.

Article 4
Freedom of Movement

1. Upon completion of the interim withdrawal. each Party will permit the free movement of the nationals and vehicles of the other into and within its territory according to the general rules applicable to nationals and vehicles of other states. Neither Party will impose discriminatory restrictions on the free movement of persons and vehicles from its territory to the territory of the other.

2. Mutual unimpeded access to places of religious and historical significance will be provided on a non-discriminatory basis.

Article 5
Cooperation for Development and Good Neighborly Relations

1. The Parties recognize a mutuality of interest in good neighborly relations and agree to consider means to promote such relations.

2. The Parties will cooperate in promoting peace, stability and development in their region. Each agrees to consider proposals the other may wish to make to this end.

3. The Parties shall seek to foster mutual understanding and tolerance and will, accordingly, abstain from hostile propaganda against each other.

Article 6
Transportation and Telecommunications

1. The Parties recognize as applicable to each other the rights, privileges and obligations provided for by the aviation agreements to which they are both party, particularly by the Convention on International Civil Aviation, 1944 ("The Chicago Convention") and the International Air Services Transit Agreement, 1944.

2. Upon completion of the interim withdrawal any declaration of national emergency by a party under Article 89 of the Chicago Convention will not be applied to the other party on a discriminatory basis.

3. Egypt agrees that the use of airfields left by Israel near El Arish, Rafah, Ras El Nagb and Sharm El Sheikh shall be for civilian purposes only, including possible commercial use by all nations.

4. As soon as possible and not later than six months after the completion of the interim withdrawal, the Parties shall enter into negotiations for the purpose of concluding a civil aviation agreement.

5. The Parties will reopen and maintain roads and railways between their countries and will consider further road and rail links. The Parties further agree that a highway will be constructed and maintained between Egypt, Israel and Jordan near Eilat with guaranteed free and peaceful passage of persons, vehicles and goods between Egypt and Jordan, without prejudice to their sovereignty over that part of the highway which falls within their respective territory.

6. Upon completion of the interim withdrawal, normal postal, telephone, telex, data facsimile, wireless and cable communications and television relay services by cable, radio and satellite shall be established between the two Parties in accordance with all relevant international conventions and regulations.

7. Upon completion of the interim withdrawal, each Party shall grant normal access to its ports for vessels and cargoes of the other, as well as vessels and cargoes destined for or coming from the other. Such access shall be granted on the same conditions generally applicable to vessels and cargoes of other nations. Article 5 of the Treaty of Peace will be implemented upon the exchange of instruments of ratification of the aforementioned treaty.

Article 7
Enjoyment of Human Rights

The Parties affirm their commitment to respect and observe human rights and fundamental freedoms for all, and they will promote these rights and freedoms in accordance with the United Nations Charter.

Article 8
Territorial Seas

Without prejudice to the provisions of Article 5 of the Treaty of Peace each Party recognizes the right of the vessels of the other Party to innocent passage through its territorial sea in accordance with the rules of international law.

Agreed Minutes

ARTICLE I

Egypt's resumption of the exercise of full sovereignty over the Sinai provided for in paragraph 2 of Article I shall occur with regard to each area upon Israel's withdrawal from the area.

ARTICLE IV

It is agreed between the parties that the review provided for in Article IV (4) will be undertaken when requested by either party, commencing within three months of such a request, but that any amendment can be made only by mutual agreement of both parties.

ARTICLE V

The second sentence of paragraph 2 of Article V shall not be construed as limiting the first sentence of that paragraph. The foregoing is not to be construed as contravening the second sentence of paragraph 2 of Article V, which reads as follows:

"The Parties will respect each other's right to navigation and overflight for access to either country through the Strait of Tiran and the Gulf of Aqaba."

ARTICLE VI (2)

The provisions of Article VI shall not be construed in contradiction to the provisions of the framework for peace in the Middle East agreed at Camp David. The foregoing is not to be construed as contravening the provisions of Article VI (2) of the Treaty, which reads as follows:

> "The Parties undertake to fulfill in good faith their obligations under this Treaty, without regard to action of any other Party and independently of any instrument external to this Treaty."

ARTICLE VI (5)

It is agreed by the Parties that there is no assertion that this Treaty prevails over other Treaties or agreements or that other Treaties or agreements prevail over this Treaty. The foregoing is not to be construed as contravening the provisions of Article VI (5) of the Treaty, which reads as follows:

> "Subject to Article 103 of the United Nations Charter, in the event of a conflict between the obligations of the Parties under the present Treaty and any of their other obligations, the obligations under this Treaty will be binding and implemented."

ANNEX I

Article VI, Paragraph 8, of Annex I provides as follows:

"The Parties shall agree on the nations from which the United Nations forces and observers will be drawn. They will be drawn from nations other than those which are permanent members of the United Nations Security Council.

The Parties have agree as follows:

"With respect to the provisions of paragraph 8, Article VI, of Annex I, if no agreement is reached between the Parties, they will accept or support a U.S. proposal concerning the composition of the United Nations force and observers."

ANNEX III

The Treaty of Peace and Annex III thereto provide for establishing normal economic relations between the Parties. In accordance herewith, it is agreed that such relations will include normal commercial sales of oil by Egypt to Israel, and that Israel shall be fully entitled to make bids for Egyptian-origin oil not needed for Egyptian domestic oil consumption, and Egypt and its oil concessionaries will entertain bids made by Israel, on the same basis and terms as apply to other bidders for such oil.

For the Government of the Arab Republic of Egypt

For the Government of Israel:

Witnessed by:

Jimmy Carter, *President of the United States of America*

The Jaffee Center for Strategic Studies (JCSS)

The Center for Strategic Studies was established at Tel Aviv University at the end of 1977. In 1983 it was named the Jaffee Center for Strategic Studies in honor of Mr. & Mrs. Mel Jaffee. The objective of the Center is to contribute to the expansion of knowledge on strategic subjects and to promote public understanding of and pluralistic thought on matters of national and international security.

The Center relates to the concept of strategy in its broadest meaning, namely, the complex of processes involved in the identification, mobilization and application of resources in peace and war, in order to solidify and strengthen national and international security.

JCSS International Board of Trustees

JCSS Publications

JCSS Publications present the findings and assessments of the Center's research staff. Each paper represents the work of a single investigator or a team. Such teams may also include research fellows who are not members of the Center's staff. Views expressed in the Center's publications are those of the authors and do not necessarily reflect the views of the Center, its trustees, officers, or other staff members or the organizations and individuals that support its research. Thus the publication of a work by JCSS signifies that it is deemed worthy of public consideration but does not imply endorsement of conclusions or recommendations.

The Jaffee Center for Strategic Studies
Recent Publications in English

1993-1994 Subscription Series

Study no. 21 Aryeh Shalev, *The Israel-Syria Armistice Regime 1949-1955.*

Study no. 22 Aharon Klieman and Ariel Levite, eds., *Deterrence in the Middle East: Where Theory and Practice Converge.*

Study no. 23 Shai Feldman and Ariel Levite, eds., *Arms Control and the New Middle East Security Environment.*

Study no. 24 Aryeh Shalev, *Israel and Syria: Peace and Security on the Golan.*

Study no. 25 Shai Feldman, ed., *Confidence Building and Verification: Prospects in the Middle East.*

The Middle East Military Balance 1993-1994
Edited by Shlomo Gazit; with Zeev Eytan.

1991-1992 Subscription Series

Study no. 18 Mark A. Heller, *The Dynamics of Soviet Policy in the Middle East: Between Old Thinking and New.*

Study no. 19 Dore Gold, *Israel as an American Non-NATO Ally: Parameters of Defense-Industrial Cooperation.*

Study no. 20 Karen L. Puschel, *US-Israeli Strategic Cooperation in the Post-Cold War Era: An American Perspective.*

War in the Gulf: Implications for Israel
Report of a JCSS Study Group. Edited by Joseph Alpher.

The Middle East Military Balance 1992-1993
Edited by Shlomo Gazit; with Zeev Eytan, and Amos Gilboa.

Books

Abraham Ben-Zvi, *The United States and Israel: The Limits of the Special Relationship* (New York: Columbia Univ. Press, 1993).